Scotland's Parliament

Triumph and Disaster

For Pam, Stephen and Alistair

Scotland's Parliament
Triumph and Disaster

BRIAN TAYLOR

Edinburgh University Press

All illustrations kindly supplied by The Scotsman Publications Ltd,
with the exception of that on page 315, kindly supplied by PA News Ltd.

© Brian Taylor, 2002

Edinburgh University Press Ltd
22, George Square, Edinburgh

Typeset in Bembo by
Pioneer Associates, Perthshire, and
Printed and bound in Great Britain by
The Cromwell Press, Trowbridge, Wilts

A CIP Record for this book is available from the British Library

ISBN 1 902930 41 X (paperback)

The right of Brian Taylor
to be identified as author of this work
has been asserted in accordance with
the Copyright, Designs and Patents Act 1988.

Contents

Preface

To those who read my first published effort, snappily titled *The Scottish Parliament*, welcome back, friends. To those who did not, similarly, welcome.

I wrote a book about the Scottish Parliament in 1999 to coincide with the first elections. As a journalist, I had covered the long-running devolution debate: the partisan dispute; the Convention which set out a detailed scheme for Scottish self-government; the referendum, White Paper and Act, which broadly implemented that scheme; the Parliament itself, Executive and Opposition. My aim was to tell that story from the inside, but also to explain the various motivations which underpinned the debate.

In 2002, Edinburgh University Press approached me with a proposal for a second edition. The objective was to update that first text, including more recent developments, but also still incorporating the core of the original edition. I readily agreed, and eventually produced a draft. It met all the stated aims, blending the earlier work with new material. The snag was there was rather a *lot* of new material. A lot had happened in the Scottish Parliament since it was first elected.

Peering gamely over the mountainous summit of the submitted draft, my editor gently suggested that perhaps two books might be appropriate. Thus it was decided. My original first edition has been revised and reissued as *The Road to the Scottish Parliament*, standing alone as a detailed account of the establishment of Scotland's Parliament, with fresh insight into the controversies which dogged the road to devolution. The new material has formed an entirely new book, *Scotland's Parliament: Triumph and Disaster*, a companion volume to that earlier work. That is the book you have in your hand.

This second book tells the inside story of the turbulent first session of the new Parliament. The death of Donald Dewar, the resignation of Henry McLeish, the accession of Jack McConnell. The rows and reconciliations. The Holyrood building, Section 28, money, Europe, relations with London. This book offers a fresh look at events, frequently disclosing new details for the first time.

There is, inevitably, a little overlap between the two volumes. However, that has been kept to an absolute minimum. Book One traces the road to the Parliament, as well as painting a picture of how devolution looked and felt when MSPs were first elected. Book Two – this book – analyses how things have turned out, how the devolved world looks as we near the close of that Parliament's first session. Please, read and enjoy.

1 Towsy Times – a Trio of First Ministers

'The First Minister will see you now.' Suitably summoned, the visitor headed for Henry McLeish's office, bumping into Jim Wallace on the way. A few pleasantries were exchanged. Progress into the office resumed.

The venue was St Andrew's House, the forbidding yet magnificent headquarters of the Scottish Executive on Edinburgh's Regent Road, directly opposite the old Royal High School, which had once been intended to house Scotland's new Parliament. St Andrew's House provokes a range of emotions. Many dislike its looming, functional Bauhaus exterior. Perhaps it reminds them of the prison that formerly occupied the site. Perhaps it is a little too reminiscent of East European state architecture: power resides here and don't you forget it.

For myself, I love it. I like the sense of self-awareness, I like the grand entrance with its slightly kitsch statues. Above all, I like the way the formality of the lay-out is leavened by elegant ministerial offices with their polished woodwork and art-deco lighting.

Our visitor, however, was not preoccupied with architecture. Conor O'Riordan had come to present his credentials as the newly appointed Consul General of Ireland in Edinburgh. O'Riordan is a highly intelligent, urbane and affable individual. He arrived well aware that the Irish Consulate had developed a remarkably high profile in its short existence. He knew that his predecessor Dan Mulhall – the very first consul – had built a huge personal reputation before departing to an ambassadorship.

He knew that from a standing start Mulhall had become the doyen of the Scottish consular corps. He knew that Mulhall's farewell party – replete with songs in Gaelic, Irish and Scots – was now the stuff of media legend. He knew the importance that Dublin attaches to the Edinburgh link. He wanted, understandably, to make a strong impression from the outset. So, as he waited in the First Minister's outer office, he ran through the issues that might emerge. Certainly, there was an extensive potential list. The economy and job creation, undoubtedly. Perhaps Scotland's place in the newly emerging political structure of the islands of Britain and Ireland, north and south. Perhaps shared action on issues like drugs.

Would there be any need to visit again that unfortunate episode when the Irish Taoiseach had been obliged to postpone a visit to the Lanarkshire memorial to the Irish famine for fear of sectarian trouble following an Old Firm game? The visit had subsequently gone ahead, and was a big success. Surely that was done with?

The Consul General need not have worried. The meeting with the First Minister went well, very well. As anticipated, Henry McLeish was anxious to discuss the economy and other interests shared between Scotland and Ireland. The two men talked for more than half an hour.

McLeish mapped out future plans, suggesting that he would like to pay a formal visit to Ireland early in the New Year. The First Minister said that he valued Scotland's links with Ireland, and was anxious to sustain these through frequent, informal exchanges of information and opinions on contemporary issues.

Henry McLeish was apparently full of ideas. O'Riordan left satisfied, no doubt to report to Dublin. This was the afternoon of Wednesday, 7 November 2001. The following morning, Henry McLeish resigned as First Minister of Scotland.

He quit after a turbulent year in charge of the Scottish Executive. He quit because of his failure to close down inquiries about his previous office cash allowances while an MP at Westminster. He quit in ignominy after an episode that only added to the problems of the self-government project.

Supporters of devolution feared for the future of the fledgling

Parliament. Sceptics smiled knowingly, their prophecies seemingly borne out. As the resignation news broke – and MSPs streamed emotionally from the Chamber into the Royal Mile – I sprinted after them, hauling on my jacket as I hurried down the circular stone stairs at the Parliament's Lawnmarket media centre.

Hijacking a standby BBC cameraman, I sought instant reaction. One MSP, Labour's Maureen McMillan, told me tearfully that a good man had been 'murdered by the media'. Others were sympathetic, undoubtedly. The prevailing emotion was pity, not scorn. However, most thought that good man, Henry McLeish, had caused his own downfall. His supporters, even a few critics, commented that he had been forced out of office just as he was beginning to make a real impact, to indicate that he might be on top of the job. Many, perhaps the majority, felt that he might have survived had he handled matters more adroitly. Many felt – and still feel – that the office-allowances row, while serious, was not sufficient, in itself, to bring down the elected head of a government.

That still left the predominant view: that it was Henry McLeish's response, the First Minister's own reactions, which mattered. To be categorical, he had been tested – severely tested – and had failed. He had failed to provide adequate answers, sufficiently quickly. He had failed to tackle Parliamentary challenges on the issue, sounding first defiant then slightly self-pitying. He had performed lamentably under interrogation on the BBC's *Question Time*. He had failed. He had lost confidence: the confidence of others in his administration but, more significantly, confidence in himself.

To be fair, Henry McLeish is keenly, bitingly aware of all this. I have spoken to him a number of times since his resignation. Even months on, the emotions were still near the surface. He could seem assured, perhaps talking of future writing or lecturing plans. Then turn to the topic of his downfall, and he sometimes seemed close to tears, almost instantly. Time has moved on, and McLeish has begun to look to the future again. Yet, he remains angry at events, angry at his advisers, angry that he is no longer in charge, with his ambition of a confident, compassionate and competitive Scotland. However, mostly he is angry with himself. He knows – believe me, he knows – that he let himself down badly.

On that day when he quit, however, the departing leader's self-recrimination was not the primary concern for Scotland. The

Scottish Parliament had to choose a successor to lead the Executive. Scotland had waited three centuries for self-government to be restored, and then, in under three years, had required three First Ministers. Tragic death had taken Donald Dewar, tortuous dithering had ousted Henry McLeish and talented determination was to elevate Jack McConnell.

Politicians are like the rest of us. However much they plot, however much they plan, their actions are shaped by mishap, tragedy, blunder and farce. Yet, there is a narrative here. The story of these three First Ministers is one of apparently linear change, a change that may be said to match the maturing of the Parliament itself.

Dewar was the bridge. An MP of long standing, a towering intellect and remarkable personality, he gave the new institution the confidence to assume power. He offered continuity in the midst of potential turmoil. McLeish was also a former Westminster politician, but he appeared to chafe at the continuing Westminster constraints, to seek occasional confrontation, to stretch the freedom of the new Parliament. McConnell, by contrast, has no Westminster background and minimal continuing links with the big players in the UK government. In that sense, he may be said to represent the future: in that politicians will head directly to the Scottish Parliament from the Scottish party system. It is not that McConnell disregards Westminster: as a pragmatic politician, he is careful to factor the UK dimension into his decisions. However, he has no immersion in Westminster custom and practice to influence his thinking, nor any need to kick loose from a Westminster past with defiant gestures of autonomy.

This book contains the story of those three First Ministers. How did they come to power? How did they behave in office? How did their colleagues behave? It is also the story of Scotland's new Parliament. What has it done well? Where has it gone wrong? My aim is to give an accurate, informed account based upon my own observations and extensive off-the-record conversations with political insiders.

Further, drawing on new information from the first few years of the Parliament, I intend to examine what I regard as structural problems in the new settlement – finance, Europe and the impact on England. I will profile the parties – and party leaders. Finally, I hope to provide a few pointers to the future.

My main interest, then, is in the structure, the framework of Scottish self-government. However, the basic narrative is fascinating too, even startling on occasion. I should confess that, frankly, I enjoy gossip. Politicians and political journalists who say they do not are, probably, being 'economical with the truth'. It may relieve readers, however, to know that I do not intend to replicate every dot and comma of those first few years. I hope to offer edited highlights rather than a slow-motion replay.

From being a relatively minor participant in a Westminster Parliament, Scotland has been transformed. Alongside that Westminster link, Scotland now has its own Parliament again – the first since Union with England in 1707 ended or, strictly, 'adjourned' the ancient, independent Scottish Parliament.

The new devolved Parliament is responsible – solely responsible – for most domestic affairs in Scotland. For the health service, for schools, colleges and universities, for the law courts and criminal justice, for the legal system practised in those courts, for the environment, for tourism, for the arts, for industrial promotion, for local government and all its many services, for the roads, for farming, for fishing.

Devolution, though, is not independence. Westminster retains responsibility for macro-economics, for foreign affairs, for defence, for the welfare system, for energy, for the Crown, for the constitution. At least, those are among its UK responsibilities. It also has the small matter of governing England to be getting on with. We shall look later at the possible problems caused by that division of power.

For now, though, back to Scotland. The new Scottish Parliament was elected in 1999 by a proportional voting system, different from Westminster's 'winner takes all' approach. Those Scottish elections produced, ultimately, a devolved, coalition government between Labour and the Liberal Democrats.

Donald Dewar, however, was definitely the boss, plainly in command of his new Cabinet. There they stood on the steps of Bute House, forming a neat, isosceles triangle around Dewar. Henry McLeish and the Liberal Democrat leader Jim Wallace at the apex, Sam Galbraith and Tom McCabe one step down, Jack McConnell and Susan Deacon on the next rung, Ross Finnie and the Lord Advocate, Lord Hardie, below that, and finally, at street level next to Dewar, Wendy Alexander and Sarah Boyack.

That evening, accompanied by John Rafferty, the First Minister's special adviser, the eleven Cabinet members sat down to dine together in Bute House. A little nervous, a little unsure. They signed each other's menus – like school students autographing souvenir photographs. Most, I imagine, still have them. Most are no longer in the Cabinet. Only three around that table are still there. Jack McConnell is Labour's sole survivor. Only the two ever-present Liberal Democrats are in the same jobs.

That evening, Dewar expressed or feigned astonishment that many of his Labour colleagues appeared to know each other well from student days. He had appointed individuals and ended up with a club, a generation. Deacon, McConnell, Alexander and Boyack were part of a bright, argumentative network of young Scottish Labour politicians for whom Home Rule and reform were paramount.

Dewar, though, was the boss. He was the big-league politician, the only one present who had been a Westminster Cabinet Minister, the one with status on the UK stage. He was the last Scottish Secretary before devolution. Indeed, one or two were inclined to whisper that he still acted a little like a Scottish Secretary even *after* devolution.

The convenient fiction is that a Cabinet leader is 'primus inter pares', first among equals, that all Cabinet Ministers have comparable clout, with just a bit on top for the boss. That Ministers are in sole command of their individual departments, within the principle of collective responsibility.

Such a description scarcely works for Tony Blair's UK Cabinet. Other than Gordon Brown, no-one comes near him for political power. It did not remotely apply in the early days of Dewar's devolved administration. Civil servants who had worked for Dewar as Scottish Secretary were inclined to act initially as if little had changed. Dewar was still in complete command with a team of juniors as helpers. Policy approval meant Dewar approval. To be fair, this was not remotely dictatorship by Dewar. He made every effort to involve his colleagues. If they advanced policy ideas, he would subject them to fierce, forensic examination; a combination of withering satire and intellectual scrutiny. If the ideas surmounted that substantial hurdle, he would back them completely.

It was simply that, in the initial phase at least, the gulf in experience was so huge. For many in the Cabinet, this was the very first time they had been elected to national public office of any kind. Dewar first became an MP in 1966.

So from the start it was Dewar and the rest, although lines of personal and political liaison emerged, as always happens. Naturally, the LibDem pair – Jim Wallace and Ross Finnie – were somewhat apart. They had not been appointed by Dewar: Wallace was there in his own right as leader of the Scottish Liberal Democrats; Finnie was nominated by Wallace. However, the LibDems – and perhaps most especially Ross Finnie – acted from the outset as the glue in the Cabinet. They would intervene between Labour colleagues, forming ad-hoc liaisons to sort out individual issues, free from ideology and internal party competition. They promoted their *own* party policies and advantage, of course. Equally, they gained a reputation as peace-makers and problem-solvers. I intend to look at this more closely later in a scrutiny of Scottish coalition politics.

One insider suggested to me that the Labour Ministers in Dewar's Cabinet could be very broadly divided into three groups. First, there was Dewar himself, Sam Galbraith and Henry McLeish – all Westminster MPs and formerly Ministers at the old pre-devolution Scottish Office.

Second, there was Jack McConnell and Tom McCabe, both former council leaders, both now MSPs from Lanarkshire, the heartland synonymous with Labour machine politics. This left Susan Deacon, Sarah Boyack and Wendy Alexander as the least experienced in elected politics, although each had considerable talent in their own fields and Alexander had previously been Dewar's special adviser.

The astute reader will have noticed that these last three also share another characteristic – gender. This led to talk in the early days of a male cabal freezing out the women. Male sources are, understandably, inclined to discount this, saying that the structure emerged for reasons of common background and experience. Suspicions linger among Labour women. This depiction is, of course, only one version. Political groupings are fluid. Your big buddy over one issue will be your sworn enemy over the next. There are also significant caveats to be attached to this map of the Dewar Cabinet.

For one, Dewar and McLeish were not chums. They had minimal rapport, one with the other. They were personally very different: Dewar was the cultured intellectual with a biting line in wit; McLeish was the more prosaic, even mechanistic politician. In addition,

Dewar had given a number of indications that he did not particularly rate McLeish, at least not above other Cabinet colleagues. McLeish had been Minister of State at the Scottish Office, but Dewar never made him his deputy, neither before nor after devolution. Self-evidently, that rankled with McLeish – as did the inevitable consequence of coalition, which was that Jim Wallace, the leader of Labour's LibDem partners, became deputy First Minister, second in Cabinet rank to Dewar himself.

One Cabinet insider said that McLeish, as ambitious as any other ranking politician, was 'plainly hugely disenchanted' as a result of this history. Another said that, consequently, McLeish 'tended to operate apart in Cabinet, to go his own way'. To be fair, McLeish never allowed this factor to overshadow his day-to-day efforts, neither departmentally nor in Cabinet. In addition, although Wallace's pre-eminence may have irked him personally, McLeish adhered firmly to the concept of coalition government. Dewar, too, worked closely and well with Jim Wallace. Little surprise, given that the pair had worked together in Opposition while the Constitutional Convention was preparing the path to devolution. However, leaders normally form a 'kitchen cabinet', a small coterie of trusted supporters.

Other than personal staff, Dewar's closest Labour colleagues were Wendy Alexander, Tom McCabe and Sam Galbraith. Alexander, his mega-bright former special adviser, had worked by his side at the Scottish Office. McCabe, the ultra-loyal and discreet fixer who kept his mind firmly on the job in hand. Galbraith, a close personal friend of Dewar, a former neuro-surgeon who combined dedication with a healthy disdain for gesture politics. Each had a key role to play. It is fair to say, though, that Dewar relied most upon Sam Galbraith as a source of experienced advice. Galbraith was his pal – and the political colleague that he trusted most. In Cabinet and elsewhere, Galbraith would give his views frankly, bluntly, and frequently in decidedly colourful language. Ministerial and civil-service sources both say that, in the early days in particular, if you wanted a policy endorsed, you needed Galbraith on your side.

As education minister, Sam Galbraith ultimately ran into trouble when the Scottish Qualifications Authority (SQA) made a mess of the school exams in August 2000, delivering the Higher results late and incomplete. Galbraith later moved to another remit and stepped down from Parliament on health grounds in March the following year. A survivor of a lung transplant, no-one grudged him his retirement.

Strictly speaking, the SQA fell within the remit of Henry McLeish. He headed the SQA's sponsoring Executive department, Enterprise and Lifelong Learning. Technically, that was because the SQA covered both schools and further-education colleges. But the public and media spotlight was very firmly upon the problems faced by Scotland's schools. Parents, teachers and pupils understandably wanted someone to blame – and Sam Galbraith, as Education Minister, fitted the bill. Indeed, he was initially criticised for not sounding sufficiently humble and apologetic. He did, however, take the heat, while McLeish stayed mostly in the background.

With neat symmetry, when McLeish became First Minister, he announced that the Education Department would now handle the SQA directly, and he handed the task of sorting out the troubled organisation to Jack McConnell, who had challenged him for the top job. Far from crumbling under the challenge, McConnell increased his reputation by a swift and decisive programme of action.

The SQA was very far from the only problem faced during Donald Dewar's spell as First Minister. Indeed, he had a notably difficult time, as cumulative 'events', Harold Macmillan's legendary bane of political life, added to the organisational problems inevitably associated with a new structure. From instinct and experience, Dewar was cautious. Some of his colleagues found him overcautious, reluctant to take the radical action they occasionally felt necessary.

There are those who still regret that the Dewar administration did not prepare a definite programme of early action for, say, the first one hundred days of devolution. One insider from the time told me: 'We were elected, we spent the first six weeks in limbo, as shadow Ministers, arguing about allowances. The Queen formally opened Parliament on 1 July – we took full power and then we went on holiday! Or at least that's how it looked to the public at the time.'

It is acknowledged that 'hitting the ground running' would have been decidedly difficult. The Parliament was elected in May, but did not assume power from Westminster until July. There were strict, legal limits on what could be done. Even so, it is argued by several insiders that more should have been put in place to give, at least, the impression of an administration itching for action. To be fair, however, Donald Dewar was keenly aware that the expectations of the public, post-devolution, were high. He knew those expectations had been artificially inflated by the political need to talk up, in advance, the potency of the new Parliament. Despite that, Dewar was determined to resist the temptation to meet those expectations with hastily formed policy announcements. He knew that hasty policy often unravelled, or failed to produce genuine change, further increasing public disenchantment. However much it frustrated his most eager colleagues, he would not be deflected.

It was, though, an uneasy time. In the very earliest phase of the Parliament, in 1999, there were damaging 'housekeeping' rows over issues like allowances for political parties. There was evidence of conflict with Westminster, including the newly formed Scotland Office, which was intended to represent Scottish interests in the UK Cabinet.

The press grew restless – and, arguably, hostile. A combination of factors contributed to this. First, the early months of the Parliament, particularly the transition period, did not provide enough in the way of substantial news stories to placate the journalists. That left more room for knocking copy, particularly for those newspapers inimical or sceptical towards devolution. At the same time, it meant a dearth of ammunition for those papers that might have felt inclined to support the new institution.

Second – and this is hard to quantify – there was a collective view abroad that the press had been corralled for too long into the pro-devolution camp. Journalists are seldom comfortable when they can be depicted as a claque, marshalled by cheerleaders. Instinctively for some, it felt like time to kick out.

Third, there is a pack instinct in reporting. Manipulative politicians will try to divert the pack with new or even false scents. Are the press baying at your heels over some politician's misdemeanours? Throw them something equally juicy: perhaps a new and contro-versial policy. Find a scandal in another party.

In the early days of Holyrood, the pack scented trouble, and nothing emerged, or could be contrived, to get them off that scent. Developments that might have played as minor slips became major blunders, contributing to the general atmosphere of muddle and malaise. For example, on 1 September 1999, the Parliament issued commemorative coins to members. The story? Useless politicians give themselves medals.

On it went. There were the lobbying allegations surrounding Jack McConnell, which we shall examine later. He was completely cleared, but damage was done. On again. In December 1999, Donald Dewar was forced, after vacillating, to dismiss his senior adviser John Rafferty, who had been accused of giving misleading information to newspapers about non-existent death threats to the Health Minister following a speech she made on abortion and family planning. The same month, Labour's Ian Welsh resigned as an MSP, implying that he was disenchanted as a backbencher in the new Parliament and had wielded more power as a leading figure in local government.

Dewar appeared at the mercy of events, beset by hurtful, personal criticism of his performance which would previously have been unthinkable. To be blunt, one factor contributing to the First Minister's problems was his age. By the end of 1999, he was 62. A mere slip of a lad compared, for example, to Gladstone, who was still cheerfully governing in his eighties.

However, the millennial obsession was with youth and new beginnings. The First Minister's spokesman, David Whitton, repeatedly insisted that his boss had no intention of stepping down. Most presumed that Donald Dewar would not continue as First Minister much beyond the next Scottish elections. Crucially, those making that presumption included his Cabinet colleagues.

At the same time as he was battling to get on top of events, his colleagues – to varying degrees – were privately measuring their own prospects of obtaining the top job. It, inevitably, affected their thinking and their behaviour. It contributed to tension within Labour. It sparked debilitating leaks to the press from Ministers seeking to pursue their own agenda. Such is politics.

These problems, however, were as nothing compared to two issues that continue to resonate now, to varying degrees: the Holyrood building project and Section 28. Donald Dewar had personally headed the expert team which chose a former brewery site opposite Holyrood Palace as the venue for the new Scottish Parliament building. He and his team chose the Barcelona architect Enric Miralles to design the building in conjunction with Edinburgh partners. Crucially, these decisions were both taken in 1998, a year before MSPs were elected.

I confess I have somewhat altered my view of the building row over time. I thought the initial complaints about the increasing cost and delays were serious, and duly covered them extensively. I believed, however, that the discontent would evaporate relatively speedily. I was wrong. Resentment about the Holyrood building has become something of an icon for those with a grudge against the Scottish Parliament or politics more generally. In these cynical, sceptical days, that includes a fair proportion of the populace.

In a similar way, the Millennium Dome at Greenwich became a totem for those who felt there was a vacuous core below the superficial sheen of Blairite New Labour. The two building projects fulfilled a similar function. Both became standing jokes. More seriously, both contrived to give solid form to nebulous public discontent.

Try a test. Ask people what they think of 'the Scottish Parliament'. Some may talk about MSPs, about the First Minister, about policies, about legislation. A fair number – I know, because I have tried this out – bypass the substance of devolution and head straight for the Holyrood building project.

They may not know the details. They may not know the cost estimate. They may not know the justification for the over-run. They do know, however, that they are angry, seriously angry, about the money seemingly being wasted on a grandiose construction at the foot of Edinburgh's Royal Mile.

If I am right, this anger with a building is, literally, a concrete substitute for discontent with devolution. People expected more. Dewar was right to fear that expectations had been unnaturally high. People feel an imprecise sense of disillusionment with politics generally and, perhaps particularly, with a new politics that had promised to be different.

Donald Dewar took the early criticism of the Holyrood project very badly indeed. I recall arriving in his Edinburgh office one day to interview him on some transient controversy or other. Dewar could not focus on the matter in hand for thinking about that day's press coverage of the building project's rising costs. On another occasion, as the coverage grew particularly savage, a Cabinet colleague recalls the First Minister wailing in despair: 'Why are they doing this?' He felt politically and personally besieged.

As I write, the cost of the project is put at £280 million, including landscaping and road work. The projected completion date is May 2003, with MSPs due to 'migrate' into the new building over

Making a point: Donald Dewar and Enric Miralles discuss the Holyrood building project.

the summer, gaining full access from September. The original price put upon supplying a home for the new Parliament was, risibly, £10 to £40 million. That was in the government White Paper spelling out plans for devolution. The original completion date for the Holyrood project was autumn 2001.

This has been a long, tortuous story. For example, the original figures are now largely played down as guesstimates with no substance. It is widely presumed that they did not include key additional cost factors. We are encouraged to avoid comparisons between those early figures and the eventual estimates.

However, such an approach is not entirely justified. I have a copy of a letter, which has not previously been published, that stresses that the original costings were 'notional', certainly, but indicates that they featured more detail than has subsequently been implied. The letter is from Muir Russell, the Permanent Secretary to the Executive, to David McLetchie, the Conservative leader, and is dated 24 October 2000. McLetchie had queried the status of those original costings.

The Permanent Secretary notes that the 'lower end' of the cost scale, £10 million, might have paid for refurbishment of the old Royal High School – a notion which was swiftly, and I believe rightly, abandoned as impractical. Muir Russell adds: 'The £40 million figure related to a new build (at Leith) on a brownfield site to a reasonable modern standard. The costings for this were obviously on a notional basis rather than being built up from detailed design elements, but, having checked our records, I can say that this figure was intended to include not only construction works but also fees, fitting out, furniture, VAT and land acquisition.' So these figures were rough, but they were not as rough as all that, they were not completely devoid of content. In particular, the £40 million figure – at the top of this early cost range – included specified, added costs. Muir Russell notes that the next formal estimate which surfaced – that of £50 million – did *not* include those added burdens. It was for construction only, with fees and other costs on top.

The relevant dates are instructive. The estimate of £10 to £40 million was published in the Scottish Office White Paper in July 1997, in the run-up to the 11 September referendum when the people of Scotland were asked to endorse devolution. It was published, in other words, when the UK government wanted to win popular consent for the new Parliament. It can be presumed that Ministers were scarcely keen, at that point, to scare the citizenry with wild talk of costly building projects. Indeed, to the cynic, it is slightly puzzling that they felt obliged to mention cost at all.

The higher figure of £50 million – plus costs – only emerged around November 1997 when detailed feasibility studies were being carried out into three Edinburgh sites: Leith, Haymarket and Calton Hill. The higher figure emerged not long after the referendum was successfully completed.

Holyrood emerged as a fourth option in December, and was chosen by Donald Dewar on 9 January 1998. From then on, it was said that the cost for the Holyrood project was around £90 million including VAT, fees and fittings; more than twice the highest figure from the White Paper of six months earlier.

It will no doubt be said – with some justification – that I am not comparing like with like, that the Parliament might have been housed in relatively simple accommodation, at relatively little cost, on a brownfield site. Or that private finance might have been deployed. Both such options seemingly vanished when a full-scale architectural competition was announced, which explains the apparent leap in cost.

However, it is difficult to avoid the conclusion that the original White Paper estimates were unreasonably low. It is difficult to avoid commenting that those low-cost estimates coincided with a period when those advocating devolution were seeking popular support for a new Parliament in a referendum. It is difficult to avoid the conclusion that at least one downside of devolution was deliberately underplayed. It is difficult to avoid concluding that much of the subsequent image problem for the project stems from those early estimates. Further, I believe the core political problem has been that the decision was taken by Donald Dewar before the Scottish Parliament was elected. The motivation was obvious and understandable: Dewar felt the building project could not be delayed. However, it caused political, indeed almost psychological, problems.

The Parliament's own corporate body assumed control of the project from June 1999. But MSPs simply inherited a chosen site, a chosen architect and a 'handover price' which was, by then, £62 million plus costs: a total figure of £109 million. As a consequence, it was difficult for them to feel 'ownership' of the project in any real sense. This gave scope to the vocal critics – like Margo MacDonald and Donald Gorrie – while depressing support. Other than Dewar, individual MSPs had played no personal part in picking the building plan. Why should they stick their necks out?

This issue of 'ownership' was crucial. The corporate body, chaired by the Presiding Officer, was in charge. From June 1999, it was strictly nothing to do with Ministers. Yet the Executive was ultimately paying the bills, and taking the flak. The decision-making structure was unclear. Eventually, much later, a Progress Group was appointed to take daily charge. The row worsened. An expert report queried that handover figure of £62 million plus costs, noting that officials had prepared 'design uncertainty' estimates of £89 million plus. Donald Dewar was obliged to confirm to MSPs that he had not been told about this higher figure. He defended his officials, saying that they had been right to withhold figures from him which were not 'robust'. It was not, to be frank, the finest moment for the First Minister nor his administration.

Since then, there has been a catalogue of controversies – and

blame – surrounding the project. MSPs blame the project man-
agers/contractors for delays. In retort, it is claimed that MSPs have
caused problems by expanding the scheme and dithering over
details. Everyone blames everyone else for the rising cost.

In short, pretty well everything that could have gone wrong has
gone wrong. We have yet to discover that the building site is
actually the location of an ancient Pictish burial ground, and should
never have been disturbed. Or that a species of bat – unique in
Europe – regards Holyrood as its natural habitat and will perish,
whimpering, anywhere else. No doubt, however, these developments
are just around the corner.

With hindsight, the initial low estimates were a tactical mistake.
With hindsight, the choice of site should have been left to the
members of the new Parliament. With hindsight, the command
structure for the project should have been more clearly defined
from a much earlier stage. However, we all know what hindsight is
worth.

So what now? There is no alternative but to make Holyrood
work and work well. Frankly, I also think, with all the caveats lodged
above, that it was the right choice. I was initially attracted to the
open space – and unstuffy image – that the docklands of Leith would
have offered. But I am convinced by horrified Edinburgh citizens
who assure me that this would have meant 'moving out of the
capital'.

Haymarket had few serious advocates. The location was unim-
pressive, with few countervailing advantages. Finally, this left Calton
Hill, looming confidently over Princes Street, and offering the twin
options of converting St Andrew's House and/or the old Royal
High School.

First, I do not believe that it would have been possible to con-
vert the old school. Yes, it is a proud and majestic building. Yes, the
debating chamber was reasonably attractive, although nowhere near
as good as the present 'temporary' home on the Mound. However,
back-up space to provide modern office accommodation was limited,
and it would have been extremely difficult (and costly) to transform
a historic, protected building without running up against severely
restrictive regulations.

Further, I am told that Donald Dewar personally disliked the idea
of extending St Andrew's House. It was previously suggested that one

Minister (not Dewar) thought the Royal High School had become a Nationalist symbol. Dewar, apparently, felt that St Andrew's House, across the road from the school, offered exactly the opposite. It was 'too colonial', too reminiscent of remote rule from London, and would send out the wrong symbols.

Dewar felt further that the work on St Andrew's House would prove more difficult than anticipated and that it could only be done by disrupting – and possibly ruining – an already magnificent architectural area of the city.

It was said by some that the Parliament would be best placed on the elevated site afforded by Calton Hill. But should a people's Parliament be a palace on a hill, set above them? Should it not, arguably, mingle among the people themselves?

I am reluctant to offer prophecies on this issue. I was wrong before when I thought the fuss would die down relatively quickly. However, I believe – I *think* – that Holyrood will eventually be a rewarding building on a historic site. I *think* we will end up proud of it. I *think* there are signs that people are slightly appeased by the evidence of substantial construction on site, by the emerging shape of an intriguing design. However, much damage has undoubtedly been done.

The same must be said about the abolition of Section 28. This was the legal clause which prohibited councils from intentionally promoting homosexuality and prohibited schools from teaching pupils about homosexuality as if it were a 'pretended family relationship'. Executive Ministers advocated abolition on the grounds that the law as it stood was intolerably prejudiced against a section of society.

Arguably, this statute – introduced by the Conservatives – had minimal practical impact upon councils and schools while it was in force. Arguably, its abolition has likewise had minimal impact. Despite that, it stirred a simply ferocious row: a blend of ministerial myopia, hysterical reaction and genuine, although perhaps not totally well-founded, parental concern. The more zealous – on either side of the argument – will tell you otherwise: that this was an issue of real substance. I am inclined, however, to think that this was a debate about principle, not practice. That does not mean abolition was futile. Nor that those advocating retention of the clause were not genuinely motivated. We should, however, bear in mind that this was, arguably, a clash of cultures, not a clash over a precise legal clause.

I have seldom witnessed such an astonishing political row; all the more vitriolic, perhaps, for its very lack of substance. Every fear, every anxiety in Scottish parents was stirred because the legislation was so imprecise and the objectives of abolition likewise. The two sides could scarcely compromise. The topic was so nebulous – so scary to some – that compromise was difficult to pin down.

Those who were in Dewar's Cabinet at the time all still feel bruised. Palpably, the most damage was done to Wendy Alexander, who advanced abolition as part of the Ethical Standards on Public Life Bill. She had earlier floated the notion in a university speech. She was personally criticised and reviled. Her image was used in billboard advertising by the campaign funded by Brian Souter, the millionaire businessman who founded Stagecoach. She was frequently singled out for attack in newspaper coverage, for example in the *Daily Record*, which took an extremely strong and uncompromising stand against abolition.

The abolition of Section 28 had long been sought by gay and lesbian groups. They wanted it scrapped for the whole of the UK, but advised Wendy Alexander that the Scottish Parliament had the power to act for Scotland alone. Alexander had, apparently, not considered this option previously. She did so now, and mentioned the prospect in the back of a ministerial car while travelling to an official engagement with Donald Dewar.

That story – which is reasonably well known – has led to comment to the effect that she did not clear abolition fully within Cabinet. This is not correct. The Cabinet was consulted – and gave its support. The problem – according to supporters of abolition – was that Alexander did not then appear to have a strategy for managing abolition and coping with the predictable reaction. One Minister has suggested to me that she played down the problem in Scotland while simultaneously suggesting that parallel abolition in England was further advanced in UK government thinking than was actually the case.

However, she infuriated her colleagues: those who backed abolition and those who harboured considerable doubts. Equally, though, there is criticism of the tactics deployed by the doubters – the so-called 'Big Macs' – Tom McCabe, Henry McLeish and Jack

McConnell. Their line is that they argued in Cabinet against the timing, against the handling of the issue, and not against the substance of abolition. They voiced concern for the impact upon the average Labour family voter.

One insider told me that Section 28 was Donald Dewar's 'gays in the military'. On assuming the US Presidency, Bill Clinton had tried to end the formal ban on homosexuals serving in the armed forces. The policy provoked an outcry – arguably giving the Clinton administration a bad start for minimal measurable gain.

By this analysis, the timing of the Section 28 debate was wrong. Dewar and Alexander should have established their administration more securely, essayed a few populist measures first before turning to minority rights. Those taking this line say Dewar's Executive ended up with a 'siege mentality' because of Section 28.

Critics of that stance, though, say the administration would never have got round to abolishing Section 28 with such an attitude. They argue there is never a comfortable or convenient time to take on prejudice. There are differing opinions, too, on the impact of the alterations suggested by those who distrusted Alexander's approach. They insist that they were trying to make her policy work, that they were not trying to water it down, still less to block abolition. However, others say their attempts to 'make the policy work' amounted to guidelines to schools which might have ended up effectively reintroducing Section 28 by another avenue. The Health Minister Susan Deacon told one Cabinet meeting: 'The *Daily Record* doesn't run this country and we mustn't give the impression that it does.' Her comment was immediately leaked to the *Record*.

Brian Souter's campaign, Keep the Clause, ran hard and effectively. They organised a ballot, delivering 3,652,602 voting papers to the citizenry of Scotland. Of those returned, 1,094,440 wanted to retain Section 28 while 166,406 wanted to scrap it. It should be said the abolitionists had, ultimately, advocated abstention.

The result was declared at a packed news conference in Edinburgh's Balmoral Hotel. Souter stood in his customary open-necked shirt and voiced his vigorous opposition to the Executive's planned reform. 'We didnae vote for it and we're no' havin' it!', he stamped. It was a magnificent and forceful soundbite – even if it did cause one or two to wonder just who had elected Brian Souter as the nation's moral guardian.

At the same time, the late Cardinal Thomas Winning of the Roman Catholic Church was similarly outspoken: in defence of family values or in open hostility to homosexuals, according to your standpoint.

Indeed, both took their comments a stage further. Keep the Clause activists appeared to be on the verge of forming a wider movement, a Scottish Moral Majority, perhaps. The Cardinal, I believe rather rashly, extended his particular criticism of Section 28 into condemning the Parliament as 'an utter failure' in general, despite his long history of support for devolution. The political advocates of abolition looked and sounded lost. They did not appear to know how to handle either of their principal critics. Occasionally, there would be unwise mutterings that Brian Souter should stick to his transport business. It is never sensible to attempt to counter an opponent, particularly a feisty opponent with apparent popular support, by questioning his right to speak out. Few dared attempt a similar tactic with the Cardinal. Instead, Executive Ministers talked about the intolerance and prejudice inherent in Section 28. They havered about the safeguards which would be built into school education while getting into a guddle over whether these would be statutory or voluntary.

It was, frankly, too late for such legalistic reassurances. By then, a significant section of the population had concluded – or been persuaded to conclude – that something vaguely dodgy was afoot. There was no ground of common knowledge, common perceptions, upon which compromise could be based.

The core difficulty, I think, was that abolition of Section 28 was a badge that Labour activists had worn for more than a decade, since the law was first instituted by the Conservative government at Westminster in 1986. Those Labour activists were now Ministers in Dewar's Cabinet. For them, it was a given, a standard, something the Labour movement would get round to in due course. They did not feel the need to evangelise for abolition. Didn't everyone agree that Section 28 was intolerant and prejudiced? Certainly, all their friends and associates did. The snag was that the vast bulk of the population had never even heard of Section 28 until its abolition was proposed. They did not know it existed, they had never contemplated invoking it in their schools. They knew nothing about it.

Abolition brought it to their attention. Abolition made them think about the issue for the first time. Confronted abruptly in this fashion, they reacted defensively and with hostility. Arguably, the issue played a part in Labour's defeat by the Tories in the Ayr by-election on 16 March 2000. This is not to say abolition could have been 'sold' to the public by preparation. Many would have remained sceptical or hostile. Several of Wendy Alexander's colleagues, however, believe that the ground should have been better prepared. To be fair, others think that the row was unavoidable, that Scotland needed to confront its own moral dilemma.

In the end, the issue was settled by sense and Sam Galbraith. His folksy populism – 'Trust me, I'm a dad' – perhaps tried the patience a little. Maybe, though, it was time that the Executive sounded as if it at least understood parental fears, however much it felt those were misplaced. Equally, sources inside Souter's Keep the Clause campaign partly blame Galbraith for resisting a compromise at an earlier stage. They say they sent signals to the Executive that a deal was possible, which is confirmed by Cabinet sources. Galbraith's supporters say he was adamant that the Executive should not simply give way, however tempting the prospect of ending a damaging row.

I believe that timing was critical: that this was a clash of cultures, that a pragmatic deal was simply not possible until every aspect had been minutely examined, until the two combatants slumped together like two exhausted boxers, all fight gone. Importantly, Galbraith backed up his appeals for principled trust with solid, practical action. His Education Department endorsed new guidance to schools on sex education. A legal 'hook' was devised to make the guidance mandatory.

Finally, on 16 June 2000 – after five months of vitriolic conflict – the issue was deflated when Galbraith announced that the aims of sex education should 'include the responsibilities of parenthood and marriage'. Keep the Clause gave this a cautious welcome, and subsided. Both sides were intellectually and emotionally exhausted. The row was over.

By now, this chapter makes it sound as if Donald Dewar's administration staggered from one crisis to another. To a certain extent, his tenure as First Minister – tragically cut short – did feel a little like that at the time. The highlights were closely pursued by low notes. However, that would be an incomplete impression to leave. Donald

Dewar's friends and colleagues would point to a record of achieve-
ment by his coalition executive, a record often drowned out by the
cacophony of political conflict. Certainly, not every objective was
attained. There were Bills delayed, such as land reform. There were
measures only partly fulfilled and measures deferred. Critics would
point to gaps.

But friends would point to the expansion of the nursery school
sector, to the establishment of a drug-enforcement agency, to the
scrapping of upfront student tuition fees, to the new health promotion fund, to the new help for carers, to the new social justice
strategy, to the extra assistance for rough sleepers, to the new code
for local councils and to the law abolishing feudal tenure.

Dewar, however, cannot be counted simply by a sum of parts. He
was not, like other politicians, merely a litany of legislation and
initiatives, tediously repeated. His place in history, his assured place
in Scottish history, will not depend upon the soundbite of everyday
politics nor the fury which accompanied Section 28. Rather, he
will be remembered as the political leader who, more than any
other, brought the new Scottish Parliament into being. He will be
remembered too as the leader who cajoled that Parliament through
its extremely difficult transitional phase from Westminster control to
shared power: a period Dewar himself ironically understated as
'towsy'.

Perhaps above all he should be remembered as a political and
personal character. When he died, when his life support machine
was switched off on 11 October 2000, at eighteen minutes past
twelve, I was quickly on air offering a televised appraisal. To the
credit of my BBC Scotland bosses, we tore up the television
schedule and stayed with the story, the dignified, emotive
announcement by David Whitton, the reaction, the grief.

Displaying the paranoia which attaches itself to most broadcasters,
I was anxious that I was sounding just a little *too* effusive, just a little
too chummy. Even at moments of tragedy, political journalists are
aware of tone, of the need to maintain a certain distance. During
brief breaks, I asked colleagues: 'Is this okay? Does it sound okay?'
They assured me the tone was fine. Then I thought: 'Damn it all, I
did admire Donald Dewar as a person. I'm going to say what I like.
I'm going to describe the man I knew.' Scotland's first, First Minister
was a charming individual who inspired warm affection across a

wide range of Scottish society. He could also be an utter pest, on occasion, but equally, he built a very Scottish reputation for his determination to remain underwhelmed. Nothing was permitted to stir an extravagant response. We all know the caricature, the Scot resigned to setbacks who will bask in the sunshine, discern a tiny cloud in the distance and observe: 'Aye, looks like rain.'

Dewar's party colleagues became accustomed to operating according to the law of inverse responses. If Donald appeared glum, things were generally okay, and trundling along. If he was bestowing smiles on one and all, start worrying. Dewar, of course, was considerably more complex than this whimsical rule of thumb would indicate.

His wit could be satirical and his conversation, occasionally, even a little hurtful. He could appear oblivious to the reaction he sometimes provoked. I once sat behind him at a wedding ceremony during which – there is no other word for it – he heckled under his breath, apparently disinclined to make concessions to solemnity.

Equally, though, I have watched him evince the most genuine concern for colleagues, or indeed for strangers encountered in the course of political canvassing. Dewar did not press the flesh with a fixed, televisual grin. Indeed, he cordially loathed photo-calls, particularly when they forced him into an uncomfortable environment. On one occasion, I caught him staring with undisguised horror at a dumper truck which an eager PR officer suggested he might care to steer.

Dewar's manner – his occasional abruptness in both social and political life – was, I feel certain, at least partly a defence mechanism, forestalling high expectations for fear, presumably, of subsequent disappointment. He had suffered deep, personal sadness himself: his wife Alison, mother of his two children, left him for Derry Irvine, later to become Lord Chancellor in Tony Blair's government. Yet, at the same time, he could be charming company both at public events and in the society of close friends. He was highly intelligent, extremely well read, extremely witty and with a range of observation and understanding far beyond the narrow party focus occupied by so many in politics. Dewar was a character, forged by his easily tolerable foibles. He was a quite remarkable blend: a professed pessimist, perhaps, without remotely being a misanthropist. An admirer of humanity, alert to its faults.

Most in the Labour Party were ardent Dewar fans. A few privately called him 'Big Donald', a deliberate parody of a casual, back-slapping approach, which, of course, sat ill with the restrained recipient. Some, however, felt that he was out of touch with the party's roots: with the trades union and council bedrock. They found his more arcane pronouncements irritating. More fool them, say I. Scotland has had no shortage of political parrots, spitting out tedious twaddle as if it were revealed gospel. Scotland's drone reservoir shows no sign of exhaustion.

Dewar was not remotely the model of a modern political leader. For one thing, he defied the categorisation which seems to be obligatory in these simplistic, pigeon-holed times. Try thinking of him as New Labour or as Old Labour and discover how futile the endeavour is. Learning a little about Donald Dewar is, however, a dangerous thing. The caricature says he was utterly uncomfortable in leisure mode. Certainly, one wicked newspaper diarist once offered a prize for the first authenticated sighting of Dewar incontestably on vacation and demonstrably enjoying himself. As far as I am aware, the reward went unclaimed. D. Dewar was not the wow of the beachside karaoke set.

He could, however, relax. Along with other journalists, I accompanied him on a trip to Barcelona, where he held talks with Jordi Pujol, the political leader of Catalonia. The serious business done, we gathered in the ancient courtyard of Pujol's HQ, sipping cava – the Catalan answer to champagne – under the gently waving orange trees. Dewar seemed and sounded decidedly content, a man reborn, a man who had concluded there is more to life than checking the minutes of the Constitutional Convention.

This was a man who looked ascetic but had a healthy appetite, an art-loving solicitor who, nonetheless, had a keen and genuine interest in football. Some even claimed to see him as a species of brooding romantic, a Kelvinside Heathcliff.

A keen sense of the absurd and a reluctance to appear overblown perhaps prevented him from being a stunning party conference orator. He always appeared to draw back from the fatuous phrase which seems necessary to stir the political blood of the contemporary, undiscriminating audience. By contrast, he was an excellent debater, alert to sharp cross-party exchanges, and a brilliant after-dinner speaker, with comic timing which would not have disgraced Les Dawson. In a mock mournful voice, he would describe, for example, sharing a Commons office with a newly elected MP, one Tony Blair. The youthful Blair was, apparently, wont to burst in and yell excitedly: 'Morning, DD,' to the anguish of his less effervescent colleague.

Born on 21 August 1937, Donald Dewar first demonstrated his wit and discursive skills in the student debating chamber at Glasgow University; the academic home of John Smith, Menzies Campbell, John Mackay and Charles Kennedy among many others. He had previously attended Glasgow Academy.

Dewar was MP for the notoriously marginal Westminster seat of South Aberdeen from 1966 to 1970. He returned to the Commons via the Glasgow Garscadden by-election of 1978. He became Scottish Secretary after the 1997 General Election and then, of course, opted to continue his career through the Scottish Parliament. On Thursday, 13 May 1999, he was elected First Minister.

Dewar could appear unworldly, either inadvertently or by deliberate contrivance. He once asked Michael Connarty – a fellow MP with a distinctly neat hairstyle – how he achieved his remarkable coiffure. Connarty said he used mousse. 'But', said Dewar, 'isn't mousse something you eat?'

He was a modern-day Manichean, a combination of contradictions. Perhaps that was fitting in a party which has historically swithered over its attitude to Scottish self-government. For Labour – even the Scottish party that Dewar led – is not an instinctive party of devolution, as we shall discuss later. Dewar's commitment to the cause of Scottish self-government, however, was unwavering and undimmed by the years of frustrated failure. He advocated devolution when it was virtually a fringe pursuit within the Labour Party. He helped form detailed plans for reform. He was the UK Minister who legislated for that reform. He was the First Minister who led the newly devolved administration.

On 25 April 2000, he entered hospital for cardiac tests. On 8 May, he had an operation to replace a leaky aortic valve. On 17 May, he left hospital for his Glasgow home. On 14 August, he returned formally to work, having immersed himself in government papers while at home.

On 10 October, he was taken ill again, falling outside Bute House. He suffered a brain haemorrhage. The following day, he died, his daughter and son by his hospital bedside. His memorial

Scotland's grief: the crowd at Donald Dewar's funeral.

service on 18 October in Glasgow Cathedral was like the man himself, deeply Scottish and a magnificent blend of solemnity and humour.

BBC Scotland relayed coverage of the service to the whole of the UK. Few who were there – or who watched that television coverage – will easily forget: the family, bowed, in the front pew of the large, medieval cathedral; the rows of politicians from every party; Gordon Brown's soaring tribute; Ruth Wishart's wit; the service itself, uplifting yet still and gentle. For myself, I remember mostly the crowds of people outside the Cathedral. The children, a little bemused yet suitably solemn. The elderly woman who stood for nearly an hour, her head tilted forward in silent prayer. She knew little, I would imagine, of Donald Dewar's foibles nor the internal machinations of politics. She had come to mourn a good man gone.

After his death, it became common practice to use a description which, I feel sure, he would have cordially loathed. I shall, however, try it out again. Donald Dewar was the father of devolution. What was that? Just what *was* that loud, chortling snort of disdain?

2 The Succession Battle

Donald Dewar's death slowed and quietened the nation. For Scotland's Cabinet, the impact was more immediate, more direct. Driven by the relentless momentum of government, they were obliged to meet on the day the First Minister died. They gathered in St Andrew's House, mute, emotionally exhausted, mourning. Mumbled words, clasped hands. Equally, though, they knew government must continue, they knew they had to confirm Jim Wallace's deputising role, they knew the law provided just twenty-eight days in which to elect a new First Minister. So, inevitably, insidiously, one or two meandering thoughts of the succession drifted into the distraught tumulus of grief.

This was Wednesday, 11 October 2000, the day the First Minister was declared dead, the day his life-support machine was switched off. Ten minutes before that tragic event was formally announced, Labour MSPs were simultaneously paged with the news. However, several senior politicians had known the night before that Donald Dewar's brain haemorrhage would prove fatal. I had known as much myself and had adapted our broadcast news coverage and preparations accordingly. Our viewers and listeners were told the gravity of the situation. However, I did not want my reports – or those of my colleagues – to pre-empt death itself. My customary cool dispersed,

I recall bustling about the BBC newsroom late on the night of the 10th, yelling 'present tense, present tense' to no-one in particular. By that I meant reports should say: 'Donald Dewar *is* . . .' and not 'Donald Dewar *was* . . .'

The future tense also intruded at the margins, for me and for Ministers. So, when the Cabinet gathered on the 11th, the succession was beginning to surface for some. It was not remotely on the agenda. It was not openly discussed, even briefly. However, it was there. In researching this book, I have frequently felt like the mysterious detective in J. B. Priestley's play, *An Inspector Calls*. Like him, I found that different people remember the same event in different ways. It depends upon their perspective, it depends upon what mattered to them. So one source told me it was obvious on the 11th that there had been 'heavy work overnight' to guarantee the succession for Henry McLeish. The source told me that the immediate line was that there should be no contest. I was told it was even suggested that Dewar had implied, days earlier, that he favoured McLeish to succeed him.

Others have a different memory. They concede that there was a London-backed, heavyweight push for McLeish, but they question whether it emerged as quickly as overnight. And they dispute that Dewar was ever cited as favouring McLeish. One source told me: 'Donald favoured none of them. Certainly not Henry – and he dreaded the prospect of Jack succeeding him.' The same source claimed that, in Labour circles, the earliest response emerged from the McConnell camp. I was told: 'Their carefully planned strategy had been blown away by Donald's death. They knew that it was too early for them. Jack didn't hide it very well.' McConnell's supporters, of course, counter that depiction vigorously.

As a detached observer, I think it certain that both of the main contenders were weighing up their prospects from an early stage. They would scarcely be human if the thought did not cross their minds. However, there was no question of an all-out leadership contest before the nation had paid its tribute to the late First Minister.

Indeed, several influential figures made plain that they did not want a contest at all. There were efforts – encouraged by Gordon Brown and others – to anoint McLeish, to settle the succession smoothly upon the most experienced Minister. There was pressure on other potential contenders, notably McConnell, to stand aside.

Gordon Brown retains an extremely close interest in Scottish politics. He is, after all, a Scot with a Scottish constituency. Scotland is one of the key powerbases that the Chancellor nurtures carefully. He intervened directly to bolster Labour's campaign in the 1999 Scottish elections. To listen to some, he twitches every single string, he manipulates every lever. Every development, certainly every Scottish Labour development, is credited by some, sooner or later, to the Chancellor. However, I feel this can be exaggerated somewhat. I suspect there may, just, have been one or two Scottish political decisions which were not taken personally by Gordon Brown. Perhaps he was busy at the Treasury those days.

Certainly, though, he had three big reasons for trying to influence the Scottish leadership. For one, as outlined above, he has a considerable personal and political stake in Scottish Labour. Problems in his 'home patch' can impact upon his UK standing, only fractionally, but fractions matter. Second, Brown likes to keep his friends close – and Henry McLeish is a friend, a political neighbour of the Chancellor in Fife where local loyalties matter. Third, the Chancellor deeply distrusts Jack McConnell. As one source put it: 'Gordon hates Jack with a vengeance.'

This mistrust has an obvious impact on contemporary relationships between the Executive and Downing Street, and I intend to look at that later. For now, though, it is enough to note: Gordon wanted Henry, and Gordon definitely did not want Jack. That message was plainly conveyed to key Labour opinion formers like the *Daily Record*.

Others played their part. As Scottish Secretary at the time, John Reid was in a central position to influence events. Other than Brown, he was the ranking Labour politician in Scotland outside the Executive; he was free to cajole but ruled out, as a Westminster politician, from becoming First Minister himself. He was instrumental in devising the truncated procedure whereby a party vote was possible within the 28-day legal deadline.

Tom McCabe – Dewar's trusted fixer-in-chief – spoke to McConnell directly and urged him not to stand, arguing that the party needed unity. McConnell listened, but heeded his own advisers and his own instinct. He decided to stand. He lost narrowly but, a year later, his boldness was rewarded when he was in prime position to succeed McLeish.

This leaves us with another question. Did Donald Dewar have a chosen successor in mind? From my own impressions and from speaking to a number of insiders, I think not, or at least not from among the ranks of immediate contenders. Naturally, he anticipated that the principal challengers – if it came to a choice – might well be McLeish and McConnell. Dewar, apparently, told one Cabinet colleague: 'In a straight choice between Henry and Jack, I'd opt for Henry – and I can't stand Henry!' Another said that, particularly after he became ill, Dewar sought to persuade Sam Galbraith to consider putting himself forward, to provide a sense of continuity. Galbraith, we know, declined.

More than one source suggested to me that Dewar really wanted to skip a generation, to look for a leader from Jackie Baillie or Wendy Alexander or Susan Deacon or Angus Mackay or Iain Gray. I think that analysis is accurate but, of course, tragic circumstance dictated that Dewar never had the time to groom a potential successor. Quite probably, he did not want to. Few leaders welcome the prospect of considering seriously their own departure from the scene.

The succession had long been pondered, privately and sometimes not so privately. The formal campaign, when it came, lasted less than

'A word in your ear': Henry McLeish, after his election as First Minister, with his rival for the post, Jack McConnell.

three days. Donald Dewar's funeral was on Wednesday, 18 October. McLeish and McConnell declared they were standing the following day, Thursday. The vote was on Saturday, 21 October. McLeish won by 44 votes to 36, a majority of 8.

Strictly speaking, Henry McLeish was elected interim leader that Saturday. This was a short-cut vote, to meet the tight Parliamentary timetable. Only Labour MSPs and the 27 members of the party's Executive Committee were entitled to vote at this stage. It was due to be ratified later in a wider ballot. Everyone knew, however, that this was purely a device. Certainly, Jack McConnell recognised that. He withdrew from the race after this 'interim' contest.

Henry McLeish, then, was Labour's candidate for First Minister. That narrow victory, though, was to pose him problems. Ostensibly, he had virtually uniform support among existing Ministers. Frank McAveety swithered, finally opted for McConnell – and was later sacked as a consequence.

The ministerial support, however, partly reflected the momentum behind the McLeish campaign. Ministers thought that experience and big-name backing meant McLeish was going to win and, with careers to protect, they did not want to be on the losing side. More than one Minister has told me privately they thought then – and they think now – that McConnell is the more capable politician.

There were also Ministers who mistrusted McConnell. Much of this mistrust, as we shall discuss later, can be traced back to his period as a high-profile General Secretary at Scottish party headquarters. Running a party machine, especially one as intricate and stubbornly resistant as the Labour Party, is scarcely the way to win friends.

So, one way or another, Henry McLeish had the backing of Scottish Ministers, but it scarcely amounted to a complete, personal endorsement. McLeish had firm, committed adherents, but he also had declared support from those who wanted to stop McConnell and those who simply wanted to back the likely winner. This was practical politics, not adulation. At the same time, the numbers indicated that the back benches of the Parliamentary party contained a phalanx of McConnell supporters. That factor, brought into the open by the election, was to prove a standing problem for Henry McLeish.

McLeish's supporters from the time are adamant that he would have won comfortably had the full ballot, involving party members and unions, been held. They say McConnell would have had very little union support. They say this would have entrenched McLeish more firmly from the start. McConnell's team dispute the arithmetic, but, frankly, it scarcely matters. What counted in terms of day-to-day politics for the new First Minister was the endorsement of the Parliamentary party.

Henry McLeish had won but it was not a comfortable victory, it was not decisive. Jack McConnell gallantly raised his rival's arm in the Stirling council chambers that Saturday, and delivered a beatific, McConnell smile, not the fixed smile of defeat but the delicious grin of anticipation. Scottish Labour had now acquired a new king and a crown prince in the same ballot.

So began Henry McLeish's year in office as First Minister. It was a year, frankly, characterised by trauma. Much of that can be sourced to the novelty of the institution, to a body politic still suffering birth pains. However, much of it must also be traced to Henry McLeish.

His period as First Minister may be remembered for the battle over free personal care for the elderly. It may be remembered for his verbal mishaps, the 'McLeishés' lampooned by the press. It may be remembered for his determination to secure a higher profile for Scotland, within the UK and internationally. For myself, I picture a First Minister who palpably lacked confidence in the job. This will come as no great shock to those who think of his nervous cough, or his occasional facial twitch. As his term in office progressed, he had begun to conquer these outward signs of inward stress. The cough and the twitch returned after his fall.

So it will surprise no-one when I say that Henry McLeish was under strain. I believe, however, that less attention has been paid to the possible cause of his underlying anxiety. It was not purely the pressure of external events, the stresses of life which we all endure, to varying degree. The First Minister doubted, intrinsically, that he was up to the task. I well recall a slightly surreal conversation with Henry McLeish, not long after he became First Minister. He was weighed down with the challenge of succeeding Donald Dewar, a mega-bright politician of huge standing. He bemoaned the fact that he was surrounded by highly intellectual civil servants like Muir Russell and Robert Gordon, each with a string of academic and professional qualifications.

Rather diffidently, I attempted to assuage the blues which had evidently gripped the First Minister that night. I argued that Jim Callaghan had felt no such insecurity, surrounded as he was by Whitehall mandarins of the highest intellect and by polymath Cabinet colleagues like Michael Foot and Denis Healey. The boss was the boss and nothing else mattered. The First Minister would not be swayed. He felt – there is no other word – inferior. He felt he was out of his depth. Maybe he was particularly down that evening. Perhaps it had been an especially bad day, perhaps he had a tough policy question on his mind that he could not immediately share with me.

I believe, however, that this was a core and lasting problem. Henry McLeish lacked the intellectual and psychological confidence necessary to move to the top job. Whether he might have built up that confidence, given time and a slightly fairer wind, is open to argument. What is certain is that he struggled in the transition from Cabinet Minister to Cabinet leader. As Enterprise Minister, he had appeared calm, tackling chamber questions seemingly without notes, exchanging witticisms and pleasantries with his SNP opposite number, John Swinney. As First Minister, he stumbled and mumbled from the start. He gripped his briefing papers at the despatch box and mangled his replies.

His colleagues, with some exceptions, are privately blunt in their assessment of McLeish. One told me: 'He simply wasn't up to the number one job – and it showed.' Another said: 'He was promoted one rung too high.' Indeed, that is a view that is widely shared. Another said, acidly, that they had expected McLeish to 'smile and open the factories' while the remainder of the Cabinet got on with the work. In the event, this source said, the First Minister's grasp of the job was 'atrocious'.

Henry McLeish readily concedes that the opening period of his tenure as First Minister was poor, marred by unnecessary conflicts, such as the silly row over whether Labour backbenchers would have access to civil servants. McLeish had suggested they might but this was later 'clarified' – or, in other words, completely overturned to stress that paid public servants worked for the Executive not the party.

He believes, however, that he was not given a fair run by the press nor by colleagues at Westminster, including those who still resented devolution. The McLeish view is that he sought an ambitiously high profile for the Parliament and the Executive, and that he was slapped down as a consequence. There is, certainly, some evidence to support that. On 9 January 2001, at a media briefing in St Andrew's House, Tom McCabe hinted that the Executive might prefer to be known in future as 'the government'. It was only a hint but it emerged later that it had the firm backing of the First Minister, that this was a strategy rather than an unguarded remark. The Westminster response was vitriolic. Residual bile, previously choked back, poured out from politicians who made plain that there was only one 'government', that the Edinburgh administration was but a pale shadow, a mechanistic subset of Downing Street. 'They can call themselves the White Heather Club,' one Minister testily told the press. Real government resided elsewhere.

Others poured scorn upon McLeish personally. In one comment given to the press, he was said to be 'thick and friendless'. Not surprisingly, McLeish found that comment particularly hurtful. Given his own self-doubts, he needed external defence and bolstering. He got exactly the opposite.

After three days, McLeish ended the row over nomenclature by declaring in the chamber: 'We *are* a government.' Note that indefinite article, 'a' not 'the'. He told MSPs he had discussed the controversy with the Prime Minister, who was decidedly relaxed about the issue. A year later, Jack McConnell spoke of his 'government' without the faintest blush or fuss. Perhaps, just perhaps, this row was part of Holyrood's maturing process. Certainly, it is fair to say that Henry McLeish attempted to advance the agenda of devolution, to offer a bolder approach than Donald Dewar. Arguably, he extended the reach of the devolved Parliament and Executive, entrenching its status under the gaze of Westminster's permanently anxious eye.

His vision was plainly stated. In one speech, he said he wanted 'a confident Scotland – confident in its future, confident in its constitutional relations, confident in its own capacities.'[1] He wanted further 'a compassionate Scotland – a fair and caring and tolerant Scotland, where everyone matters. A competitive Scotland – taking tough decisions for the long term, spending money wisely, building an economy to compete in global matters.' To achieve these objectives, he said in the same speech that 'what matters is what works', adding that 'in any conflict between pragmatism and ideology, pragmatism will always prevail'.

McLeish's loyalty was unquestionably to the 'project', to the new institution. He was incontestably a post-devolution First Minister. He sought to make devolution work in the interests of Scotland and believed, with some justification, that it was necessary to challenge Westminster and Whitehall power to achieve that aim. To borrow a phrase from the SNP, he stood for Scotland.

He is also a pleasant, decent man. Born in Methil in Fife in 1948, he played professional football with East Fife, plus a brief stint as a youth at Leeds United. He then studied at Heriot Watt University, qualifying to work as a local authority planning officer. His political career followed the classic path of talent and ambition: councillor, council leader, MP, Minister. In 1999 he was one of the Westminster team who opted for Holyrood, joining Donald Dewar's Cabinet.

However, he struggled as First Minister. One sympathetic Scottish Minister told me that Cabinet colleagues had let Henry McLeish down. They should have seen his isolation, the challenge he was facing, and rallied round much more supportively. Instead, the Cabinet was focused upon inter-departmental policy rows and factional conflict.

Others are much less forgiving. They say that McLeish undermined any claim for support by regularly leaking to the press, as Enterprise Minister and as First Minister. One said he was 'congenitally incapable' of keeping things to himself – and that this infuriated colleagues. This analysis would appear to be borne out by Peter McMahon, McLeish's press adviser, in the series of articles he wrote for *The Scotsman*. In one, McMahon writes of McLeish: 'He had made his way throughout his time in politics by feeding stories and it seemed almost like a drug to him.'[2]

More seriously, several senior sources say that McLeish was unwilling to address controversy, to close issues down. He would give the impression that he agreed or sympathised with the person to whom he was talking at the time. The result was confusion, with the Cabinet and civil servants uncertain what had been decided, what line to pursue. Insiders say this was the most common source of frustration, and argue that it is the key difference between McLeish and Scotland's other First Ministers. Dewar perhaps took his time, but he was focused and, ultimately, decisive. McConnell is the boss. You may not always agree but you know exactly where you stand.

Henry McLeish and Wendy Alexander sort out the line to take
in the row over his Cabinet reshuffle.

By contrast, one source after another told me that McLeish would dodge conflict. He would skate over tricky issues in Cabinet, suggesting that they could be sorted out later, between the principal combatants. Without leadership from the top, without open, hard–edged discussion, such issues tendered to fester rather than be resolved. One senior insider told me: 'Henry would avoid conversations that involved conflict. This was a serious flaw. He would simply walk away.' Another was more brutal still, noting that 'Henry tended to bear the imprint of the last backside that sat upon him.'

Several point to the episode in March 2001 when McLeish had to reshuffle his Cabinet team after Sam Galbraith stood down. He had wanted to transfer responsibility for the politically sensitive water industry to Wendy Alexander. Indeed, McLeish apparently thought that the deal was done. He authorised his press spokesman Peter McMahon to inform journalists of this decision at the daily briefing for the media held in the Government Room above the chamber on the Mound.

Wendy Alexander, however, had a different take on events. She did not accept she had agreed to take the new portfolio. She thought she had enough in her ministerial briefcase without taking on water. According to one Minister, she 'went ballistic, phoning everybody in protest, including the Chancellor'.

McMahon's account[3] is that 'British politics almost ground to a halt' as Alexander pursued her grievance, volubly. McLeish gave in, considerably undermining his authority, according to McMahon. Certainly, other sources say he seemed nervous and unsure when he confessed to colleagues that he had let Wendy Alexander have her way. One Minister told me: 'That episode was the beginning of the end for Henry, he had lost credibility and shown himself to be weak.'

Politics and controversy are permanent companions – and Henry McLeish's year as First Minister was no exception. There was the foot and mouth outbreak, the row over road maintenance contracts, the dispute over fisheries, the 'cull' of quangos, the efforts to prevent further problems with school exams, standing conflict over health care, measures to contain sectarianism, and more, much more. It was the year, above all, of the terrorist attack on the World Trade Center and the Pentagon. It was the year of the UK General Election and a second, successive landslide victory for Tony Blair. Inevitably, all this had significant consequences for Scotland and for Henry McLeish's governance.

However, the policy issue linked most firmly with Henry McLeish is smaller in scale than such UK and global events. It is an issue where, I believe, he contrived to show both his inherent strength and his weakness. That is the issue of free personal care for the elderly. To recap, the expert committee chaired by Sir Stewart (now Lord) Sutherland, then Principal of Edinburgh University, had suggested in March 1999 that frail elderly people should not have to pay if they needed help with personal tasks such as washing themselves. Such assistance should be equated with nursing care. It should be provided free, regardless of income or savings, in the interests of dignity and equity.

The Sutherland Committee reported to Westminster, but devolution meant that responsibility for this issue in Scotland rested with the Scottish Executive and Parliament. North and south of the border, however, the initial response was comparable. Tony Blair's government in London decided that the cost of the full Sutherland package was prohibitive. They introduced various measures but not free personal care. Donald Dewar's Executive took broadly the same line. Free personal care could not be afforded. It would have to wait.

Enter Henry McLeish. Virtually upon taking office as First Minister in October 2000, McLeish indicated that he was minded to think again. He made plain that he expected this rethink to feature in the review of policy which Cabinet members were to undertake. One colleague, speculating about McLeish's motivation, told me: 'Cherchez la femme.' I was invited to conclude that the First Minister was heavily influenced by his wife Julie, a senior social worker specialising in the care of the elderly.

Certainly, Henry McLeish adores, idolises and trusts his wife – and I feel sure that is a substantial element of the story. However, I also believe that McLeish instinctively felt free personal care to be right, to be humane. Further, I am sure he was tempted at least in part by the notion of developing a distinctive policy. He wanted to do something that Westminster would not do, that Donald Dewar had not done. He wanted to make his mark. Such a motivation is far from dishonourable, especially when in pursuit of providing assistance to the weaker members of society. Colleagues did not question his motives. They did, however, question his methods and the outcome of the policy.

McLeish can be an instinctive politician. Look at his 'gut feeling' bid for Scotland to host golf's Ryder Cup. Look at his stance, too, on Euro 2008. Had McLeish still been First Minister, Scotland would have been bidding for the football tournament alone, not in partnership with Ireland. That does not make his style better or worse: it makes it different. The positive side of such an approach is an ability to look beyond the balance sheet, to seize the moment. One supporter insists that the Glasgow housing stock transfer, among the most radical plans pursued by the Executive, is down to McLeish, that he pushed ahead instinctively when the financial figures were incomplete. It should be said that others dispute the extent of his involvement.

Earlier, as Minister for Enterprise and Lifelong Learning, he sliced through the endless numerical haggling to cut a deal with the Liberal Democrats over the abolition of upfront tuition fees and the reform of student finance. One insider said: 'There was a key moment when Henry just looked up and said, "Okay, we're doing this."'

There is, however, a negative side to intuitive politics, and it came sharply to the fore in the Cabinet's bitter internal debate over free personal care. First, critics say McLeish was inclined to slide over the problems, to decline to confront the cost implications of the policy. Second, it is said that – in pursuit of his aims – he was not always entirely open with colleagues, that his stance varied.

Few in McLeish's Cabinet backed free personal care. These were, after all, virtually the same Ministers who had backed Dewar's line that the policy could not be afforded. Even the LibDems – who supported free care – had resigned themselves to sidelining the policy, at least in the interim.

For Labour Ministers, there were two objections. There were those who thought that it would be impossible to quantify the costs, that demand might increase exponentially, that the Cabinet might be signing a sizeable blank cheque. Frankly, some still hold that view, even now that the deal is done.

Second, there was a more fundamental issue. Personal care was previously means tested. That is, it was free to those of very limited means while those with earnings or savings above a certain level were obliged to pay. By definition, that meant that extending free personal care to all was helping those who were already relatively – I stress, relatively – well off. For those on the Left, it seemed like an unwarranted subsidy for the middle class.

In Cabinet, the Health Minister Susan Deacon was opposed to McLeish's policy. She could see the appeal of the case which had been made by the Sutherland Committee and she acknowledged that, in ideal circumstances, such care should be freely available. She agreed to review the position, but she believed that McLeish's policy was not a prudent use of limited resources. She opposed the policy at all points.

Indeed, all the Labour Ministers shared her reservations to varying degrees. Some were more persuaded by the Sutherland Report. Some were more inclined to give ground to the First Minister. Virtually no-one on the Labour side acclaimed the policy without reservation. At the same time, there was almost complete hostility to the move from Westminster and Whitehall.

McLeish came under persistent pressure from the Treasury and from Alistair Darling at social security to back down. Supporters of the First Minister say this opposition derived from two motives: one, that London was worried it would be obliged to follow suit, facing the expense of providing free personal care for England; and, two, that there was still a residual feeling in Whitehall that Scotland had a cheek devising its own policies. One source told me that, when McLeish persisted, the Treasury threatened to re-examine the extent of the funding available to Scotland. If the Scottish Executive could even contemplate free personal care, it plainly had too much disposable cash.

The pressure on McLeish, then, was enormous, but he stood his ground, courageously or foolishly, according to your view of the policy. He had one ace – and it was the same factor which had featured in the earlier debate over tuition fees.

The Liberal Democrats backed free personal care. So did the Nationalists. So did the Scottish Tories – contrary to the position taken by the party in England. There was, in short, a majority for free personal care in the Scottish Parliament, even without Labour. It could be argued that Labour could either implement free personal care voluntarily – and take what credit was going – or have the policy foisted upon the party by the votes of others. Provoking such an outcome was, of course, not practical politics for McLeish. It would have infuriated the Labour group and left him politically isolated in his own party. However, it was the unstated, underlying reality. Labour was potentially outvoted.

This did not forestall sharp dispute in Cabinet. Indeed, Cabinet Ministers felt that McLeish was not playing entirely straight with them. They felt, at various times, that he was saying one thing to one Minister, with a markedly different version of events being relayed to another.

In particular, that impinged upon the coalition with the Liberal Democrats. They felt that they were not getting a full and accurate picture of the Labour perspective. They felt, to be blunt, that McLeish was not being honest with them. As the internal Cabinet row reached crisis point, the Liberal Democrats began to take detailed notes of what was being said on both sides. They apparently thought the coalition might break, and they wanted to have evidence ready to present their side of the story.

However, Labour Ministers also felt aggrieved. I was told that, on one occasion in Cabinet, Wendy Alexander effectively accused the First Minister of lying as she confronted him over the care question.

Others felt he dithered, that he was 'watery' as to the detailed content and implementation of the policy.

There was anger and residual discontent. However, the First Minister was determined. It is important to recall the context. Henry McLeish was under general attack. The free personal care debate came to a head shortly after the testing, if ludicrous, row over whether the Executive might call itself a government. McLeish needed a victory, and he saw that victory in helping Scotland's elderly.

He believed in the policy, passionately. He advanced the argument, consistently. In addition, though, he saw political and personal advantage. His Labour critics wanted him to back down. The press predicted he might well back down. By standing firm, he was able to confound both his internal and external opponents at one and the same time. For McLeish, this was too good an opportunity to miss.

In the end, it came down to hard political reality. McLeish was determined to implement free personal care. He had only been in office for three months: a new First Minister was unthinkable. Therefore, his Cabinet critics could either live with the policy or resign. Understandably, they chose to stay. Remember that the argument was over whether this policy was a suitable and sensible use of resources. No-one disputed that free personal care was, intrinsically, a good thing if it could be achieved without problems elsewhere. Cabinet Ministers do not generally resign in protest at intrinsically good things. Such gestures are inevitably a little difficult to explain to the voters.

Susan Deacon delivered a statement on Sutherland on Wednesday, 24 January. She had announced a £100 million package of assistance for the elderly the previous October. This time, she emphasised the priority attached to care of the elderly and detailed a series of initiatives, such as an improved assessment system and extra aid for dementia sufferers. But there were no firm words on free personal care.

Events moved exceptionally swiftly. The LibDems were unhappy with Deacon's statement and immediately tabled a motion calling for free personal care. It fell to the Nationalists to pick the topic for debate in Parliament the very next day, Thursday, the 25th. They adopted the LibDem motion.

On the eve of the debate, LibDem and Labour Ministers – with civil-service advisers – met in the fifth-floor government suite of offices at Parliamentary headquarters, the hideous modern block on George IV Bridge which has housed MSPs since the 1999 election. The aim was to reach a deal on the issue which would avoid an open split in the coalition in the coming Parliamentary debate. But the talks were tetchy – and, finally, at 11 o'clock the Liberal Democrats walked out, declaring that no further negotiation was possible.

According to LibDem insiders, the civil servants who were present naturally congregated around Labour, as if they, solely, were the government and in need of assistance while the LibDems were to be viewed as interlopers or opponents. This intensely angered the LibDems. The perceived slight was later resolved by a civil-service apology.

Inside the Liberal Democrat group itself, however, there was a further element provoking tension. Jim Wallace had previously tried to broker a deal, urging his colleagues to reflect upon the gravity of their stance, to consider the threat they were posing to the entire future of the coalition. At its most basic, he was aware that the policy of free personal care had only minority support in the Cabinet.

The LibDem group was having none of it. They insisted on a clear statement that free personal care would be implemented. Otherwise, they made plain they would vote with the Opposition parties and against the Executive. Wallace had no option but to advance that case to his Labour colleagues. Insiders stress he was well aware of the views of his group, but was determined to push the issue to the limits, to stress the seriousness of the dispute. That, then, was the background to the ministerial talks which ended in failure. The following morning, Thursday, 25 January, ahead of the debate, Henry McLeish phoned Jim Wallace personally and said: 'We've got to sort this out.' Frantic negotiations continued throughout the day.

If those talks were tense, then the debate itself was taut and passionate. Speaking from the back benches, Labour MSP Richard Simpson moved an amendment to the SNP/LibDem motion, accusing others of deliberating confusing the issue. In particular, he said the LibDems must 'accept the responsibilities and disciplines of government'. His phrasing and tone went down exceptionally badly on the Liberal Democrat benches. They felt they had expended endless energy trying to broker a responsible deal. With delicious irony, Richard Simpson later accepted the disciplines of government as deputy Justice Minister. His boss? Jim Wallace, the Liberal Democrat leader.

Susan Deacon delivered a powerful and impressive defence of her position. Her objective, she said, was better care for the elderly. Acknowledging the apparent attractiveness of free personal care, she went on: 'I do not want to tell someone that they will receive free personal care if I cannot have the confidence to say that the services are in place to deliver that care. I do not want to tell people that they are going to have free personal care if I cannot say when or how they will receive that care. I do not want to say to people that they will receive free personal care if the consequence of that promise is that other services may ultimately need to be cut.'

From her standpoint, it was a coherent, well-argued case. The issue, however, had moved on. The Liberal Democrats were now determined to secure free personal care. They had been tempted up the hill by Henry McLeish and were not disposed to slink down again without success.

LibDem backbencher Donald Gorrie wryly reminded Labour that the elementary Parliamentary arithmetic was against them when he said: 'I know that it is difficult for people who have been brought up in the Labour Party tradition to accept losing votes. I have spent my whole life losing votes. I have probably lost more votes than anyone in recorded history.' The debate closed just after noon, at 12.34. The vote, however, was not due until Decision Time at five o'clock, following the standard practice in the Scottish Parliament. The haggling and negotiations continued in the corridors around the chamber all day.

The formal subject for debate in the afternoon was finance, the Scottish budget. Frankly, attention was elsewhere. In the chair, the deputy Presiding Officer George Reid remarked acerbically that the debate could not be heard because of 'private conversations' in and around the chamber.

Those conversations were also, in a way, about finance, but they were rather more urgent than the exchanges on the chamber floor. For the coalition partners, this was raw politics: how to strike a deal on funding care for the elderly before that vote at five. With ten minutes to go before the vote was due to be held, there were furious points of order to the effect that the media had been tipped off about an impending Executive statement. (Quite right, we had.) Then there were further complaints that the information supposedly contained in the statement had not been brought before MSPs in the earlier debate. (Bogus point, the Executive's position had changed.)

Finally, Tom McCabe rose from his seat at seven minutes past five. It was plain that the Health Minister – who had criticised free personal care only a few hours previously – felt unable or unwilling to announce the U-turn in person. Struggling to be heard above the cheers and catcalls, McCabe announced that the Executive would bring forward 'as soon as practicable' proposals for the implementation of free personal care for all. He noted this would be 'accompanied by an analysis of the costs and implications of so doing', a phrase that was later picked apart for hidden meaning. The Liberal Democrats, however, were satisfied and were able to vote with their Labour colleagues. One LibDem MSP told me their cheers were utterly genuine: until that very last moment they had not been certain that sufficient agreement had been reached.

Alongside those cheers, though, there was some irritation at the manner of the deal. Keith Raffan resigned as LibDem health spokesman, arguing that the issue should have been openly settled within the Executive, rather than being fixed minutes before a key vote. One source suggested he was also frustrated at being cut out of the serious, off-stage talks.

MSPs headed out into the High Street, to be pestered there by people like me. There was, however, one more item of business. This was 25 January – Burns Night – and Tory MSP David Mundell had secured time for a brief debate to mark the birthday of the Bard. He imagined Robert Burns 'looking down with a roguish smile' on the Scottish Parliament and perhaps murmuring to himself:

> O wad some Pow'r the giftie gie us
> To see oursels as ithers see us.

But how will others see this episode? Free personal care has since been taken forward by Malcolm Chisholm, Deacon's successor as Health Minister. How will people judge Henry McLeish's determined pursuit of this policy? I imagine they will use McLeish's own nostrum: what matters is what works.

If free personal care works well, without biting too much into other sections of the budget, then Henry McLeish will be praised as far-sighted. If it goes awry and becomes a significant burden on the Scottish finances, without adequate return, then Henry McLeish will be condemned as stubborn and foolish. Either way – and regardless of his wider reputation – this forms part of his legacy.

Whitehall's opposition to free personal care has endured. One consequence of the new policy in Scotland is that people who receive the new assistance will in future be prevented from getting attendance allowance from the social-security budget administered by the Department of Work and Pensions. The money will have to be provided by the Executive.

The relevant Minister, Alistair Darling, has refused repeated requests to transfer the benefit cash, equivalent to some £20 million, to the Executive. To be fair, Darling has a point. It is part of the devolution settlement that Scotland must take the financial conse-quences of its own decisions. Darling argued that he was protecting the integrity of the UK benefits system. Equally, however, the polit-ical background meant that he was scarcely motivated to seek a solution.

The argument was hard-fought. One insider said Scottish civil servants cheered loudly as they listened into a telephone conversation, relayed by speaker, in which an Executive special adviser angrily berated a Whitehall counterpart over the refusal to transfer attendance allowance.

Some insiders believe that the Executive should have taken this to the wire, that they should have insisted upon implementing the Joint Ministerial Committee (JMC) structure which is precisely designed to resolve such disputes. One told me: 'If the JMC isn't used for this, what on earth is it for?' This would have brought together Ministers from London and Edinburgh in an effort to hammer out a deal.

By the time this particular issue arose, Jack McConnell was First Minister. He decided that it was not worth picking a fight that he was certain to lose: the Treasury were against him. Further, everyone knew that free personal care was associated with Henry McLeish. McConnell concluded that if he were to go head to head with Whitehall, it would be over an issue in which he had direct personal investment.

Henry McLeish, then, pushed through a significant change in the treatment of Scotland's elderly. He did so in the face of scepticism from Labour colleagues in his own Cabinet and hostility from members of the UK Cabinet. He persisted and survived, only to stumble and fall over the question of his own constituency office expenses.

Notes

1. Speech by the First Minister Henry McLeish, Glasgow University, 20 August 2001.
2. Article by Peter McMahon, *The Scotsman*, 25 January 2002.
3. Article by Peter McMahon, *The Scotsman*, 26 January 2002.

3 Officegate – Rent Must be Paid

Andrew Duncan is a man with a grievance. For twenty years, assisted latterly by his local MP, he pursued a property dispute relating to his house in Fife. The origin of the problem lay in feudal title – Scotland's ancient system of determining and registering land ownership. Such disputes were not uncommon. Many householders who tacked a loft bedroom onto their bungalow later found they should have obtained permission from – and paid a fee to – their feudal superior. The system has since been completely reformed by the Scottish Parliament. Mr Duncan's case was a little different. First, it was particularly long-running. Second, it led to the downfall of the First Minister.

Without going into detail, Andrew Duncan felt aggrieved, and believed that the actions of others had left him substantially out of pocket. He blamed his troubles on Fife Council and on the well-established law firm Digby Brown. They disagreed. As the row wore on, Mr Duncan continued to brief his MP, Henry McLeish.

Digby Brown are regarded as being close to the Labour Party on the grounds that much of their work is for trades union clients. One or two Labour politicians previously worked for them. The company has offices in Glasgow, Edinburgh and Dundee. This might have remained a local property dispute but for one discovery. In

For a while, the most photographed doorway in Scotland: Henry McLeish's Glenrothes office.

1998, Andrew Duncan learned that Digby Brown also had a small office in the Fife new town of Glenrothes. He immediately went to draw this to the attention of Henry McLeish at the MP's constituency office, 14 Hanover Court, Glenrothes.

As he entered the MP's office, he spotted a sign indicating a tenant on the premises. That was when he learned that Digby Brown, the law firm he regarded as his adversaries, did indeed have an office in Glenrothes. They leased it from Henry McLeish MP. Mr Duncan told me he was 'hopping mad'. He said he felt 'betrayed' that his MP had apparently helped him pursue a dispute involving Digby Brown while, at the same time, maintaining a link with the law firm. He told me: 'It all just made me want to dig, to find out what was going on.'

And so dig he did, assiduously. McLeish commented at one point that it was 'deeply regrettable' that a constituent he had tried to help 'for many years' should now seek to make an issue of his office arrangements. Mr Duncan was unimpressed and remains so now. He told me the MP had 'behaved badly' by failing to disclose his connection with Digby Brown. So, undeterred, the retired builder set out to investigate his MP's financial arrangements, learning subsequently that Fife Council had also been tenants of Henry McLeish for a spell. After further close inquiries, the story was eventually broken by the *Mail on Sunday* on 1 April 2001. By then, Henry McLeish was First Minister in the Scottish Parliament. He was, temporarily, an MSP as well as an MP.

The core issue was that while an MP, he had not declared the income from the sublets as he should have done under Commons rules. Henry McLeish responded. He approached Elizabeth Filkin, the Westminster Standards Commissioner, the following day. Then, acting upon advice, he added the income from the office sublets to his listing in the Members' Register of Interests.

McLeish hoped that was the end of the matter and, for a time, it seemed that he might be right. But the Tories at Westminster were pursuing the issue. Elizabeth Filkin, meanwhile, had referred the issue to the Commons Fees Office, which handles allowances for MPs. The issue lay largely dormant for some months until – on 23 October – McLeish confirmed that he was to pay £9,000 to the Fees Office in settlement. This was an agreed sum, out of his own pocket, intended to reflect the money that his office had raised from sublets without formal declaration. McLeish said the Fees Office regarded the matter as closed.

The Westminster system operated by allowing Honourable Members to claim an allowance, up to a maximum sum, for running an office in their constituency. The cash was to help them provide a local advice service and deal with constituents' problems. Henry McLeish became the MP for Central Fife in 1987. At that time, as he later explained, the maximum office allowance for Members was £21,302. He stepped down as an MP at the General Election in June 2001, to concentrate entirely on his work at Holyrood. By then, the allowance was £52,760.

McLeish later explained that he ran a particularly active constituency office, that he always spent beyond the maximum allowance.[1] The excess was covered by the money raised from renting out space on the upper floor of his office. At no time had he claimed any more than the fixed sum from the Commons. The public purse, in other words, had not been picked. At no time had the money from rent gone on anything other than office costs. It had been kept in a separate business account, with no financial gain to himself of any sort.

This latter point is open to a certain degree of quibbling. Arguably, an MP who runs a particularly active office does so in the hope that his constituents will reward him with re-election. It is not, therefore, entirely a selfless act for an MP to boost the budget devoted to local work on behalf of his electors. Such subtlety, however, was overlooked as the row rolled on. Perhaps inevitably, it was billed 'Officegate'.

To cut to the chase. In the Scottish Parliament, on Thursday, 25 October, Sir David Steel blocked the Conservative leader David McLetchie from asking questions about the affair on the grounds that it was a Westminster issue. He was technically correct but, as he later appeared to acknowledge, wrong by any commonsense standard.

On 28 October, Fife police confirmed that they had received a complaint about the offices row which they were investigating. On 29 October, there were new accusations that the Hanover Court address had been listed by Labour on election leaflets, contrary to rules. McLeish stressed the office had not been used as an election headquarters. Labour reminded all local parties of the rules which prevent public money being diverted to party purposes.

On Thursday, 1 November, there was a full-scale confrontation over the issue in the Scottish Parliament. That evening, the First Minister appeared on the BBC's *Question Time*, from Glasgow. He struggled badly.

Over the following weekend, McLeish and his advisers finally tried to pin down every single detail of the rental income. On Tuesday, 6 November, McLeish published those details, listing five sublets. A sixth sublet subsequently came to light and, on Thursday, 8 November 2001, Henry McLeish resigned as First Minister.

Few people think this was a story of political corruption. Even the First Minister's sharpest critics tend to accept Henry McLeish's assertion that he made no personal gain. It was, he said in an interview with me and on other occasions, 'a muddle not a fiddle'. The muddle, however, was major. This was a story of persistent questions – and increasingly inadequate answers. It also contains longer term lessons.

First, it is important to understand that the dispute related to McLeish's allowances while an MP at Westminster. It had nothing to do, strictly, with the Scottish Parliament. The rules at Westminster were notoriously lax, although they have since been tightened. One

MP told me: 'You could use your office as a brothel on the side and nobody would care.' I have no evidence that any MP actually offered this particular service to constituents. By contrast, the cash rules in the Scottish Parliament were strict from the start.

It is at least arguable that Holyrood exposed a Westminster problem: that the closer scrutiny operating in the Scottish Parliament brought a degree of Commons laxity to light. Other MPs, including Nigel Griffiths, a government Minister, had their constituency office arrangements questioned as a result. All defended themselves robustly, but it is a reasonable bet that every member has quietly reviewed and, if necessary, revised arrangements as a consequence of the McLeish row.

Politicians can sometimes be reluctant to challenge the financial arrangements of rival parties. This is prompted not by cross-party comradeship but by quivering thoughts of glass-houses and stones. They do not want to jeer at their rivals – only to find that one of their own buddies has been up to exactly the same wheeze. This, perhaps, explains the initially cautious approach adopted by Labour's opponents, with the exception of the Tories.

The Scottish Tories had a certain advantage in this regard. When they first began to pursue Henry McLeish over his Westminster allowances in April 2001, they had the best possible defence against any counter-attack. They had absolutely no fears that any of their MPs might crumple under close scrutiny. They had none. The Scottish Conservatives did not have to trouble the Commons Fees Office since they lost every seat in Scotland in 1997.

To be completely fair, David McLetchie hunted Henry McLeish with a masterly combination of biting satire, rhetoric and persistence. He was careful to avoid lodging allegations or accusations, confining himself to inviting the First Minister to answer specific questions and clarify matters.

As the hunt closed upon him, the First Minister tried various tactics. He swithered between condemning the pursuit as an evil smear or a trivial distraction. Neither tactic worked as McLetchie, an Edinburgh lawyer, swept aside the protests and simply returned again and again to apparent gaps in the First Minister's account.

Finally, McLeish rounded upon McLetchie directly. On 1 November, during questions in the Scottish Parliament, the First Minister said that, 'with the Presiding Officer's indulgence', he would deal with the Tory leader's role 'in this tawdry attack'. McLeish listed his ministerial efforts over the week and contrasted that with McLetchie who had been 'grubbing around the gutter'.

It was a good try – but it backfired disastrously. David McLetchie rose slowly and shook his head slightly before saying: 'The First Minister should not kid himself. It is his blackest hour and, from the way he has conducted himself, everyone in the country knows that.' McLetchie went on to depict the First Minister scrambling for excuses, lampooning him wickedly as a dodgy kid trying to wriggle away from responsibility: 'I didnae ken, it wisnae me, a big boy did it and ran away.'

Earlier, in the same question session, the SNP leader John Swinney had challenged the First Minister over the Digby Brown sublet. Apparently, the company had neither telephone nor fax in the Glenrothes office which they leased from McLeish. Digby Brown later explained they used the office solely to allow visiting lawyers to meet Fife clients.

It was a substantive attack – but it was McLetchie's words which hit home. They were delivered with just the right blend of anger and scorn. Above all, they rang true: they represented the First Minister's plight accurately. He did appear to be offering excuses rather than answers. As McLetchie spoke, you only had to look at the faces on the Labour back benches to know they felt the same.

That night, Henry McLeish fulfilled a long-standing engagement to appear on the BBC's *Question Time*, presented by David Dimbleby from Glasgow. Dimbleby and his producer each telephoned me in advance for a briefing on current Scottish events and, above all, 'Officegate'.

I said that the Digby Brown sublet had been extensively discussed in Parliament and the media. Dimbleby asked me what had yet to come out, what might be worth pursuing. I replied that Henry McLeish had yet to specify the full extent of his previous sublets, and how much cash they had raised for his office.

By common consent, McLeish's performance on the programme was woeful. His press adviser Peter McMahon said in his *Scotsman* series that it had been 'appalling'. Senior insiders questioned later whether the First Minister should have been advised to withdraw from the programme, citing urgent Executive business. That is, of course, with hindsight. In advance, it seemed, rightly, that pulling out would look weak and evasive.

As the questions from the audience piled in, David Dimbleby asked the First Minister to specify how much his office had raised from previous sublets. McLeish waffled. Dimbleby persisted and the First Minister was obliged to confess that he did not know.

Henry McLeish had faced months of media and political questioning over his office finances. He had been cross-examined in the Scottish Parliament that very day. And yet he was simply unable to say how much the sublets had raised. For the First Minister, this was calamitous. Unfairly or not, he looked and sounded shifty, ill at ease. Viewing colleagues said they groaned with a mixture of sympathy and despair.

I think there was a key factor at play here, a factor which later proved crucial in the case of the sixth, undisclosed sublet. Henry McLeish appeared indefensibly casual about the entire affair. Yes, he realised that the controversy had become grave: how could he other? But insiders all say that he was reluctant to focus upon the core point: the sublets and the detailed questions arising. He could not, would not accept that he had anything to answer, and so he did not, would not attempt to come up with answers. When he did, it was too late – and the details were incomplete.

I believe that the sixth sublet tells us more than the others. It speaks eloquently of a casual attitude not just to political questions but to the business of running public services. It tells of a party, the Labour Party, that is so entrenched in local power that internal deals can end up replacing external scrutiny.

After the *Question Time* appearance, Henry McLeish and his key political advisers spent the weekend in Bute House trying, finally, to pin down the precise details of the sublets. By dinner time on Sunday – fish suppers and Chardonnay – they believed they had mustered all the facts. The upper floor at 14 Hanover Court had been let five times between 1987 and 2001: to Honeywell-Shield, a security systems company; to Capital Copiers; to Fife Council; to a law firm, Thompsons; and finally to Digby Brown.

The total value of the sublets – the figure McLeish had been unable to give on television – was £36,000. The First Minister announced this figure on Tuesday, 6 November. He also said he had

now invited the Fees Office to look again at the affair, and added
that he was willing, if necessary, to pay back this entire sum.

Henry McLeish carried out contrite media interviews, he faced
the press at a news conference. It was all out in the open. There were
five sublets. Exhausted advisers knew they would take a roasting in
the media, but they began, tentatively, to think of the future, to think
of the Cabinet meeting scheduled for that afternoon.

John McTernan, the First Minister's senior political adviser,
decided to block all possible avenues for things going awry. He
phoned key Labour figures – in Parliament, party headquarters and
Fife – advising them to keep quiet, to close down the story, to refuse
requests for media interviews.

All was going well until he phoned Lynda Struthers from
McLeish's constituency team. She had absolutely no problem with
closing down the story. Full co-operation there. No disagreement
whatsoever. No more to be said about the five sublets. It was just,
well . . . it now turned out there had been six lets, not five. A care
agency known as the Third Age had leased the front office on
the ground floor at Hanover Court. This was quite separate from the
five lets of the upper floor. Crucially, it had not featured in McLeish's
statement to the media, which was now exposed as incomplete.

McTernan drew Peter McMahon aside and muttered: 'Can I have
a quiet word?' As the implications sank in, McTernan and McMahon
sat slumped on the elegant, steep, circular staircase of Bute House,
where Henry McLeish had posed for pictures with his new Cabinet
just a year earlier. It looked all over for their boss.

They went to Cabinet, paying little or no attention to the topics
under discussion. Their notebooks – normally filled with scribbled
reminders of questions to raise, things to follow up – were virtually
blank.

They did not discuss the crisis properly with McLeish until the
following day, Wednesday, 7 November. By then there were three
options: say nothing and simply hope the issue would go away; disclose the new information immediately to the media; incorporate
the sixth sublet into the statement which McLeish was already due
to make in the Scottish Parliament on Thursday.

Option one was impossible. The media would eventually find
out: indeed, *The Herald* newspaper was believed to be sniffing
around the story although, in the event, they did not publish in

advance of the First Minister's resignation. As things turned out, it was left to me to disclose on television that it was an extra let that had brought down the First Minister. As Team McLeish considered their options, they feared that political rivals might find out, and confront the First Minister in Parliament. Specifically, the Scottish Socialists were thought to know about the sixth let. So Option one – silence – was out.

Option two was desperately limp. 'Okay, guys, I know I told you that my statement was full and final closure of this affair. But – and I know you're gonna laugh – turns out there was a sixth let! Another muddle! What are we like, eh?' You see the problem. Scarcely impressive.

Downing Street, numbers 10 and 11, were apparently urging Option Three. Disclose the sixth sublet in the chamber on Thursday, apologise profusely, then tough it out, hoping that the baying ranks of Labour MSPs could shout more loudly than the Opposition.

Team McLeish duly had a go at Option Three. Speech-writer Colin Currie and economic adviser John McLaren drafted a statement for McLeish which incorporated disclosure of that sixth sublet. Plainly, it was going to take considerable strength of character to deliver such a humiliating admission – and endure the following flak. The problem was that it became steadily clear that Henry McLeish was not up to that task.

That evening, Wednesday, 7 November, the First Minister attended a rugby gala dinner at the Palace of Holyroodhouse in the presence of the Princess Royal. To those who were there, he seemed in good form. At midnight that night, back in Bute House, McLeish took a call from Peter McMahon and considered the options, including the evidence of renewed press interest. McLeish said he'd 'sleep on it'.

For the First Minister, alone in his official residence, there was precious little sleep that night. In the morning, it was plain that it was over. McLeish's key advisers went to St Andrew's House, to the First Minister's office. They tried to canvass options, but any residual spirit had abandoned McLeish. The fight had gone out of him utterly. It was clear that McLeish was incapable of delivering the type of battling, defiant performance that would be needed. Instead of discussing his survival, the First Minister sat slumped on his office couch, dishevelled and in tears, occasionally pacing over to glance out the window at the city.

Tony Blair and Gordon Brown were contacted, and tried to dis-
suade McLeish from resigning. But nothing worked. One insider
told me: 'He couldn't see any end to it. He was required to prove a
negative – that he hadn't benefited from the money. If he owned up
to the sixth let, the next question would be – where did the money
go?' It was, after all, a reasonable question. The sixth sublet, the
Glenrothes Third Age group, started in 1992 as a voluntary operation to help run pensioners' lunch clubs. In August 2000, its main
account was closed and the balance transferred to Age Concern. In
the intervening years, it received funding from Fife Council and the
Unemployed Voluntary Action Fund, plus income from those
attending day centres.

Douglas Sinclair, the chief executive of Fife Council, reported on
Third Age to his authority's standards and audit committee on the
8 March 2002. The report had earlier been leaked to my BBC colleague Glenn Campbell. Sinclair stressed there was no evidence of
council cash paid to the group 'being used for any purpose other
than that for which the group was established'. However, the report
tells a story of casuistry and casual attitudes to public money. This is
not white-hot corruption. Instead, it is cosy and insidious, reflecting
Labour's entrenched local power, eliding the divisions which ought
to exist between party and public service.

Sinclair talks of one Labour insider taking part in the interview
which led to another Labour insider being appointed to a job co-
ordinating the charity's work in Fife. He adds: 'A clear conflict of
interest existed and in my view she should not have participated in
the interview.' He talks of the party insider, connected to McLeish,
who played a part in the arrangement which turned Third Age into
tenants of the former First Minister. The report notes: 'She should
have asked herself the question "how would the average man or
woman have perceived my involvement in the negotiation of a lease
between the Third Age group and Henry McLeish." The answer
should have been obvious.'

Then there is the question of Julie Fulton, McLeish's wife.
Sinclair's report does not specify a direct role for her in the running
or financing of Third Age. Equally, though, he finds that as a senior
social worker specialising in care of the elderly, she was at least partly
responsible for relations with a charity which had been established
precisely to enhance services for older people in Fife.

Specifically, Sinclair says that she played a part in the decision to continue funding the charity's work of providing lunch clubs after the Third Age management committee had stopped functioning. He says that, on 26 March 1999, three senior council managers, including Julie Fulton, approved a report recommending payment of cash to a group, the Third Age, which they knew had formally ceased to exist, although its work continued. This was, he notes, 'unacceptable'.

Sinclair stresses again that there was no improper use of council money. The public funds continued to provide services for the elderly. That was later confirmed by a report from Audit Scotland – on 3 May 2002 – which said that the grants of £98,000 to Third Age from the council were 'in all material respects used for the purpose intended despite a lack of monitoring by the Council'.

That latter point, however, is key. Sinclair had earlier pointed to a 'substantial crossover between management of the Labour Party, the Third Age co-ordinators, membership of the Management Committee and Social Work employees in supporting the group.' Again, cosy and insidious, rather than overtly corrupt. Hopefully, this report, and particularly the enormously high profile attached to it because of the link to McLeish, will help provide a remedy to the malaise it describes, and will infuse the sugar of sweet, internal deals with the saline bite of open scrutiny. More to our present purpose, though, is the impact of the Third Age upon McLeish.

Insiders tell of his reluctance to get down to hard facts in attempting to clear up the confusion surrounding his office sublets. But why? Did he genuinely forget about his ground-floor tenants, the Third Age group, when he listed five sublets on the upper floor? Or was he apprehensive that particularly close scrutiny of the Third Age let would bring his wife into focus?

Certainly, the impact upon Julie Fulton has been severe. From the emergence of Third Age as an issue, she was on prolonged sick leave, suffering from stress. Douglas Sinclair notes that he was unable to interview her for his report as a consequence. She later rallied sufficiently to begin a defence of her actions at the council. Henry McLeish feels bitter about the media treatment he has received. However, that response is as nothing compared to his defence of his wife. He is furious beyond measure at the thought that she has been dragged into the controversy.

Intriguingly, his first wife Margaret also featured in one or two insider conversations. Before she died, she ran McLeish's Glenrothes office. At various points in the emerging controversy, insiders would mutter behind their hands that Margaret was in charge of constituency finance. Any mumbled, private suggestion that this might be brought into the open was met by Henry McLeish with a cold stare. Those making the suggestion knew not to try again. In the case of the Third Age issue, it is feasible that McLeish believed he was protecting his wife Julie from media and public attention. Whether that was his motivation, or whether he genuinely forgot about the sixth let, the result was the same; microscopic scrutiny of Henry McLeish and his wife.

The outcome, of course, was that McLeish resigned as First Minister. On the morning of Thursday, 8 November, shortly before eleven o'clock, the Conservative leader David McLetchie was on his way to Parliament to continue his pursuit. He was due to table a motion on the conduct of the First Minister, and had a suitably robust speech ready, which he clutched firmly as he hurried up the Royal Mile.

His pager buzzed with a message asking him to return to the MSPs office block urgently for talks with Tom McCabe. There, he was informed of the First Minister's intention to resign, told that McCabe would break the news and told further that McLeish would make a personal statement. McLetchie was left with the impression that actual delivery of this planned statement was conditional upon the First Minister being up to the ordeal. McLetchie left the office quietly, pausing at the door only to add: 'It was nothing personal, you know.'

Shortly after eleven o'clock, McCabe stood up in Parliament and announced: 'I inform the Chamber that the First Minister has this morning written to Her Majesty the Queen and to the Presiding Officer indicating that he intends to tender his resignation.' McLetchie withdrew his motion on the First Minister's conduct, and MSPs streamed out into the Royal Mile.

I have written earlier of the reaction of MSPs, varying from shock to anguish. David McLetchie, the prosecutor in chief, was notably measured. Partly this was because he believed then and he believes now that McLeish had indeed made no personal gain from his 'muddle', that he could have resolved the row with firm handling.

*Stepping down: Henry McLeish leaves Parliament with his wife, Julie,
after resigning as First Minister.*

Partly, though, it was because at that precise moment he was unsure
as to McLeish's emotional state – and did not want to add to his
personal distress.

Henry McLeish was indeed in a mess, emotionally, tearful and
self-recriminatory. Encouraged by his friends and colleagues, he rallied, rehearsing the statement at a makeshift despatch box. Fortified

by a bridie and chips – plus a stiff malt whisky – he headed for Parliament to resign.

In the statement, heard in silence, he apologised again for the mistakes surrounding his constituency office costs. He spoke of his pride in the project of devolution. Then he added:

> I did not come to Parliament simply as some kind of career choice. I did not enter Parliament because it was some kind of family tradition. I came to Parliament to work for the people I know and grew up with and to serve them. That has been my purpose since the day and the hour that I was elected.
>
> I came to Parliament, and eventually to the office of First Minister, to serve my constituents and, eventually, all the people of Scotland. If I have let them down in this matter, I hope that I have served them well in many others.

The statement itself was a success, combining both humility and pride. Despite the advance worries, McLeish delivered it well, without stumbling. At the close, he was led out directly past the silent Tory front bench. Pausing briefly for a word with the Presiding Officer, he joined his wife Julie in the black-and-white, tiled corridor outside the chamber, headed down the stairs into a waiting car and was gone.

Note
1. Statement by Henry McLeish, 6 November 2001.

4 Jack the Lad

Few things try the soul quite so much as corporate bonding. It appears, however, that bright, chaotic individualism cannot be permitted to exist in our interwired era. So it was that on Monday, 11 March 2002, officials from the Scottish Labour Party found themselves in deepest Kinross.

This was scarcely a political down time. The report by Fife's chief executive into the Third Age had just been published. Over the weekend, Labour's party executive had declined to offer immediate endorsement to Henry McLeish as a candidate for the next Scottish elections. However, callers to Labour's HQ that Monday were politely informed by recorded message that the party was shut. The team members were elsewhere. In Kinross. Bonding. With varying degrees of enthusiasm, Labour's bonders essayed their main task, which was to find a golden globe intended, apparently, to represent a scrap of nuclear waste. They failed miserably. Perhaps, understandably, they felt distracted, unable to give full attention to this vital endeavour.

Other exercises seemingly involved using blindfolds and tying each other up. An overzealous interpretation of the term 'bonding', perhaps, by a keen corporate guru. In any event, it is a pity that Labour's happy band did not attempt to take their Cabinet colleagues along with them. In the aftermath of Henry McLeish's resignation, they were definitely in need of a little bonding. Or they were fit to be tied.

The key question, of course, was who would succeed Henry McLeish. This needed calm, measured consideration, give and take on all sides, intelligent discussion of what was best for the party, the Executive and the nation. Needless to say, it was not forthcoming. In its stead, querulous conflict, Machiavellian scheming and mutual recrimination.

Jack McConnell was palpably in the field. Indeed, it could be said he had been in the field since the Scottish Parliament was first elected. Jack the Lad – as he is frequently styled – does not lack self-confidence or a capacity for self-advancement. Former Cabinet colleagues of McConnell are, mostly, vitriolic about the manner of his long-term rise to power. One told me: 'Jack's behaviour was utterly disgraceful under both Donald and Henry. He pursued his own agenda, with no sense of corporate or collegiate responsibility.' Another said: 'Jack was out for himself from Day One.' The core allegation is that, in Cabinet, McConnell tailored his actions to his own ends, rather than those of the Executive as a whole. Colleagues recall him 'grandstanding' on issues where he could take the lead, while belittling initiatives which came from other departments and other Ministers.

More than one, for example, pointed me in the direction of the pay deal for teachers, reached while McConnell was Education Minister after scrutiny by the McCrone Committee. McConnell's colleagues claim that he paid out too much money while exaggerating the return in terms of changes to teachers' conditions of employment. The allegation is that McConnell saw an opportunity for a grand gesture which would improve his standing, but that the necessary details have subsequently unravelled somewhat. McConnell's supporters deny this, saying that he struck a reasonable deal which was vital for progress in education. However, Jack McConnell has admitted privately to friends that he was 'a bit daft' in the early days of the Dewar Cabinet, perhaps a little too close to the press, who were seeking insider gossip.

Understandably, McConnell was severely shocked by the Lobby-gate allegations in September 1999, when two lobbyists, working for a public affairs firm, were taped by *The Observer* newspaper, claiming that they had privileged access to McConnell, who had previously been connected with their firm before becoming an MSP. McConnell was exonerated by the Parliament's Standards Committee of any improper behaviour, but colleagues say he took note and ditched his 'daft' behaviour as a consequence, narrowing his focus to concentrate upon ministerial and Executive matters. Others insist that McConnell was far from the only Cabinet Minister to look out for Number One in the Dewar and McLeish Cabinets. They say that Susan Deacon and Wendy Alexander, among others, also advanced their own agendas, recalling that Dewar had to chide Deacon and McConnell for briefing against each other in a squabble over departmental cash.

Jack McConnell, however, was in a league apart. Other Ministers might fancy their chances of advancement, and tailor their actions accordingly. McConnell had a squad of supporters in place. There is a rather pleasant restaurant called Omar Khayyam in Edinburgh's Haymarket. McConnell and his sympathisers – one might call them the Jackobites – met there regularly and in other venues for curry and confidential chat.

The chief Jackobites were Tricia Ferguson and Andy Kerr. Both were promoted to the Cabinet along with Mike Watson. Other acolytes mentioned at various times include Karen Whitefield, Frank McAveety, Michael McMahon, Kate McLean and Cathy Craigie. The list is inevitably imprecise – and some may dispute their 'membership'. This was not a secret, signed-up conspiracy, an underground plot to destabilise the Executive. Other Ministers were very well aware that McConnell had his informal team. Equally, McConnell behaved in public as a model Minister, giving McLeish minimal scope for sustainable complaints about disloyalty.

McLeish's supporters say the McConnell camp weakened their man by underhand briefings or, at the very least, by withholding praise and support. I feel that is overstated and partly reflects internal Cabinet tension and McLeish's own disquiet. The Jackobites scarcely wished McLeish well but they did not have to run a prolonged, pro-active campaign. Being there was enough.

They did assume, though, that their time would come. One source told me that McConnell even drafted his possible ministerial team as it became apparent that McLeish would fall. So McConnell was definitely in the running when that fall came. But who else? The divisions quickly became clear. On the morning of McLeish's resignation, as the First Minister sat slumped in despair, his Cabinet colleagues hurried to his side. Some to offer comfort, some – including Jackie Baillie – to rage at him for quitting and to plead with him to think again.

As Baillie delivered her blunt message, in came two other Cabinet Ministers: Tom McCabe and Jack McConnell. McCabe had deliberately brought McConnell along with him, to the evident fury of other Ministers. To be fair, McConnell had as much right as others to be present, but it seemed to some that McCabe, who was embroiled in solving a crisis for one Labour leader, was already looking to anoint the next.

Certainly, McCabe moved quickly to back McConnell in the private arguments over who should succeed. But was there to be a 'Stop Jack' candidate? At first, that seemed certain. On the day McLeish resigned, the various contenders held talks on the fifth floor of the MSPs office block, the area reserved for Ministers. It appears this was not a fixed cabal, a single meeting, but rather floating negotiations involving various participants at various times. Susan Deacon privately advised her colleagues that she was not a contender: she was pregnant, expecting her second child. She was just a mite miffed to find that she was not much mentioned in press speculation about the succession in any event.

Sarah Boyack knew she was not a prospect: she had endured a relatively troubled time in Cabinet as it was. This left Jackie Baillie, Angus Mackay and Wendy Alexander. The serious discussions centred upon these three.

Mackay and Baillie were reluctant to put themselves forward. Alexander indicated she would stand. That much is agreed by all. It is at this point, however, that interpretations differ. Wendy Alexander and her personal supporters insist that she never declared, finally and irrevocably, that she would stand. Others say that is sophistry: that a campaign was up and running, that her private comments completely convinced other potential contenders such as Mackay and Baillie that they need not stand, that a candidate was in place to challenge McConnell.

In her customary fashion, Alexander dropped in and out of the talks. Certainly, by that night, if anyone was to stand, it was Wendy Alexander. One insider insisted: 'She did not have to be persuaded, she was biting my hand off to stand.'

The divisions then came to the surface via a slightly bizarre route. Labour's Cabinet members had to agree among themselves who would act as liaison officer with their LibDem coalition partners. It was a routine non-job, but it exposed the split. McConnell proposed Tom McCabe, while Wendy Alexander suggested Jackie Baillie.

One by one, the others indicated that they backed Alexander in this relatively trivial vote – and by implication in the big contest to come. To be frank, Jack McConnell had few doubts where he stood anyway but this vote operated like a dress rehearsal, delineating the precise divisions among Labour's Cabinet Ministers.

So Alexander, then, was seen as the prime challenger and, importantly, the elementary mechanics of a campaign were put in place. The following day, Friday, Alexander's supporters – including her brother Douglas – met in the Glasgow flat of MSP Pauline McNeill, Wendy Alexander's closest friend in politics. Campaign tactics were discussed. Lists of possible supporters stuck up on the wall. Strong and weak points identified. Key figures in the media briefed.

That evening, the leadership contest was the main topic of gossip at a party at Scottish Labour HQ, convened to bid farewell to a well-liked staff member. However, Wendy Alexander continued to harbour doubts. She told friends she doubted she could stand the intense lifestyle, that she had seen it 'kill Donald' – her friend and mentor Donald Dewar. They replied that they would be there for her, that they would help. 'Not at midnight in Bute House, you won't,' she retorted. She told friends that Bute House could be 'as much a prison as Barlinnie.' She continued to voice those concerns and others as she travelled with colleagues to Stirling on Saturday morning for a party policy forum. One source commented that a serious, determined candidate would have worked the room, whereas Wendy Alexander got involved in two lengthy conversations, including one with Malcolm Chisholm.

The deciding factor – according to Alexander's closest supporters – was that she calculated she might win and feared the consequences. She, apparently, felt that uncertain voters within the Labour

Parliamentary group were drifting her way and that she had growing union support. This analysis, naturally, is disputed by Team McConnell, who say their candidate was firmly in the lead.

By the Saturday night Wendy Alexander had decided not to stand. She consulted further with friends and family, announcing her decision on the Sunday. Her potential supporters were frankly furious. Several of them demanded talks with her to clear the air. One source said Alexander restated her personal anxieties, 'havering about babies and her biological clock'. All involved say personal concerns were cited. But some say Wendy Alexander's core problem was more basic. Did she want the job? Did she want to climb any further up the oleaginous ministerial pole?

Team Alexander – now leaderless – discussed 'for about five minutes' whether they could field another candidate, but they concluded it was out of the question. While Wendy Alexander was still in the frame, it was possible to argue credibly that this was a scheduled and structured campaign based on principle, seeking among other things a more collegiate style of government. Once she was out, reviving the campaign with a hurriedly arranged deputy would simply look like a desperate attempt to stop Jack McConnell at all costs.

Quite separately, there was a brief, further possibility of a contest. Malcolm Chisholm – a widely liked MSP who later became Health Minister – indicated on the Sunday that he might put his name forward. Chisholm had previously resigned as a Minister from Tony Blair's government over the issue of benefit cuts. He was, apparently, prepared to stand as a candidate of the conscientious Left with the objective, at the very least, of prompting a debate within the party about its aims and ambitions.

In the event, he assessed his potential support, found it was insufficient to merit even a principled challenge, and was kind enough to telephone me at home early on Tuesday, 13 November to enable me to break the news on *Good Morning Scotland* that he was withdrawing from the contest.

That same day, Jack McConnell was confirmed as Labour's sole nominee. That same day, he held a news conference and, with his wife Bridget by his side, confirmed what many had known for years – that he had had an affair with a party employee while he was Labour's General Secretary.

The news conference was, inevitably, tense. A packed hotel room,

Face the Press: Jack McConnell with his wife, Bridget, as the couple confirm that the new First Minister had a past affair.

political correspondents mingling with feature writers, TV camera crews, photographers, news reporters and sundry others who were there perhaps largely out of curiosity. The media crowd seemed to be collectively craning forward to see and hear.

McConnell entered, declared his intention to clear the air and admitted that he had 'let everybody down' by his affair with a colleague seven years previously. He did not name the woman involved, but the media later did; she was Maureen Smith, formerly Labour's press secretary.

Bridget McConnell gazed forwards, looking neither to right to left, never glancing at her husband as she told the media: 'Jack betrayed my trust seven years ago by having an affair. It goes without saying he hurt everyone involved.'

There was comment later to the effect that Jack McConnell had victimised his wife by obliging her to participate in an excruciating public disclosure of past problems in their marriage. I believed then – and believe now – that this analysis, while perhaps understandable, does not accord with the character of Bridget McConnell.

She had already worked through the emotional consequences of the affair, which she initially learned about not from her husband but from Maureen Smith, who turned up at the McConnell family home in Stirling. She had subsequently steeled herself to rebuild her marriage with the man who adopted and helped to raise her children.

Bridget McConnell is a talented, bright, personable, professional woman, who is in charge of cultural services for the city of Glasgow. I believe it is wrong to imagine that she would agree to act utterly against her will. The couple had discussed over the weekend the prospect that full disclosure might be necessary in the event that McConnell was nominated for the leadership. They concluded, jointly, that the press would investigate and revisit the affair in any case, that it was better to confront the issue openly and upfront. Whether it was entirely fair to Maureen Smith is another matter. McConnell alerted her to his intentions and, arguably, she would have faced scrutiny in any event, given that several journalists knew the basics of the story. He pleaded for the privacy of all involved to be respected.

Events then hurried to a conclusion. On Saturday, 17 November, McConnell – the sole nominee – was confirmed as Labour's choice for First Minister at a party ballot meeting held in Glasgow. On Tuesday, 20 November, he won the backing of the Liberal Democrats after promising them action on voting reform for local government. On Thursday, 22 November, he was elected First Minister by the Scottish Parliament. On Sunday, 25 November, he reached a private agreement with Wendy Alexander as to the portfolio she would carry in Cabinet. The following day, he was appointed formally to the post of First Minister by the Queen at Buckingham Palace. On Tuesday, 27 November, he reshuffled his Cabinet.

That reshuffle was brutal – all the more so because Jack McConnell had indicated in advance that he would be moderate. He had told the media and, much more importantly, the Labour group that there would be no 'night of the long knives'. He had indicated that he was seeking a government of all the talents. What few guessed was that he meant all the talents of his own campaign team.

Almost all, myself included, were gulled. Some had taken McConnell at his word without examining the details. I had less of an excuse. In one item for *Reporting Scotland*, I had reported the 'government of all the talents' pledge while simultaneously going through the Ministers who could face the sack.

I only got one wrong: I thought that Angus Mackay would survive. (I believed that Susan Deacon would be offered a place. She was, but declined.) Yet, even as I ticked off the possible victims on my fingers, I still contrived to give a certain amount of credence to the line that the reshuffle would be consensual. In my defence, I can only say that the 'government of all the talents' promise was widely and repeatedly delivered. That 'possible victim' does not equate to 'certain sacking'. I might add that no-one else predicted a clear-out. Those who say now that they knew all along what McConnell was planning are exercising hindsight. No doubt they had excellent reasons for keeping their inner knowledge to themselves at the time.

McConnell met his ministerial colleagues one by one and delivered his verdict. He sacked Jackie Baillie, a politician of talent but a long-standing adversary of the new First Minister. She had chaired the Labour Party while he was General Secretary and the pair had developed a mutual antipathy then and since. In the words of one insider: 'They used to lob grenades at each other in Cabinet; it was no surprise at all when she was sacked.'

He sacked Angus Mackay, a palpably able and thoughtful Minister. Mackay, however, had been closely and directly associated with McLeish. He had, arguably, agitated just a little too eagerly for an alternative candidate. McConnell, apparently, felt he could not trust him. He dispensed with Tom McCabe, who had worked long and hard for both Dewar and McLeish. Political life had not been made easier for McCabe by a long-running feud between himself and the *Daily Record*.

McConnell asked McCabe, who had supported him for the leadership: 'Do you want a break?' He offered him a move to a junior ministerial post or even a committee convenership, presumably aware that such a demotion would be insupportable. McCabe decided to stand down entirely, replying: 'A break is a break.' The formal letter to him was markedly warmer than the others.

He sacked Sarah Boyack, to the regret of some but, frankly, the surprise of no-one, including probably herself. Fairly or not, she had appeared to struggle on occasion, notably over the issue of private road maintenance contracts. Her chief critic then was Labour MSP Andy Kerr, who entered McConnell's Cabinet as Finance Minister.

So the chief architects of Wendy Alexander's non-campaign were all sacked. Wendy Alexander herself was reappointed, but with a massive new remit covering Transport, Enterprise and Lifelong Learning. McConnell calculated she was too able, too entrenched to dismiss. He wanted her as a Minister. However, he was determined to show her who was the boss in a manner that had eluded Henry McLeish. Later, as we shall see, she cast off her 'Minister for Everything' remit and resigned from Cabinet.

He definitely wanted Susan Deacon to remain in his Cabinet, but he asked her to move from Health to Social Justice. I believe McConnell had two motives for this. The private, internal sugges-tion was that Deacon had partly lost the confidence of the medical profession after a series of controversies. The other motive is that McConnell needed to demonstrate firm leadership, to shape his own Cabinet entirely to his own mould. In any event, Deacon refused. She argued that, given her pregnancy, it made no sense to move her to an entirely different remit where she would have to spend time acquiring the details of the new brief, only to leave office to give birth.

She insisted she could handle Health admirably, with additional junior ministerial back-up. Further, her friends vigorously deny that she had lost the confidence of the medical world, arguing that pol-icy controversy is intrinsic to political and public life. McConnell tried again, confident that the challenge of combining ministerial office with pregnancy would prove too tempting for such a capable woman. He was wrong. Susan Deacon refused once more, and chose to leave the Cabinet.

McConnell's supporters defend the reshuffle. They say, first, that a united Cabinet was vital after the anguish of the final McLeish period, that McConnell consequently needed his own team in place. He certainly achieved that, elevating Andy Kerr, Patricia Ferguson, Mike Watson and Cathy Jamieson to the Cabinet. Kerr, Watson and Jamieson came from the back benches. Ferguson had been deputy Presiding Officer. They were joined by Iain Gray and Malcolm Chisholm, promoted from the junior ministerial ranks.

Second, McConnell's aides say that the reshuffle would not have looked so sweeping if Susan Deacon had taken the offer of a new post. Third, they insist that McConnell had to tell the back benches that there would be 'no night of the long knives'. They argue he had to offer temporary reassurance, to buy time to effect the transition.

I would dispute that third point. I believe that McConnell was unwise to deliver a promise which he was unwilling or unable to fulfil. Even if Susan Deacon had stayed in Cabinet, this would have been a substantial clear-out of the McLeish team. Rather than leave a misleading impression, he would have been better advised to say nothing in advance about his Cabinet plans. But then perhaps I am just sore because, in company with others, I bought the line. One way or another, McConnell had ended up parting company with every one of his Labour Cabinet colleagues, except for Wendy Alexander, the Minister who had looked like being his principal rival. Jack the Lad had a new nickname: Jack the Knife.

5 New Politics? The Coalition

To many, the new politics in Scotland seems very like the old. Internal party conflict and overblown rhetoric. Certainly, that is the decidedly tarnished and peeling surface, the tedious veneer that settles on public affairs, dulling the senses and depressing the turnout at elections. Listen to question time on a Thursday and you might gain the impression that little has changed from Westminster days. Admittedly, there is none of the pomposity associated with the (Right) Honourable, Learned and Gallant members, facing each other two bold sword lengths apart.

The questions, however, are the customary mix. The genuine seekers after truth are too often matched in number by sycophants seeking advancement on the Executive side, together with synthetic indignation from the Opposition parties. Questions to the First Minister from his SNP and Conservative opponents have become formulaic: an open inquiry (when will he next meet the Scottish Secretary or whatever) followed by a burst of scripted outrage from the interrogators and a litany of Executive achievements from the First Minister.

Yes, there are variations. Perhaps a joke, often from David McLetchie. Perhaps a little diversion when the answering Ministers lose their notes and have to rely on their native intellect. These joys, however, tend to be sprinkled in a pasture pungent with the familiar manure of political name-calling. We must search for the new politics elsewhere, and, thankfully, I think it can be found. Look at the relative openness of the Scottish Parliament, look at successful innovations like the petitions committee, look at the committee system more generally, look at the well-attended and well-structured debates, look at the new relationships with the civil service, with London. Look, perhaps above all, at coalition politics.

Scotland has had to get used to shared power, to close inter-party policy scrutiny, to Parliamentary votes that cannot be guaranteed, to opposition that requires subtlety to deal with the new structure. Each, I would argue, has played a part in improving the health of the body politic.

Labour has faced the biggest culture change. Many Labour MSPs, particularly from the west of Scotland, simply had not encountered other parties, other ways of working. One told me: 'I thought Tories were a breed apart, I couldn't conceive of working alongside them. And I didn't know any Liberals at all.'

These Labour MSPs took time getting accustomed to the new politics. They had been used to squaring matters internally. Now they had to argue their case with coalition partners and in open Parliament. They found a puzzling absence of horns upon Tory heads, they listened to Tavish Scott, Donald Gorrie or Jamie Stone and said to themselves: 'So that's a Liberal.'

The core fault-line in Scottish politics still lies between Labour on the one hand and the Scottish National Party on the other. More accurately, it is a fault-line between the largest, established party in Scotland espousing the Union with England and the principal party seeking to end that Union. However, even across that divide there can be accommodation between individual members on individual issues.

Coalition government, however, is the most palpable demonstration of new politics. It was presaged by the Constitutional Convention where Labour and the Liberal Democrats worked alongside others to produce a detailed scheme for devolution.

It was perfectly possible for Donald Dewar and Jim Wallace – fellow lawyers and friends, with Convention co-operation behind them – to form a good working relationship. That did not guarantee that the spirit of co-operation, or even of mutual understanding,

stretched to the back benches. This was definitely a political arrangement, not a marriage. For a start, there were very few areas of
Scotland where Labour and the LibDems encountered each other
politically on a significant scale. Aberdeen, parts of the Highlands,
maybe Inverclyde and sections of Edinburgh. Not the Borders,
where the LibDems are strong nor Labour's central belt powerbase.
You get to know a party by working for it – or fighting against it.
Labour and the LibDems had few points of contact.

Second, there were cultural differences. Labour is used to consulting internally, bargaining with its union and council power blocs
to agree a policy. The LibDems prefer open discussion, with fewer
set parameters, although they are not remotely averse to tough
politics where necessary. Of the two, the LibDems are marginally
more cuddly, but the gap is not wide.

Labour in Scotland derives much of its support from a proletarian
base, and responds either genuinely or with contrivance. To be fair,
mostly it is authentic concern for the condition of those with less.
Sometimes the rather strained attempts to stress a seamless bond
between Scotland's working-class past and 'New' Labour can try the
patience: pass me another Chardonnay and I'll tell you my mother's
Co-op number.

The LibDems are middle class, with a light dusting of Whig
aristocracy. Yes, I know there are LibDem councillors and activists in
the urban housing schemes, but the party's outlook is middle class. It
was no accident that the sticking point in the coalition negotiations
was the abolition of student tuition fees, which poorer families did
not pay in any case.

There is more, however. The two parties have a different concept
of politics. Not superior, one to the other, but different. Faced with
a problem, Labour will want to cut a deal, to sort it, to square it, to
move on. LibDems will want to scrutinise the problem every which
way, to examine every aspect. Even as agreement seems possible –
and Ministers are heading for the door – the cry will go up: 'But
have we thought of X.' Then back they will troop for more. This
aspect of the LibDems has frequently infuriated Labour, who feel
themselves on shifting ground, when they are used to solidity. One
senior Labour source put it succinctly when he told me: 'You think
Jim Wallace is too nice to be a politician but he must be a seriously
hard bastard to deal with those mad backbenchers of his.'

So coalition has obliged Labour to think and act differently, to accommodate the LibDem approach, although it should be said that there is little sign of any real rapprochement between the two. Again, this is political pragmatism, not true love.

It is important to realise, however, that coalition has been tricky for the Liberal Democrats too. For one thing, Jim Wallace is intrinsically suspicious of links with other parties, fearing that his own party's carefully guarded independence could be lost or that the voters might visit discontent with the Executive disproportionately upon its minority member. They might get angry with Ministers, and take it out on the LibDems.

His instinctive views are completely at odds with the enthusiasm for political realignment displayed by Paddy Ashdown, who formerly led the federal Liberal Democrat Party at Westminster. Ashdown talked eagerly of the 'project': close co-operation, even perhaps ultimately integration between Labour and the LibDems. In this, he matched the occasional rhetoric of Tony Blair, who would reflect upon the 'tragedy' that the Labour and Liberal strands of progressive thinking had become separated in the early twentieth century.

These views provoked various reactions. Frankly, most on the Labour side at Westminster were suspicious or hostile. If they thought of the LibDems at all, they thought of them as a handy but potentially troublesome fall-back should Labour fail to gain a majority at Westminster. The 'project' left them cold.

Among LibDems, some like Lord Jenkins – a former Labour Cabinet Minister and SDP founder – were enthusiastic. Others questioned the Blairite analysis, arguing that there was more dividing the parties than historical or electoral accident. Others again were inherently and deeply suspicious. That last band included Jim Wallace.

The issue provoked an angry row between Wallace and his federal leader. In June 1997, Wallace was an MP and Scottish LibDem spokesman. He learned from another colleague that Ashdown was planning to agree with Labour that the two parties should form a Joint Cabinet Committee on the constitution. This, apparently, was to form the prelude to a possible Westminster coalition despite Labour's huge majority. The project was definitely moving forward.

Wallace was livid that he knew nothing about the plan. He believed he was entitled to know, as Scottish leader, not least because the proposed committee on the constitution was bound to be dominated, in these early stages of the new Labour government, by Scottish devolution. Angrily, he stomped down to the federal leader's Westminster office and confronted Ashdown. Equally angrily, Ashdown demanded to know how Wallace had come by his information. There was a furious shouting match, which, according to one observer, nearly came to blows. My source wryly observed: 'It's just as well they stuck to shouting. Paddy is a former marine and could probably have killed Jim with his bare hands!'

This episode had an impact on the coalition talks in Scotland. Wallace, instinctively cautious about the wider Lib/Lab project, was decidedly cool when Ashdown intervened, trying to 'run the coalition negotiations by remote control from London', as one source put it. To be fair, Ashdown plainly saw the opportunity to give that wider project of cross-party co-operation a significant practical and psychological boost. No doubt encouraged by Ashdown, Tony Blair phoned Jim Wallace at one point during the talks to offer encouraging words. Wallace, however, insisted on handling the negotiations on his own terms – with Donald Dewar. The two declined to act as proxies for London dreams.

At all points, then, there has been structural tension within the coalition. When first formed, there was close personal liaison between Dewar and Wallace, but little rapport below that, between the aides and special advisers on either side. Other countries are more used to coalition government, and have developed mechanisms to deal with the inevitable strains of conjoining parties who are political rivals. An Irish government source told me that successful coalition required three main elements: an agreed, detailed and precise programme for government; close links between the leaders; and a team of bipartisan advisers whose principal job was to preclude tension, to spot problems and tackle them before they got out of hand.

Scottish Executive members had studied the Irish experience, and broadly endorsed that analysis. They had the detailed deal, exhaustively negotiated. They had the close links at the top between Dewar and Wallace. However, they did not have the problem-solving machinery. If anything, the advisers on each side acted in separate cabals. Arguably, John Rafferty – Dewar's chief adviser until his early departure in December 1999 – attempted to resolve that. LibDem sources say they were wary of his Machiavellian reputation but they appreciated his efforts to negotiate seriously, for example over tuition fees. That guarded praise is privately endorsed by civil servants who say Rafferty was focused on policy delivery by contrast with one or two others who tended to be fire-fighters driven by media coverage.

In return, Labour sources say that LibDem demands were frequently unreasonable in relation to their voting strength. They were, in short, looking for more out of the coalition than they were bringing to the bargaining table. These structural complaints on either side have largely persisted, although mitigated by custom, practice and necessity. Labour and the LibDems have learned for the most part to live with each other.

Originally, Labour perhaps thought of themselves as the landlord – with a truculent tenant. The landlord did not particularly like the arrangement – and would definitely have preferred sole occupancy – but needed the rent. Now it feels more like a flat share. The two are not exactly buddies: comradely nights out are few and far between. But they get along. They are Scotland's answer to the Odd Couple.

There has been a change in attitude, which can probably be traced to a particular event. In April 2000, Jim Wallace took questions in the chamber in place of Donald Dewar, who had entered hospital for tests. By common consent, Wallace was excellent, dealing effectively with the challenges from the SNP's Alex Salmond and the Tories' David McLetchie. Labour's backbenchers had been briefed in advance to applaud the stand-in. After a few exchanges, they did not need to be prompted: their enthusiasm was obvious. Sources trace the substantial improvement in off-stage relations between the coalition partners to that event. They say that in the early phase Labour advisers would very much take the lead, if not the sole position, in briefing Dewar prior to questions in the chamber. Naturally, when Wallace deputised, LibDems were closely involved. That arrangement – using the expertise of both sides – has persisted since on a regular basis.

However, mutual incomprehension persists too. The story is told that Tom McCabe, while Labour's business manager and Minister for Parliament, was growing increasingly irritated with the LibDems. His background in Lanarkshire, the natural home of ingrained

Labour machine politics, left him antipathetic to a party which appeared to him to be vacillating on issues for no good reason.

McCabe demanded to know why LibDem Ministers could not simply tell their backbenchers the plain facts, and insist upon a deal. Tavish Scott, then his LibDem counterpart, responded with a wry grin then made him an offer: come to a LibDem group meeting. Just come and listen.

Duly invited, McCabe came, looked, listened and learned. Perhaps he witnessed Donald Gorrie or John Farquhar Munro in full, unstoppable, liberal spate. Perhaps he sat, rapt, as Mike Rumbles listed a few practical problems with the latest Executive Bill. Perhaps he enjoyed a little thespian oratory from Jamie Stone. Whatever, McCabe left chastened and enlightened.

There have been episodes that add to the strain. On 8 March 2001, the Executive lost a vote in Parliament over an aid package for the fishing industry. In essence, Ministers had offered long-term support, but the Tories and the SNP plus some on the LibDem benches were also demanding short-term, emergency assistance for the fleet.

The debate was prompted by a Tory motion urging that short-term package. The final vote on whether to endorse the Tory plan was tied 55–55. But the Executive had previously lost an attempt to amend the Tory motion. The Presiding Officer, Sir David Steel, therefore ruled that the Tory motion had effectively become the status quo. As a consequence, after the tie, he gave his casting vote to the demand for emergency aid for the fishing industry. The vote was overturned the following week, but there was immediate political fall-out. Labour's Scottish conference, which opened the day after the controversial vote, was dominated by talk of tension in the coalition. Tavish Scott, a notably capable LibDem MSP, was obliged to resign as his party's whip, arguing that the confusion prompted by the Executive's stance compromised his position in his Shetland constituency with its substantial fishing fleet.

I believe the row typified the tensions in this coalition. To be blunt, Labour simply did not appreciate the seriousness of the issue for the LibDems. Several central belt MSPs were heard muttering that fishing was getting far too much attention – and far too much money. They plainly wanted the focus switched back to urban Scotland. This position is arguable. What it failed to take account of, however, is the totemic political importance of the fishing industry to rural communities, particularly in the north-east, the eastern Borders and the islands: classic LibDem territory. For Eyemouth or Peterhead, fishing is the equivalent of Ravenscraig, the defunct Motherwell steel complex which came to symbolise industrial central Scotland. The fishing industry has a symbolic importance beyond jobs and investment, beyond the arguments over aid. It is a sense of community, of origin, of shared experience. Politicians neglect that factor at their peril.

At the same time, Labour resented the Liberal Democrat back-bench stance over this issue. Four LibDem MSPs voted with the Opposition parties to contribute to the Executive's defeat. Labour felt some LibDem backbenchers were too casual about the conse-quences of their actions. They felt further that the LibDem approach attached too little importance to the concessions announced by the Minister, Rhona Brankin, a Labour member.

The LibDems say misfortune and muddle compounded the prob-lem. Labour's troops were not all in place by the time of the votes, which came half an hour earlier than usual. Further, the LibDems claim that a last-minute deal might have been possible at an emer-gency Cabinet meeting on the morning of the vote, but that Henry McLeish was delayed, stuck in traffic.

By the time he arrived, Rhona Brankin was already on her feet in the chamber, outlining the long-term aid package, without the additional short-term measures which might have forestalled defeat.

I do not believe that is an argument which can be pushed too far. Had a deal been possible or thought necessary, it could have been announced before the vote – as was done with free personal care – and sold as a response to the views expressed in the debate.

To be fair, the LibDem leadership privately admit that their back benches must bear a substantial degree of responsibility for the row. One source said that the leadership would 'never forgive those MSPs who ambushed the coalition' over the issue.

Yet the coalition has held together – and arguably strengthened. There are fewer efforts now by Opposition parties to prise the coalition members apart: they know from experience it tends to backfire. Labour members have learned the habit of co-existence. The LibDem dissidents privately admit that the coalition has worked better than they expected, which translates as saying that the LibDems have got their way on a number of key issues.

Labour's attitude has changed with the change of First Ministers. Donald Dewar actively sought a partnership and worked closely with Jim Wallace, but, equally, his experience and stature tended to place him out on his own, ahead of the team.

Henry McLeish was arguably the most enthusiastic for the concept of coalition. Cynics might say that was because he lacked whole-hearted support from his Labour Cabinet colleagues. By contrast, I believe that McLeish genuinely grasped and espoused the concept of a new Scotland, outwith narrow confines. In particular, he understood that Scottish patriotism, adherence to Scotland, did not rest with any one party.

McConnell is 'coalition pragmatic', to borrow a phrase from a senior LibDem source. The LibDems were initially apprehensive: they detected an early tendency for McConnell to announce or signal policies without fully considering the sensitivities of his coalition partners. For example, not long after McConnell took over, it was announced that the Executive intended to consult on increasing the Scottish age of criminal responsibility, in keeping with European standards. The line fed to the media, with the First Minister's approval, was that this change would not be made without concrete guarantees that the safety of the public would be protected at all times.

All well and good, apparently. Except that the LibDems had been led to understand that a fully open consultation would be announced, that the Executive would not close down any avenues for potential reform in this area. This was not in itself a significant internal row but it was a pointer to the tension within the coalition which was later to emerge over the self-same issue of youth crime.

The LibDems suspect this early tendency to foster an impression of solitary power by the First Minister was silently encouraged by the civil service, anxious for a return to firm government. In the event, the LibDem fears have proved groundless. McConnell is reform-minded and works hard to preserve the coalition. Labour to his core, he nevertheless understands the need for partnership. A former maths teacher, he can count: he knows that Labour cannot govern alone, at least not without the daily risk of defeat and a daily challenge to the stability of the Executive. Further, he had gained valuable experience of consensus when he worked within the Convention as Labour's General Secretary.

So, when McConnell was obliged to reshuffle his team in May 2002 after the resignation of Wendy Alexander, he turned to Jim Wallace for advice, and indeed made a point of announcing that he would be fully consulting his LibDem counterpart. On an earlier occasion, a Cabinet reshuffle had produced inter-party tensions. In October 2000, as the newly elected First Minister, Henry McLeish had privately signalled to Labour his intention to increase by one the size of his Cabinet.

The snag was that the addition of an extra Labour member would disadvantage the LibDems, tipping the arithmetical balance of the Cabinet in Labour's favour. The LibDems were decidedly upset and convened an emergency group meeting. The row was eventually finessed, but it heightened LibDem suspicion.

So McConnell consulted Jim Wallace at an early stage – and made a show of doing so. Ironically, one option McConnell floated was moving Wallace from Justice to fill Wendy Alexander's Enterprise brief. Wallace declined, preferring his own high-profile remit to what might be seen as a hand-me-down, albeit a powerful hand-me-down. Equally, he was reluctant to move to an entirely new department where he would have to learn an entirely new remit, while, simultaneously, leading his party into the final year of Parliament before the next round of elections. The story of Wallace's stand was duly leaked in an effort, no doubt, to show the LibDems' relative clout within the Cabinet.

McConnell considered moving Mike Watson but ruled this out because he was closely and personally involved in Scotland's bid to host the Euro 2008 football championship. Similarly, McConnell decided against moving Andy Kerr from Finance because he had just begun the process of settling the next departmental spending round. Another option included promotion from the junior ministerial ranks for Peter Peacock.

There were press reports to the effect that Andy Kerr blocked an early return to government for Angus Mackay. To the contrary, I believe that any objections to such a notion would have come from the First Minister, who would be aware that he had only just despatched Mackay from his Cabinet.

In the event, McConnell moved Iain Gray from Social Justice to Enterprise, promoting Gray's deputy Margaret Curran to the Cabinet role. He completed his reshuffle by moving Hugh Henry to deputise at social justice and rehabilitating Frank McAveety as a junior Health Minister. McAveety had been sacked by Henry McLeish.

The promotion of Margaret Curran is significant. Yes, McConnell's options were relatively limited. Yes, he needed another woman in his Cabinet to replace Wendy Alexander. But Curran is very far from being a Jackobite, remote from any taint of sycophancy. She had, however, shown herself to be decidedly able, first as a back-bencher and then as a deputy Minister. Curran was promoted for talent, helping McConnell to rebut claims that he only rewards toadying.

So movement in this reshuffle was confined to Labour ranks, with the LibDems staying resolutely put. Privately, McConnell's team insisted that the First Minister had a Cabinet of his choice and was more than content. Certainly, the First Minister managed to reassert his authority swiftly. In mid-May, the week after the new ministerial team was endorsed by Parliament, Labour contrived to make plain that it was eminently capable of pursuing its own agenda, distinct from coalition aims.

On 15 May, the First Minister announced that he would person-ally chair a new Cabinet subcommittee investigation into youth crime. The initiative was a response to disquiet in Labour back-bench ranks about the extent of teenage disorder in urban Scotland. The move was interpreted by the press as a snub to Wallace, the Justice Minister. It was pointed out that McConnell was not muscling in on his colleague's territory. Youth crime was part of Cathy Jamieson's remit as the Minister for Children and Education.

However, matters moved on. The very same day, I was able to inform an astonished nation on *Reporting Scotland* that Labour was considering the establishment of new youth courts, following the model of specialised courts dealing with drugs offences. The plan reflected concern that the respected Children's Hearing system was simply too soft on persistent offenders. It had, according to one source, 'too much of a social work ethos'.

This was a deliberate move by Labour to advance its own pro-posals on an issue which deeply worried its core support. It was not a break with the coalition but a political recognition that, with elec-tions in the offing, the two Executive parties had to begin setting out their own distinctive proposals. Most observers had expected the minority party, the LibDems, to be the first to produce a policy which departed from coalition consensus. But Labour got there ahead of their partners.

It is important to understand that the issue of youth crime was carefully chosen for this purpose. First, it resonated with Labour voters who are resolutely sick of teenage yobs ruining their neighbourhoods. Second, it was virtually guaranteed to diverge from the LibDem perspective. On crime and punishment, Labour could rely upon the LibDems to be . . . well, liberal.

The LibDems duly responded, voicing support for the concept of Children's Hearings with their emphasis on rehabilitation and their remoteness from formal court procedure. The controversy grew. On Thursday, 16 May, Jim Wallace was interrogated by police superintendents at their conference in Peebles as he defended Executive plans to extend the Hearings system to older, first-time minor offenders. The same day, Wallace sat in obligatory silence in Parliament as Jack McConnell expounded his line on youth crime at First Minister's questions.

Wallace was understandably irked, not least because, according to one source, he had briefly floated the notion of youth courts with McConnell. He had been told it was under consideration as a possible Labour manifesto idea, but had not expected early public disclosure. As Wallace walked back down the Royal Mile from Parliament that day, the party's able media officer Neil Mackinnon consoled him, arguing that the row was purely a consequence of electoral politics.

To be fair, Wallace was well aware of that. The First Minister and his deputy easily resolved any lingering irritation over the issue, recognising that there would be more and more occasions when the parties required to diverge fractionally from the established Executive line. As one source put it, they ended up 'almost laughing together' over the whole affair. Note that 'almost'.

On 22 May, the Cabinet subcommittee on youth crime held its first meeting, with Jack McConnell in the chair alongside Jim Wallace, Cathy Jamieson, Margaret Curran and the Lord Advocate. There had been advance press reports suggesting that Labour – and McConnell in particular – favoured jailing parents who persistently failed to subdue their errant offspring or oblige them to attend school from time to time.

However, at the media briefing afterwards, Cathy Jamieson repeatedly distanced the Executive from this notion, stressing that Ministers wanted to examine other options such as making better use of existing powers within the Hearings system and, if necessary, extending the powers available by legislation. She confirmed that youth courts would feature on the agenda.

It appeared that the liberal – and, arguably, the Liberal – perspective on crime had made a comeback. However, the LibDems were disinclined to crow, claiming privately that the idea of throwing parents in the slammer had never been a runner in the first place, that it was only discussed by the subcommittee in terms of how to handle the inevitable media questions. The row resurfaced on 13 June 2002. MSPs were debating a proposal to pilot an extension of the Children's Hearings system to cover youngsters aged 16 and 17. The Conservative leader David McLetchie was getting right up ministerial noses, noting acidly that such a plan would mean that a 17-year-old husband could theoretically go before a Children's Panel for beating up his wife.

Ministers angrily disputed that, stressing that the panels would only be used for minor offences where it was felt that the ethos of the Hearings system might be appropriate. Deputy Justice Minister Richard Simpson went a little further, arguing that alternatives to Children's Panels did not work, that the juvenile court system in England, for example, was 'an absolute disaster'.

This was fine as a slab of rhetoric to slap down a pestilential Opposition critic. The snag was that it appeared to run completely contrary to Jack McConnell's stated enthusiasm for the concept of youth courts in Scotland. The Executive issued a statement in an attempt to 'clarify' matters. Hilariously, this said that the Minister had been 'in no way inferring that the English system was inappropriate (i.e. a disaster)' which, of course, cleared everything up instantly. Presumably, the Minister had been using the word 'disaster' in its positive, upbeat sense.

More sensibly, the statement further argued that what worked south of the border would not necessarily work in Scotland. Ministers were seeking a distinctively Scottish solution. To be absolutely fair, I think this spat derived from honourable efforts – on all sides – to find a solution to a seemingly intractable problem. There is no right and wrong here, no clear-cut fight between Executive and

Opposition. Rather, all politicians are ranged across a broad policy spectrum from liberalism to lock 'em up.

The issue of teenage crime is desperately serious and is receiving serious attention from MSPs of all parties. As well as considering criminal behaviour, perhaps MSPs need to pay more attention to the 'order' aspects of law and order. Scotland needs to deal with the vandalism, graffiti and hooligan behaviour which disrupts normal life and, unchecked, provides fertile soil for crime.

As far as the coalition is concerned, I think there may be much less to the youth-courts row than meets the eye. Yes, there are ideological differences between Labour and the LibDems, which the youth-crime issue conveniently highlighted, but who expected anything else? As one of Wallace's colleagues told me: 'If the *Daily Mail* wants to brand me a liberal, then I'm proud to plead guilty. I joined the Liberal Party, which is a bit of a clue.'

This question of youth courts was simply the first in a series of issues designed to stress – or contrive – policy distance between Labour and the Liberal Democrats. My observation is that the two parties have both changed as a consequence of coalition – without losing their individual identities to any great extent. Further, given the electoral system, minority politics would appear to be a fixture in Scotland.

That does not, of course, guarantee coalition. For example, Labour might choose to go it alone in future, effectively challenging the Parliament on a daily basis to vote down the party's programme. The LibDems might rediscover the joys of a period in Opposition. I must confess I find neither scenario likely, given the pleasures of majority administration and the pain of hirpling along in a minority.

Alternatively, there might be a government of another hue. Remember, though, that the voting system for the Scottish Parliament was specifically designed by Labour to prevent the SNP from taking majority power with a minority, even a sizeable minority, of the popular vote. To take control, the Scottish National Party would need pals. But who? For the Nationalists, Labour or the Tories are presently inconceivable partners. The SNP has a fixed policy ruling out any dealings with the Unionist Tories. Labour is the entrenched enemy of the SNP throughout urban Scotland. The LibDems, then? The Liberal Democrat leadership has a fundamental objection to the SNP policy of a referendum on independence.

But could that seemingly solid obstacle slip? SNP strategists believe they could perhaps rely upon momentum to oblige the LibDems to obey the popular will. Even then, they might need votes from elsewhere, perhaps the Scottish Socialists and the Greens. The snag is neither of the minor parties favours formal coalition.

This all brings SNP strategists back to: what if? What if the Socialists and Greens – who both back Scottish independence – could be prevailed upon at least to work with a Nationalist-led Executive? What if the SNP has clearly moved forward in the popular vote, while Labour has lost support? In those circumstances, it is argued it would appear perverse for the LibDems to thwart that movement by allying with a party which had slipped back.

But coalition has changed the LibDems. They are a more confident party. Jim Wallace is reluctant to consider working with the SNP for three reasons. One, it would appear to disavow the good work he believes has been done in partnership with Labour. Two, he is a staunch Unionist, intuitively hostile to the SNP's main aim. Three, he knows that even speculating about such a deal might talk up the prospects for the SNP, who are the LibDems' main rivals for list votes in Glasgow and other parts of Scotland.

Longer term, there are other intriguing scenarios. If the Nationalists continue to do relatively well but cannot achieve power on their own, could they end up changing their stance and doing a deal with, for example, a revamped Tory Party? On the fringe of the Scottish Conservative conference in May 2002, Brian Monteith MSP – a thoughtful Tory libertarian – argued that his party must confront the realities of PR politics.

He said the Tories must consider advancing policies which had a chance of producing resonance on other benches, with possible coalition in mind. Monteith urged other parties to respond in kind. Specifically, he suggested that a Tory Party of the future might endorse full tax powers for the devolved Parliament and might therefore be able to find accommodation with the SNP, whose declared ambition is to extend the scope of devolution towards independence.

Monteith believes the parties might be able to resolve the question of an independence referendum. The Tories would agree to hold such a ballot, provided the SNP accepted that, if the people voted against independence, there would be no repeat of the process for perhaps a decade at least.

Right now, such a scenario seems decidedly unlikely. The Tories are quintessentially Unionists: it is part of their name in Scotland, part of their intrinsic nature. The Nationalists may have a more complex approach these days, but they remain in favour of independence. Monteith was at least partly urging his own colleagues to think outside their party box, and partly urging other parties to end the Tories' status as the political pariahs of Scotland. He wants Tory thinking to be accorded an accepted place in Scottish political debate.

So there are subtleties to be considered beyond party boundaries which are, frankly, far less rigid than puritans would wish. Look at another option. Could progressive opinion on the Labour benches work with progressive opinion on the SNP benches?

Privately, one or two Nationalists mutter that they have more in common with Labour social democrats than they have with some on their own side. Less privately, one or two Labour optimists forecast a schism in the SNP between the fundamentalists ('independence, nothing less') and the gradualists ('let's work for Scotland, regardless'). This, it is claimed, would allow the gradualists to work with Labour.

As I write, each of those alternative scenarios looks less likely, certainly in the short to medium term, than the continuation of the coalition between Labour and the LibDems. However, I referred earlier to lessons from political experience in Ireland. There is one further Irish lesson. However unlikely a coalition might appear in advance, if the voting figures point that way, it will happen. Somehow, it will happen.

6 An Uncivil Service?

It is decreed. Petitions to the Scottish Parliament 'must not contain offensive language'. For the avoidance of doubt, it is specified that means no nasty, sweary words, nor phrasing which is 'intemperate, inflammatory, sarcastic or provocative'. There is simply no joy left in politics.

Even as I reflect that our MSPs are denying linguistic licence to others which they frequently exploit for themselves, I think on. The petitions committee is a success, part of the new politics of Scotland. It should perhaps be forgiven a slightly puritanical approach. Intriguingly, public petitions apparently played a big role in the ancient, independent Scottish Parliament, and have now been revived as part of the modern, democratic structure. (For this information, incidentally, I rely upon academic research. Contrary to wicked jibes, I was not around to report upon the pre-Union Parliament.)

The theory is that any member of the public can approach the petitions committee with a grievance, and expect at least a hearing if not immediate redress. The provisos are that the petition must be serious, it must fall within the ambit of the devolved Parliament, it must not interfere with a court case, unless to suggest a longer term amendment to the law, and the petitioner must have attempted to pursue other avenues such as writing directly to the Executive.

The committee, convened by the estimable John McAllion, has had its share of teething troubles. There is at least one serial petitioner who would appear to read the morning press or listen to *Good Morning Scotland* – and pick up a pen instantly. By now, this persistent individual is probably on 'Dear John' terms with the convener. But still the committee is a success. It has genuinely contrived to provide a conduit for people to voice grievances. The very existence of the committee means that there is a body dedicated to ensuring that those grievances – perhaps imperfectly expressed, perhaps half-formed – get an answer. Maybe not the answer required, but attention. Politicians are paying attention. I glanced at the committee's website and picked a meeting at random. That particular day, the members were discussing the planning system, miscarriages of justice, the Scottish Agricultural College, budget cuts in the Borders, water boards and predatory birds. The petitions committee operates by requiring other wings of the Parliament – perhaps subject committees like education or health – to pay heed and respond, where the issue is deemed sufficiently serious. It is a filter, a monitor, but also an engine to drive forward popular concerns. For example, public anxiety over sharply disputed claims that the MMR triple vaccine might be linked to autism was channelled through the petitions committee and resulted in an official inquiry.

The other committees of the Parliament have also contrived to varying degrees to open themselves to public opinion. The Scottish committee system is definitely part of the new politics. For a start, Holyrood's committees combine legislative and evidence-gathering functions. They bring together the standing and select committee powers familiar from Westminster.

The theory is that the Scottish committees, which largely match the powers of the devolved Executive, will scrutinise planned legislation in advance, helping to determine its general shape. The same committee will then use its body of acquired expertise to process legislation line by line. Further, the committees have the power to interrogate Ministers and other witnesses, to launch inquiries into areas of concern within their subject and to initiate legislation for themselves. I believe all these functions have been carried out reasonably successfully. Individual committee members have, indeed, developed particular skills that allow them to contribute intelligently to a more elevated debate than is often possible in partisan politics.

MSPs do not leave their party cards at the door but the business-like and consensual atmosphere appears to be infectious.

There are, however, one or two significant caveats to be lodged. First, I think committees, particularly in the early days, have been far too keen to wheel in the relevant Minister for a prolonged and pointless grilling – often without any particular objective in mind. No doubt it is entertaining for Opposition members (or thwarted Executive backbenchers) to deliver a good kicking to a Minister. But, unless there is a precise agenda, this can swiftly deteriorate into formulaic and futile point-scoring.

Second, I think there is still too little emphasis on a strict evidence-based approach. There can be a slack temptation to call upon the usual suspects in a particular field: the union, the academic, the charitable pressure group. Again particularly in the early days, these witnesses were often allowed to deliver a lengthy opening statement with little related questioning. The individuals thus invited were often touchingly grateful. No-one had paid them so much attention before. This is more like it, you could see them thinking, this is what devolution is all about. I believe things have improved in that respect. Committees tend to have a sharper focus in their inquiries. They subject witnesses to closer cross-examination to establish their credentials and whether their views are representative.

If possible, the committees should extend this, attempting to gather ideas and opinions from those actually affected by proposed legislation or Executive initiatives. For example, they should talk to the people in the housing schemes directly concerned with street crime, rather than their appointed or self-appointed mouthpieces. To be fair, some already do this, using MSP rapporteurs to brief the rest of the committee on their findings.

The committees frequently complain that they are the forgotten stars of the Scottish Parliament, that they are the hard-working engine room of devolution. Certainly, with few exceptions, committee members are assiduous. The work is demanding, the workload prodigious. Members can become almost obsessive about the task of getting to the source of a particular concern.

I believe, too, that the committees are steadily gaining individual reputations within their particular fields. They are much less inclined to fall into the twin traps which ensnared them at earlier phases in the Parliament's life; taking 'expert' evidence on trust or bombarding witnesses with dogged questions without any clear objective for the interrogation. However, I remain cautious in my verdict. It is still just two cheers for the committee system. Members *are* occasionally too partisan – or intellectually bewildered. Conveners are occasionally prone to grandstand, showing off their expertise rather than directing their colleagues into more productive lines of inquiry. In general, though, the committees are working well, sometimes very well.

The Scottish system has one big plus which outweighs any lingering limitations. Scotland's Parliamentary committees are beyond the scope, beyond the control of the Executive. I have witnessed, by contrast, the law-making committees at Westminster, the standing committees, where the Commons majority is palpably in charge.

At Westminster, legislative or standing committees are convened purely for the purpose of considering a particular Bill line by line, upstairs from the main chamber in the committee corridor. The committee is therefore a transient item, not a group with its own ethos and customs. The government side will normally feature one or two Ministers plus a Whip. It takes a particular effort of will for backbenchers to challenge their dominance.

A particularly contentious issue may stir a genuine debate, and these are frequently of high calibre. But the objective of the government is to get its Bill through with the minimum of disruption. Committee members on the government side will be encouraged to sit quiet and get on with their constituency correspondence, while the Opposition benches lodge a series of frequently bogus amendments to provoke debate or waste time.

It should be stressed that these comments do not, of course, apply to the Select Committees at Westminster, which have a quite separate role. They do not consider legislation but conduct inquiries, interrogate witnesses and produce reports. They have a permanent membership and – with occasional exceptions – carry out their noble function, which is to be a pain in the collective governing backside.

Again, I would not wish to suggest that the Scottish system is without fault. Committees at Holyrood endure their share of tendentious drivel from the Opposition and tedious sycophancy from Executive supporters. But there are key differences.

First, as mentioned earlier, the committees at Holyrood are managing to develop their own expertise. An important part of the

new Scottish politics is that there is public consultation over the
basic principles of proposed changes to the law before that legislation enters the formal Parliamentary system. That consultation is
conducted by the committees who hear evidence as to whether a
Bill is needed at all and, if it is, whether the proposed Bill meets the
perceived need. It is undoubtedly helpful that the MSPs who consider legislation line by line are the very same MSPs who have
previously conducted this general investigation.

Second, the Scottish committees were deliberately created without a formal Executive membership. Executive Ministers have no
vote when the Scottish committees are considering legislation line
by line. There is no Whip on the committee, corralling the members.
The Executive can explain, plead and cajole, but it has no formal
vote.

Committee membership matches the political colour of the
chamber, and so the Executive majority is narrow. More than one
Minister and civil servant has told me privately that the Executive
is obliged to tread exceptionally carefully when committees are
considering Bills, that there are no overt levers to pull to exercise
influence and relatively few discreet ones. I would suspect that case
is perhaps a little overstated. The Executive majority, narrow though
it may be, will still tend to prevail in most cases. However, committee
ethos in Scotland creates a predisposition to subject legislation to
Parliamentary rather than purely partisan scrutiny.

Ministers and civil servants, naturally, attend committee sessions
on Executive legislation. They argue their case, but it is important to
understand the psychological distinction between a Westminster
committee effectively run from the inside by the government and a
Scottish committee, with its own ethos, inviting the Executive to
attend and comment.

This Scottish formula was deliberately devised in an effort to alter
the balance of power between Executive and Parliament. The theory
was that legislation was a matter for Parliament, that it could be
instigated by Executive, by committees or by individual members,
but that MSPs, not Ministers, would then determine its progress. I
believe the balance of power has been successfully tilted, although I
would add that the record is a little patchy on the origin of legislation. Perhaps understandably, Executive Bills still predominate. There
have been demonstrations of Parliamentary power, notably when

Street politics: one view of the fox-hunting debate.

Labour back-bench disquiet obliged the Executive to accept Tommy Sheridan's Bill to abolish warrant sales. (The acceptance was qualified by the insistence on finding an alternative scheme for debt recovery and, as I write, those qualifications are still being hotly debated.) Then there was the Bill to ban hunting with dogs, originally introduced by Mike Watson while a Labour back-bench MSP. Its prolonged progress scarcely enhanced the reputation of the committee system or Parliament.

Perhaps the Bill was badly drafted, perhaps its legislative intention was unclear, perhaps its social or class motivation was all too clear, perhaps the Parliamentary opposition to the Bill was disproportionate, perhaps the several legal challenges were unwarranted interference with Parliamentary democracy, perhaps the accusations of an anti-rural bias were overblown. On 13 February 2002, the Bill finally cornered its foxy quarry, exhausted and irritable after endless hours of committee wrangling. On that day, the Bill reached the main chamber for its third and last stage of consideration by MSPs. Civil servants muttered a discreet 'view halloo' and rode in to try to rescue Parliament from the legislative muddle.

During the lengthy session, it fell to Cathy Jamieson – then a Labour backbencher, later Education Minister – to deliver the most impassioned denunciation of the alleged horrors of hunting. It fell to Ross Finnie, as Rural Affairs Minister, to advance several amendments on behalf of the Executive designed to sort out the Bill. Finnie indicated that his role was not to judge the merits of the Bill either way, but to make it work in line with the declared will of Parliament at Stages One and Two for a ban on hunting with hounds.

Ross Finnie duly secured as many wording amendments as he could, then joined his LibDem Cabinet colleague Jim Wallace in voting against the Bill in the final division. Neither, apparently, was convinced that the Bill, even after the Executive's tender care, was in a fit state to write into the statute book.

I offer no judgement myself on whether the new law is fair and workable: that will be tested in the courts. However, setting aside for a moment the quite remarkable displays of emotion on either side, Parliament *had* plainly voiced support for a ban, and the Executive was right to attempt to remedy perceived flaws in the legislation. In the aftermath, one civil servant remarked privately to me that the confusion over fox hunting proved the need for Executive drafting and supervision of legislation. The word 'control' was not used, but that was what was meant.

Certainly the fox-hunting farce was scarcely a good advertisement for open, non-Executive law-making. Perhaps, however, Parliament has learned lessons. Perhaps, MSPs will stop asking themselves: 'What shall we do next?' Perhaps, they will increasingly say: 'How shall we do it – and why?' Either way, the fox-hunting controversy recalls another aspect of the new politics: the changing relationship between politicians and civil servants.

For a century and more, the old Scottish Office administered Scotland on behalf of London. The overall ambition, not an ignoble one in the context of defending the state, was to placate Scotland, to offer concessions to Scottish sentiment while maintaining an essentially united body of policy north and south of the border.

The relationship was frequently prickly, especially when Scotland sought to make a stand on some issue or other. Indeed, Rhodri Morgan, the First Minister of Wales, contrasted the attitude of the Scottish Office with that of the Welsh Office, where he used to work as a civil servant. He said: 'You promoted staff in the Scottish Office on the basis that they had put one over Whitehall. You promoted staff in the Welsh Office on the basis of whether they had kept their nose clean in Whitehall.'[1]

But at least the Scottish Office and Whitehall departments were part of the same government. To a large extent, they are in the same overall team still, but I believe that, beneath the surface, there has been substantial change, although the extent of that change has perhaps yet to be fully absorbed. The Executive may still look the same. It occupies the same premises as the former Scottish Office, the staff are still members of the Home Civil Service along with their colleagues in Whitehall. But, for all that, the Executive – Ministers and civil servants combined – now form a government, not a branch of government.

It is important not to push this too far. Executive civil servants know their limits. They work within Treasury rules and block spending constraints. As I shall examine later, in Chapter 14, they are careful not to overstep the mark on issues like representation in Europe. They are institutionally alert to the importance of the United Kingdom.

However, the Executive is a government. It decides priorities according to its own policy programme. It allocates spending according to presumed Scottish need. Without any obligatory reference to London, it advances a detailed programme of legislation to remedy perceived defects in the established canon of Scots law. It has a departmental structure of its own, with internal competition for funds and status.

Yes, it is constrained by UK rules and structures, but, then, arguably member states within the European Union are constrained by the rules and structures of that organisation. External constraint does not preclude a body from governing within those limits. The Scottish Executive is not *the* government, but it is *a* government.

Like governments elsewhere, there are structural tensions. One of the most significant is the emerging and developing relationship between Ministers and the civil service. To a large extent, this mirrors the controversy in Whitehall over accountability and service delivery. I intend, however, to focus upon Scotland.

Privately, some – I stress, *some* – Labour insiders can be decidedly snide about the civil service. Liberal Democrats have a different agenda, based upon concerns that they can end up sidelined in civil-service thought processes. Some Ministers profess themselves relaxed about the relationship, arguing that robust political leadership can overcome any problems with the civil service. However, discontent among Labour Ministers is relatively common. One senior Labour insider told me of the shock on first entering government to find the relatively low calibre of the civil service at junior ranks. He said: 'We knew some of the top guys like Muir Russell and Robert Gordon, and we thought the civil service was just full of incredibly bright people. Then we got in and found that the others weren't like that at all.' Another told me that the upper ranks of the service appeared 'snobbish' to Labour arrivistes, while the junior ranks often sat silent. Labour Ministers frequently talk of having to press umpteen times to get action on a particular issue. They voice their suspicions that the civil service operates to a different standing agenda. One described the senior civil servants as 'endlessly wily'.

It is important to understand that this view is ingrained in some Labour Ministers, both in London and Edinburgh. Like Thatcherite Tories before them, they instinctively suspect that civil servants are not on side, not 'one of us', not signed up to the Project. These Ministers can end up seeing themselves as heroic battlers against the internal machine, perpetually thwarted and frustrated, only winning out through superhuman effort.

Such Ministers – and, again, this is a widespread view – try to go round the civil service. They use special advisers, often with a party background, who serve as paid public officials but can offer partisan political guidance in addition to policy analysis. Alternatively, Ministers may tap in to external advice from supposed experts. They use Parliamentary devices to force the civil-service machine to act, perhaps bringing an issue into the open by asking sympathetic backbenchers to press for reform in a particular area.

I hear what is said, and I understand that it must be frustrating for an eager politician bristling with ideas to find that the standard mandarin response is: 'Well, if you're sure, Minister . . . ?' Further, civil servants do have a bit of a tendency to act as the permanent government obliged to endure, for the sake of form, a group of 'here today and gone tomorrow' Ministers, in Sir Robin Day's memorable phrase.

This clash has produced some remarkable spats inside the Executive. Often these rows have little bearing on the issue at hand. Rather, they are substitutes for the wider 'who governs' conflict. For example, in July 2001, the Executive had to find a replacement for Kenneth Mackenzie as civil-service head of the Development Department. For very good reasons, politicians are constrained from interfering too much in the selection of senior civil servants who may end up serving an administration of a different colour long after their present bosses have been ousted from office.

However, on this occasion, a couple of Ministers voiced concern. They did not seek the final say, but they wanted the shortlist for the job extended, suspecting that the Permanent Secretary, Muir Russell, had a favourite in mind. Further, they wanted to look at reshaping the department itself, matching its structure more closely to new ministerial portfolios. A significant private row produced the customary compromise: the department was left alone but the shortlist was duly altered.

Later, in June 2002, there was another bitter – and very public – row over civil-service appointments. Jack McConnell's aides briefed that the First Minister was deeply unhappy with newspaper advertisements for up to forty new policy analysts to work within the Executive. Sunday newspapers were told that McConnell had been kept in the dark, and that he intended to confront the Permanent Secretary.

I understand the First Minister's motivation. Opposition parties had complained, variously, that the Executive was grandstanding, or that the new analysts would effectively end up writing Labour's manifesto, breaching the neutrality of the civil service. Team McConnell felt they needed to squash these complaints.

This was all fair enough, but the response was disproportionate. Point one, civil-service posts are – rightly – nothing to do with politicians. Point two, thirty-two of the forty jobs were filling exist-ing vacancies: only eight were new. Point three, the money for the jobs had already been allocated: this was not freelance empire building by Muir Russell. Point four, the Opposition parties were trying it on with their complaints: they could not believe their luck when the First Minister's aides responded. Point five, the complaints could have been addressed by issuing a written rebuttal, rather than by briefing against the Executive's own top civil servant.

It would seem that, on further reflection, Jack McConnell acknowledged these points. Certainly, he moved to close the row down notably swiftly. Muir Russell returned from a brief holiday in France, and duly met the First Minister. In a low-key joint statement, the Permanent Secretary voiced his concern that the purpose of the adverts had been distorted by the media. Had he anticipated such wicked behaviour, he would of course have alerted the First Minister. In return, the First Minister withdrew any threat of a veto upon the job appointments, which ended this dispute. More generally, though, I stress again that I can understand the overall ministerial motivation. At the end of the day, Ministers must have their way. Elected politician trumps appointed official. I believe, however, that some complaints are overstated: that Ministers, some Ministers, protest too much about the civil service.

First, while it is critically important to get external advice, outwith the formal civil service, the experience to date is not wholly positive. In the early days of the Executive – and the UK Government – the political special advisers too often ended up bickering with each other on behalf of their ministers. They also had a tendency to flock together at moments of crisis, dousing the latest storm in the media rather than keeping to the medium- or long-term agenda.

To be fair, each was individually highly talented. The system – and their place within it – required definition. Matters have improved since, although there are still internal tensions. One or two civil servants privately fret that Jack McConnell has relied heavily on a small coterie of special advisers, particularly Jeane Freeman, a notably bright policy aide with a reputation for knowing what she wants. The civil servants stress their aim is *not* to push an official 'line' but to ensure that the First Minister has access to the widest possible range of advice.

This argument can produce a sceptical chortle from the corps of special advisers. They say Ministers favour their advice precisely because it blends policy options with political reality, with the electoral consequences that are critically important for every politician. I would not want to overstate this problem. Civil servants and special advisers generally contrive to work together, recognising that the overall objective is to produce the best possible policy programme for the Executive. Tensions between these two camps are probably inevitable, built into the structure. They are like competing courtiers, each seeking to catch royal attention.

So what about the alternative? What about advice sourced entirely outside government? External experts, for example in the university sector, can be brilliant in their field, without having a clue as to how to translate their expertise into a practical programme which an Executive or Parliament can implement. Sometimes, indeed, their research can appear almost perversely obscure, and remote from popular concerns. I am aware that there are key figures inside the Executive and academia who are keenly alert to this problem, and are seeking remedies. It is not suggested that academia should become a subset of public affairs. There must be room for pure research. However, we are plainly missing a trick in Scotland. We need answers to social and economic problems. Finding these answers requires expertise and time. Academics, if suitably channelled, are ideally placed to carry out that task. They would, I suspect, find it enthralling to work to a real rather than notional target.

There is in Scotland a nascent think-tank network, notably the Scottish Council Foundation, which is beginning to have an impact. There is room for more, for expansion of this sector. However, this will complement – not supplant – the civil service. It is for the Executive – civil service, special advisers and Ministers – to sift the advice coming from external sources. Equally, I feel some of the complaints directed at the civil service are the product of political frustration and motivations which are different, one from the other. Politicians are driven by electoral consequences and, sometimes, by the media. It could scarcely be otherwise. By definition, since they depend on votes, they will be reluctant to propose anything which is unpopular. Quite right too. That is the basis of popular democracy.

However, civil servants are not intuitively driven by such motivations. That is not to say they deliberately pursue unpopular policies, or thwart Ministers. Far from it: the notion of service means bailing the Minister out when things go wrong. Also, contrary to myth, civil servants are human. They like to see their Minister and their department doing well. It is good for morale, good for the mandarin soul.

Yet their motivations are different. They have to think beyond the headlines and the next election, to the next administration, to the longer term impact of a piece of legislation or an Executive initiative. Let me give you an example. Driven by popular and media pressure plus their own instincts, Ministers were understandably keen to end the situation whereby men accused of rape could cross-examine their alleged victims personally in court. There had been harrowing examples of protracted inquisitions which appeared designed to increase the suffering of the complainant.

Civil servants, apparently, raised doubts, provoking occasional ministerial irritation. I believe the civil servants were quite right – indeed, obliged – to raise doubts. Yes, the plan had noble and worthwhile aims. But did it not also risk eroding the rights of the accused, the nature of jury trial, and, arguably, the presumption of innocence? At the same time, there were concerns that the reform might breach the European Convention on Human Rights. I say again, the civil service were obliged to raise these doubts, and to keep raising them until they were satisfactorily addressed, which, in this case, they were. By such objections, new laws are tested in advance in Parliament and inside government, rather than, subsequently, in the law courts when they are challenged.

It is important to remember that civil servants do not counsel caution out of badness. The independence of the civil service is not an accident or a mandarin whim. It is a key check within the UK – and now the devolved – constitution. However, the civil service is much less defensible on the issue of service delivery. Departmental civil servants can be a whiz at writing White Papers. They appear considerably less assured when it comes to the task of turning the objectives of the White Paper into practice.

This is a problem which has confronted governments down the ages and is now confronting the Executive. Ministers say what they want done; civil servants translate that request into dense prose and endless targets for action by someone else. In the last resort, the department will announce a five-year plan. What happens then? Nothing.

This is, of course, a ludicrous and deliberate oversimplification. The law changes; local authorities are constrained to work within the Executive's declared aims; and partnerships are struck with the private sector which produce results. However, delivery can end up falling well short of aspirations. Ministers know that. To be fair, the civil service itself is well aware of this structural problem and is actively seeking remedies.

There are two principal strategic changes in hand. First, the talk is of constructing a narrative for Executive policy. Instead of simply setting short-term targets and longer term aims, the Executive wants to map out and to track progress, to recognise as part of the internal culture that White Papers are not an end in themselves.

Second, there is a drive towards more evidence-based research. Inside the Executive, the analysis, statistical and research functions have been modernised. Instead of pursuing their own ends, these functions are now integrated within the wider Executive structure, providing valuable back-up to the policy teams.

The aim must be to build similar links with external sources of advice. I believe the civil-service machine must end any lingering institutional suspicion of 'outsiders', and make use of available resources. Similarly, I believe those external sources of advice must sharpen up to deal with the exigencies of politics and government.

The Executive civil servants are well aware that things have changed. In his 'mission statement' for the Executive, the Permanent Secretary Sir Muir Russell – a talented, intellectual and astute boss – says the new set-up must be 'open and in touch'. It must earn respect and trust for its efforts to promote Scottish interests. He describes the challenge as 'a new era in the government of Scotland'. To greet that new era, the Executive civil service is led by a senior management team, matching the principal service departments.

Apart from Sir Muir himself, John Elvidge now attends Cabinet meetings as head of finance and central services, a key role at the core of government. He replaced Robert Gordon, who is chief executive at the Crown Office, helping to drive the reform programme in Scotland's creaking courts service. Nicola Munro heads the development department, with Mike Ewart at education, Eddie Frizzell at enterprise, John Graham at environment and rural affairs, Trevor Jones at health and Jim Gallagher at justice. Dr Peter Collings is the principal finance officer and Agnes Robson the principal establishment officer. Even as I write, further change is planned. The First Minister is setting up a scrutiny team to monitor executive efficiency – and Sir Muir has announced he will move in 2003 to become Principal of Glasgow University.

Of course, there is a further 'external' source of advice available to the Executive: Her Majesty's government. Westminster, Whitehall, Downing Street, all these powerbases remain firmly part of the new politics affecting Scotland. We shall look later at the relationship between the Executive and the various Whitehall departments. There is also a further liaison point which we must not neglect: the Scotland Office.

To be honest, this is rather a curious beast – a residuary body from old Scottish Office days, neither a fully-fledged Whitehall department nor truly part of the day-to-day machinery of government in devolved Scotland, which is also privately recognised by political insiders.

Post-devolution, it was decided that there should be a mechanism linking the new Scottish Executive with the UK government. Scotland had previously been represented by a Secretary of State within the UK Cabinet. This post was retained, but the role was transformed into one of liaison. The theory was that the Scotland Office would act as a go-between, reflecting the Executive to the UK government and the UK government to the Executive.

The vast bulk of Scottish Office staff transferred to the new devolved Executive. The slimline Scotland Office retains around 100 staff, a tiny cohort by comparison with the thousands who toiled at the old Scottish Office, although still far too many for the critics who say it has no role whatsoever. The Scotland Office itself says the staff are needed to prepare briefs for Cabinet and its committees where the Scottish Secretary is frequently consulted on detailed policy questions.

Intriguingly, Scottish Executive Ministers have been inclined to bypass the Scotland Office. Donald Dewar apparently felt that a department of state in Whitehall – albeit a small one like the new Scotland Office – was unnecessary. He believed any work involved could be carried out by a ministerial private office, with a handful of staff reporting directly to the Secretary of State.

The customary image of Dewar is of a politician keen to maintain links with London. Certainly, he had a Westminster background – and was institutionally leery of anything that would rock the cross-border boat – but, according to well-placed sources, he disliked the notion of a Scotland Office and adopted a 'scorched-earth' policy towards it on occasion. At a personal level, there were differences in outlook and approach between Donald Dewar and John Reid, the first post-devolution Scottish Secretary. The two had a blazing semi-public row on the fringe of a Labour conference, driven partly by claims of hostile briefing and counter-briefing.

Similarly, Reid and Henry McLeish faced difficulties in their relationship. Sources say there were even quibbles over precedence: that is, who should speak first at shared public events. The relationship – cool to begin with – plummeted several degrees more when McLeish was caught on tape in conversation with Helen Liddell at the climax of the 2001 UK General Election describing Reid as 'a patronising bastard'.

McLeish contrived to laugh it off reasonably well, tapping a microphone during his next Parliamentary appearance in a mock attempt at caution. As for John Reid, he has somehow managed to survive McLeish's criticism. He is one of the most intellectual and analytical members of Tony Blair's team, an acute observer of politics, government and people. Those skills have transferred with him to his new brief in Northern Ireland, where there is no question that the Secretary of State has a substantial continuing role.

He is extremely pleasant company and one of the wittiest speakers in politics: his annual address closing the Scottish Labour conference is simply brilliant. He can also be . . . on occasion . . . a . . . just a *tiny* bit of a . . . no, better not, maybe that microphone is live. Things have settled down with the passage of time. The division of responsibilities is clear between Jack McConnell in St Andrew's House and Helen Liddell in Dover House, the magnificent headquarters for Scottish affairs in Whitehall.

Liddell seems keen to avoid conflict, to work within her brief alongside her deputy, initially George Foulkes then, after a reshuffle, Anne McGuire. Together, the Secretary of State and deputy field questions on a monthly basis in the Commons – a rather bizarre affair when inquiries have to be phrased in a way that gets round the undoubted fact that the vast bulk of domestic Scottish power now resides elsewhere, in Edinburgh.

In addition, Scottish affairs are monitored in London by the Advocate General, Lynda Clark, who advises on the legal implications of devolution, including looking out for any instances of the

Scottish Parliament exceeding its powers. She, too, is questioned monthly in the Commons. The Scotland Office also has a representative in Westminster's Upper House, Lord McIntosh of Haringey.

The Prime Minister, apparently, is content that the early conflicts have gone. On one occasion, he greeted Helen Liddell at a reception and said: 'Are you coming to see me?' On being told that the Scotland Office had no pressing matters to raise with the Prime Minister, Blair replied, with a smile: 'Good!'

Helen Liddell keeps her views to herself but I cannot imagine that she is entirely content in a job so divorced from primary policy preparation. Yes, there is a job representing Scotland in Cabinet and its committees. Yes, the Secretary of State can plead Scotland's case on reserved issues like defence orders. There is, however, a fundamental weakness in the role of post-devolution Scottish Secretary. Domestic power over Scottish affairs lies elsewhere. The Secretary of State knows that, and, crucially for the status of her post, so does the rest of Whitehall. The Executive has tended to build its own links with individual departments in London, short-cutting the need to use the Scotland Office. The Permanent Secretary at the Executive, Sir Muir Russell, is very well connected in Whitehall.

The rather anomalous position of the Scotland Office was highlighted by a curious controversy early in 2002. George Foulkes, then Liddell's deputy, floated the notion that the Executive might not have complete control over whether to site any new nuclear plant in Scotland. Planning controls were devolved, but the need to maintain the UK's overall supply of energy was reserved to Westminster. Without going into details, Foulkes speculated that it might be seen as strange if the overall energy ambitions of the UK were thwarted by planning objections in Scotland. It was plain that the question was being internally reviewed as part of a wider study.

The nuclear issue caused a substantial political row and, eventually, the Prime Minister issued a letter stressing that planning powers, and hence control, were indeed devolved to Scotland. The desirability of cross-border co-operation was also stressed.

The further question is whether co-operation in the wider sense requires continuing lubrication from the Scotland Office, or whether the post of Scottish Secretary should vanish. I have long forecast that the post will go, perhaps subsumed within a wider remit for relations with the three devolved territories of Scotland, Wales and

Northern Ireland. Perhaps, ultimately, that role might involve links with the planned new regional bodies in England. This, however, would involve problems in that the Scottish Parliament would not remotely consider itself as having the same status as an English region and would not welcome any strengthening of Whitehall's role over Scotland.

In Scotland, only the Tories grumble at all seriously about the possible loss of Scottish influence at the UK Cabinet table. Scottish Nationalists frequently condemn the cost of the continuing Scotland Office. Liberal Democrats have openly stated that it is redundant. Labour defends the arrangement but in practice few Labour MSPs appear to cherish and nurture the Scotland Office. I doubt, frankly, whether they give much thought to it at all. At the same time, there is continuing evidence of envy from English regions like the north-east with a comparable population to that of Scotland but no separate stake in the UK Cabinet. All of that has led me to assume that the post was not long for this world, and certainly it is scarcely the greatest political prize on offer. Budding student politicians do not whisper into their pillows: 'Oh, I do so want to grow up to be Scottish Secretary!'

Yet there seems little immediate prospect that Northern Ireland is ready to dispense with the office of Secretary of State in the UK Cabinet, for this remains a very real job. Wales, which has only secondary legislative powers, arguably has a greater need for Whitehall links than Scotland. Is it credible that the post of Scottish Secretary will wither away without parallel reforms in the other devolved territories?

I know that the post of Scottish Secretary is not remotely what it was before devolution. I know that the Executive goes its own way in Whitehall and, increasingly, in Europe and around the world. Almost nothing endures in politics – except taxation and bad jokes. I do not believe that the Scotland Office will survive all that much longer. However, even within the new politics, change tends to take time in Scotland.

Note

1. Speech to the Institute of Welsh Politics, November 2001.

7 Identity – What Makes a Scot?

Do you remember the first meeting of the Scottish Convention to draw up a scheme of devolution? No, not the one which produced Scotland's present Parliament, but an earlier effort. It met on 15 November 1924. Or perhaps you remember the further Convention after the Second World War?

Do you remember when the Scottish Tories produced a strategy paper advocating increased administrative devolution to Scotland? No, not under the former Scottish Secretary Michael Forsyth. But on 3 November 1949.

Do you remember the House of Commons carrying a Scottish Home Rule motion? No, not the 1990s or even the 1970s. But on 3 April 1894.

Dipping into history, of course, can be a troublesome business for political journalists and indeed for politicians. While in office as Secretary of State, Michael Forsyth delivered a lecture at Stirling University attempting to place in context the modern Scottish Conservative preoccupation with the Union. In the course of the lecture, he reflected upon the centuries during which Scotland had vigorously asserted its independence.

In passing, he queried why Scots apparently preferred the gallant – but ultimately unsuccessful – patriotism of William Wallace to the victorious independence campaign of Robert the Bruce. The result? Headlines screaming that the Scottish Secretary had condemned Wallace as a loser. Although more than a mite apprehensive about applying ancient lessons to contemporary politics, I would stress that it is important at least to bear in mind that self-government is a long-running story in Scotland. This brings a potential upside in that politicians have a fund of earlier analysis upon which to draw. They can attempt to avoid initiatives which, while bright and shining at the time, were later seen to contain errors. Specifically and most obviously, Tony Blair's Labour government learned a lot from the problems which dogged the devolution efforts of their 1970s predecessors.

The longevity of the devolution debate, however, has had a clear downside for the advocates of change. There is a risk that the public become cynical over promises, even subjects for discussion, which they feel they have heard before. Additionally, the peculiarly protracted nature of the controversy meant that the debate over Labour's latest scheme was pursued by rival party cynicism, most notably from the Nationalists but also sporadically from others. The SNP famously declared that they 'wouldn't trust Labour to deliver a pizza – let alone a Parliament'. Labour leaders would scarcely be human if they didn't permit themselves a statesperson-like chuckle over that one in the light of subsequent developments. The Nationalists would argue, however, that they were pursuing an understandable political tactic while Labour were in Opposition: essentially, warning that devolution couldn't be guaranteed in the light of history and urging the electorate to underwrite Home Rule with SNP support. The common factor is that those who advocated devolution were aware that there was a crust of history and potential public cynicism to pierce before the dish could be presented to the voters. Before we examine the main dish – Scotland's Parliament – let us pick a little at the piecrust of history.

The standing political joke – regularly deployed by those in search of a wry, knowing laugh – is that devolution is like evolution, only it takes longer. In various forms, the campaign to restore at least a measure of Scottish Home Rule has been around since the Scottish and English Parliaments both voted to end their separate identities and to merge in 1707. That clinical description of the Act of Union between Scotland and England, of course, masks a persistent concern among sections of the Scottish public that the partnership was unequal, that the English Parliament regarded itself as simply continuing in the supposedly merged Westminster, that the previously independent Scotland was absorbed.

Such concerns were vigorously voiced by opponents of the Union when the measure was debated by the Scottish Parliament. These concerns were counteracted by the offer of guarantees for established Scottish civic and religious institutions, plus promises of general economic advancement, plus, it would appear, offers of patronage to key individuals. Historians commonly attribute the apparent decline of such overt anti-Union sentiment to a combination of economic growth in Scotland after the middle of the eighteenth century and direct or indirect efforts to play down Scottish cultural identity and foster British links. It should also be stressed that many Scots saw clear advantages in the Union. Attachment to Britain was built upon a range of motivations: the trading and colonial opportunities presented by the Empire, the maintenance of the Protestant religion and the perception of a common foreign enemy in France. Whether voluntarily or under subtle duress, Scotland in the nineteenth century showed some signs of surrendering at least the public manifestations of national identity.

Giving a lecture[1] on St Andrew's Day in 1998, Donald Dewar, then Scottish Secretary, reflected this element. He depicted Victorian Scotland – or more accurately its wealthier segment – as 'aping polite London society'. Further, he cited the concerns of Lord Cockburn whom he described as 'the great recorder of nineteenth century Scotland'. Cockburn, said Dewar, had voiced fears in the 1850s that Scotland was destined to become 'but an English county'.

Certainly, this was the era of North Britain, the North British railway, the palatial North British Hotel in Edinburgh. This was the era of partial assimilation, the era of a common role for Scots in the creation and maintenance of the Empire. However, a sense of Scottish identity survived to the present day, and it is that sense which has informed and underpinned the political initiative to devolve power to Scotland.

One argument is that civic Scotland persisted while political Scotland decamped to Westminster, that the 'high politics' of London with its concern for foreign, defence and trade matters bore little relation to the 'low politics' of everyday Scottish life with its concern for the Church, the law courts, parish education and the like. While accepting that analysis, I believe that the persistence of a sense of Scottish identity is, in many ways, a simpler, less scientific matter. As noted above, the impulse towards a sense of being British was strong and welcomed by many, including many in Scotland. Had that sense been all pervasive, the totems of Scottish identity evident in civic society might have lost their impact or their importance. The people of Scotland have simply chosen, often without assertion or demonstration, to remain Scottish.

That feeling would appear to be growing. Identity is an issue regularly tracked by academics in social-attitudes surveys covering Scotland and Britain as a whole. The most recent figures for Scotland, featuring data gathered in 2001, were presented to a conference in Edinburgh in March 2002.[2]

This survey system is particularly helpful in that it deploys questions which recognise that people in Scotland may have a range of identities. Using a standard measure, people are asked to indicate how they mostly see themselves. The latest figures indicate that, in Scotland, some 36 per cent of the people – more than a third, in other words – feel themselves to be Scottish and not British. A further 30 per cent feel more Scottish than British. Some 24 per cent regarded themselves as equally Scottish and British. Only 3 per cent felt more British than Scottish and a further 3 per cent thought themselves British and not Scottish. Four per cent opted for other identities.

It will be seen that these figures suggest that, north of the Border, the core identity – the default position, if you like – is plainly Scottish. Significantly, further data presented at the conference by analyst Catherine Bromley indicated that 'being Scottish' mattered a lot to people. It was ranked as highly important even among competing identities such as parenthood, gender and faith. Indeed, Scottish identity was only outranked in one sector: women thought their identity as a parent more important. Men, apparently, derived more of their sense of themselves from Scottishness.

Furthermore, the trend over recent years has been for Scottish identity to grow in importance, with exclusively Scottish identity moving up to the head of the list. This can be tracked through survey work done at election times, using figures which uncover both the sense of relative importance attached to varying identities and the final verdict if people are obliged by the interviewer to make a choice. Do they, in the end, feel British or Scottish? In a newspaper essay[3] based upon work in a book, Professor John Curtice tracked the change when he noted that 'the erosion of Britishness has been dramatic'. He added: 'Little more than twenty years ago, just after Scots had failed to back devolution with sufficient enthusiasm in the 1979 referendum, no less than 39 per cent of people in Scotland said they felt British more than they felt Scottish.' As recently as 1992, he noted that the same 'forced choice' question indicated that 25 per cent of people in Scotland plumped ultimately for a British identity.[4] By the year 2000, that figure had dropped to 13 per cent.

Anecdotally, I believe these figures are borne out. I have regularly had occasion to pursue this issue through 'vox pops' or interviews conducted in the streets of Scotland. (My eternal gratitude, incidentally, to those many people kind enough to stop for a shivering reporter and camera crew.) When I raise the topic of identity, the most common and unhesitating response is 'Scottish'. Indeed, the answer is often given in a tone which suggests that the respondent wonders why I feel the need to ask, whether I have taken leave of my remaining senses. During the run-up to the 1997 General Election, I was commissioned by the BBC's (then) *Nine o'clock News* programme to prepare a substantial feature item on the campaign in Scotland. The BBC, of course, covered the Scottish political contest thoroughly. The parties were far from neglected. But this was to be different.

We opted to examine the nature of Scottish identity and to feature a range of opinions and analyses, including voices from Scotland's academic and cultural sectors. I was most struck, however, by the day we spent filming in Coldstream: a small Scottish community right on the border, as close to England as it is possible to be. Virtually everyone we spoke to stressed their Scottish identity, some in the most vigorous tones. I recall the man, serving behind a bar, who dropped his voice slightly as he talked of 'over there', referring to neighbouring England a few hundred yards away as if to some form of uncharted, dangerous territory. No-one had anything against England or the English. People were simply stating that they lived in Scotland and were Scottish.

I can understand that, psychologically, people on a border may be the most assertive in defining their geographical identity. I can believe that there are Scots more generally who define their identity in negative terms, who start from the presumption that they are 'not English'. I believe, however, that national identity in Scotland has changed, as it has shifted towards the default position of Scottishness. This is also an anecdotal leap in the dark, but I believe that we in Scotland are now less aggressive about our identity. We have become comfortably Scots.

To be Scottish used to be a matter of defiance. It was loud and raucous. It was broken crossbars and purloined Wembley turf. It was: 'Here's tae us, wha's like us, gey few and they're a' deid!' At the same time, we also sustained the Scottish cringe, the balanced perspective of a chip on both shoulders, the underlying suspicion that we were somehow inferior – and that the world knew it. As we yelled, we also whined inwardly. 'Wha's like us? Wha wad want tae be?' This is not something one can track in a survey but I am convinced this has changed. Instead of acting as amateur landscapers, the Tartan Army of footballer supporters wins recognition for fun and fair play. We have become less assertive yet at the same time more confident, more relaxed about our sense of our own national identity.

I am aware, however, that this observation requires significant caveats to be lodged. Scotland remains scarred in places by bigotry and racism. These attitudes – often hideously twinned – ooze like suppurating pus through the body of living, breathing Scotland. They are nauseating, noxious attributes. They blight the lives of the target victims and disfigure the features of the host nation which acts as their carrier.

I am aware, too, that there are those who will disagree with my depiction of Scottish identity as becoming more relaxed. They may feel themselves the victim of prejudice based on identity. They may, for example, have experienced anti-English sentiment in Scotland. It will be little comfort to those people to be told that such opinions are a throwback, that they reflect the craven nation we were rather than the positive one we seek to be, that they diminish the pitiful fool who delivers them even as they hurt their intended victim. I believe, however, that sociological rules will have exceptions. I believe that more people in Scotland are becoming more relaxed about their national identity. I believe it is important to strengthen that feeling – not weaken it – in order to foster a more relaxed attitude to neighbouring or shared identities. Scots need to feel good about themselves in order to feel good about others.

Equally, prejudice is not confined to Scotland – although we do seem to have forged or adopted a particularly pestilent strain of religious bigotry. Such prejudice will not be reduced by obliging people in Scotland to pretend that they are somehow other than Scottish. It will not be reduced by attempting to confine people solely within a state identity which does not accord with their own sense of themselves.

There are politicians, often but not solely on the Right, who will rail at 'Scottish' identity or patriotism. Yet these same politicians, sometimes in the next breath, will vaunt British identity or patriotism. The contradiction never occurs to them. They see one identity as intrinsically feeble and wrong, because it does not accord with their world view. They see the other as intrinsically heroic and right, because it does. They say Scots should end division and simply be British. Yet suggest that they might become more European, and their faces will turn purple with rage. Scottish identity, it seems, is an aberration; British identity is seen as a permanent, almost divine, fixture.

Rather, identity should be seen as a choice, motivated by a combination of factors. There is nothing particularly good or bad in national identity itself – whether it be American, German, British, English or Scottish. Bigotry will not be addressed by corralling or outlawing one form of identity. Instead, one needs to tackle the ignorance, the mean spirit, the greed, the selfishness and the poverty of ambition which are the true causes of prejudice – in every nation and state.

So, I am aware of the caveats, of the distressing exceptions. I would still argue, however, that people in Scotland are becoming more relaxed about their own adoption of Scottish identity. I would argue, further, that this is not a consequence of devolution, but rather a parallel social shift. It is part of the maturing of the nation of Scotland, if one can attach a rather grand label to an extremely nebulous concept. Devolution has been a political, state response to the developing sense of Scottish identity.

Let us try to trace a little of that development. Those who are hardy enough to ascend the steps arising from Waverley Station in

Edinburgh will find an entertaining icon of Scottish identity. As they surmount the final step, defying the attendant hurricane force wind which seeks to cast them back down again, they will find that the hotel at the top is no longer named the North British, as once it was. It is now the Balmoral. North Britain, it would seem, has lost something of its force as a marketing tool.

There are obvious institutional examples of the perseverance of Scottish identity: the Church of Scotland, deliberately protected in the Act of Union and now providing temporary shelter to Scotland's new Parliamentarians in the General Assembly building on the Mound in Edinburgh; Scottish education, which has remained distinct; the Scottish legal system; Scottish banks and banknotes; and Scottish sporting teams.

However, institutions can only ultimately reflect identity. They cannot forge it where no genuine, popular attachment exists. Think, for example, of restructured local government past and present, north and south of the border. You cannot make a person talk lovingly of returning to Cleveland. You cannot persuade someone that their roots are in Strathclyde when they know they come from Ayrshire.

It is also futile to fix Scottish identity on a generic basis. Scotland, as others have commented, is a cheerfully mongrel nation: an ancient blend of Highland and Lowland, Celtic, Anglian, Viking and Roman, with just a tangy hint of Pict. There are Scots of Irish birth or descent, those who might claim a comparable attachment to England, Wales, continental Europe or elsewhere.

Then there are the more recent arrivals, notably from Asia. There cannot be a perkier Scot anywhere than my good friend Ali Abbasi, the travel guru of BBC Scotland, the author of magnificent joke books and now a student of Gaelic.

Clearly, there is a strong cultural element to identity. People may express their Scottish identity through an interest in Scottish artists or, more commonly, writers. They may find that a particular author matches their sense of themselves, perhaps through insightful description of their environment or empathy with their problems and challenges.

Frequently, Scots express their identity through the poems and songs of Robert Burns or, more accurately, through the accretion of national sentiment, both genuine and misplaced, which has been added down the years to the image of Ayrshire's finest.

Incidentally, too much is expected of Rabbie. He has been annually required at Suppers in his name to encompass the national feelings of a people who for 300 years lacked the political and constitutional machinery to share that burden. He has occasionally, as his fellow poet Hugh MacDiarmid wickedly explained, been asked to replace the experience of actually living in Scotland. I find I still grin knowingly at the line in MacDiarmid's *A Drunk Man Looks at the Thistle* which describes 'croose London Scotties wi' their braw shirt fronts' enjoying a Burns Supper.

Writers can sum up the identity of a nation, although it is unfair to expect them to bear this task alone or to be circumscribed in their work by considerations of national origin. The best writers, perhaps, contrive to relate experiences drawn from their own identity to the wider world or to more fundamental human characteristics.

Other cultural forms, too, have exemplified an increase in attention paid to matters Scottish. The reawakening over the past few decades of the interest in Scottish folk and popular song comes into this category. Most strikingly, this element has moved far beyond a self-conscious revival of culture. The key factor is that those enjoying Scottish-derived music no longer feel the need to see it almost entirely as an act of cultural solidarity or defiance. They are comfortable, casual, towards their identity.

I am very far from an expert, but it strikes me there is a welcome maturity too in the Scottish music field. Bands will make their base or their recordings in Scotland and think it no big deal. People will dance themselves silly to ceilidh music because they like the Eightsome Reel, not because they are making a cultural statement. Formal Highland Dress, once obligatory, often gives way to a relaxed kilt, rough socks and boots.

Again, though identity can be expressed through popular culture, it is not defined by it. Neither can language be relied upon as the defining characteristic.

Gaelic is an extremely important element in Scotland's cultural mix and I share the concerns of those who advocate its support. Indeed, youthful enthusiasm at university prompted me to attempt a couple of lessons in the language. The only phrase which I confess I can recall is: 'Ha an cu aig an doruis.' I may well have got this wrong but, as I remember, this means, 'There is a dog at the door.'

Scarcely the path to linguistic fluency, but handy all the same if one is in a pub in Stornoway and there is a noise of barking outside.

Then, keeping it personal, I am fond of employing Scots words familiar from the area around my native Dundee. As a correspondent at the House of Commons, I was occasionally called upon by bemused colleagues from Hansard and the Press Association to translate Scots words and phrases which diligent MPs, notably Donald Dewar, had managed to slip past the linguistic restraints of a Chamber which insists on pure and frequently stilted English.

An anguished cry of 'gey dreich', I would assure them, implied nothing more than that the Honourable Member found the proceedings 'somewhat dull'. An inadequate rendering, I know, but linguistically legal as far as Westminster was concerned.

On certain occasions, nothing – not even the imprecations of concerned friends – can prevent me from singing 'Nicky Tams' or 'The Road and the Miles to Dundee', hand clasped firmly to my right ear, nostrils working furiously.

However, Scotland's identity cannot simply be defined in terms of language. Naturally, I am aware that the history of attempted suppression of the Gaelic language and the discouragement of Scots speech were linked to efforts to mute Scottish identity. Both were to be deplored. However, there can be hazards in overreliance on any linguistic definition of identity. Those who do not speak the specified language – be it Gaelic, Scots, Welsh or Breton – can feel set apart from an identity which they would otherwise profess. Scotland's new politics must be linguistically – and ideologically – tolerant.

Then there is the Scottish identity which arises from sporting allegiance: the 'ninety-minute nationalists' of Jim Sillars' famous phrase. I yield to no-one my passion for Scotland's national football and rugby squads. Even the most polished and urbane Scot can turn into a typhoon of patriotic fervour at Hampden or Murrayfield. I once attended a rugby international in the company, among others, of a highly intelligent, sophisticated Scottish MP who had the good grace to warn us in advance that he intended to behave like an extra from *Braveheart* for the following eighty minutes. He was as good as his word.

Again, though, is it only my impression or has the nature of that sporting patriotism changed? Scots want their national squads to win as much as ever but that seems to be tinged now with a whimsical recognition of Scotland's sporting flaws. The Tartan Army of football fans seem, thankfully, in search of a good time and a good reputation: perhaps more even than a good victory. They seem less likely to be 'on the march with Ally's Army' as in the past and more inclined to be in a conga line with the local gendarmerie.

Perhaps, just perhaps, this phenomenon is a reflection of a growing maturity in the debate over Scottish national identity and its outward expression. To repeat, I believe the identity issue in Scotland has moved on. Even as people declare their Scottishness more unequivocally, they are tending to stress it less aggressively. They are Scottish, not English or Belgian or Greek. Scottish. Increasingly, not British. No big deal. They are Scottish.

Where exactly does this leave British identity? In this consideration of Scottish identity, it should of course be stressed again that there are many advocates of British identity, that there are many physical and psychological ties which bind Scots to the UK. The choice of a Scottish national identity does not preclude acceptance of a British or UK state identity. There are also of course those in Scotland who, quite clearly, consider themselves British first and foremost. Writing in *The Scotsman* on 15 August 1998, in an essay repeated from *The Spectator*, Andrew Neil complained that 'those of us who are proud to be Scottish and British have become strangers in our own land'.

Neil's point is noted, and we must perpetually guard against forms of exclusive nationality which may isolate or vilify others. For the most part, however, it is my experience that people north of the border are mostly content to label themselves Scottish or predominantly Scottish, without rancour and without question.

Particularly in Europe with its varied history and contemporary moves towards political integration, identity is often a matter of choice. We pick from a menu: Scottish, British, European, none of the above. Or perhaps we identify with our religion or class upbringing. Or perhaps we plump for alternatives, derived from music or sport or grassroots politics. All the evidence – anecdotal and statistical – is that, confronted with that menu, people in Scotland choose increasingly to be Scottish. It matters to them. It is what they are. The history of devolution is that of a people who increasingly believed they had a particular national identity and

wanted that identity expressed in political form. It is a history of
political response, not political initiative.

The Scottish people, I believe, were not crying out for a particular form of political expression. It is a familiar anecdote of canvassers
from a range of parties that voters are far less inclined than the
politicians to make sharp distinctions between devolution, independence and federalism. That does not mean they are unconcerned
about such matters. They are simply not the starting point for the
electors. The factor which motivates Home Rule is an imprecise
feeling of Scottishness, an attachment by choice to Scottish identity.
It is, if you like, Scottish patriotism.

It is the feeling which formed the Scottish National Party and
contributed to the obliteration of the Scottish Tories at the 1997
General Election through their popular identification as an English
party. It is the feeling which drove Labour's devolution reform
package and the Liberal Democrats' work in the Convention.

I do not believe there is a rigidly defined core of devolution
supporters and an entirely distinct cadre of independence advocates,
with occasional seepage at the edges. If that were so, there would be
a relatively precise match between those who tell opinion pollsters
that they favour independence and those who declare for the SNP.
By contrast, opinion polls regularly find that constitutional opinion
varies across the parties, that there are for example Labour supporters
who favour independence and SNP supporters who opt for devolution among the range of views offered to the pollsters. I would not
wish to overstate this. Self-evidently, there are party activists and
voters who do make a sharp distinction between the various constitutional options. There are people who support devolution but
fear independence. There are people who support independence
but regard devolution as a sideshow or a Unionist trap.

However, my impression – and it is first and foremost an impression – is that the starting point is identity rather than the particular
constitutional options on offer from the parties. The constitutional
gap is frequently less precise than politicians fretting about their
party's future would perhaps wish. People begin by saying: we are
Scottish. Then they implicitly challenge the political parties to offer
a response. Electoral success is partly determined by that response.

Again, that feeling of Scottish identity brought the SNP into
being. It has prompted the Labour and Liberal (or Liberal Democrat)

parties to promise devolution in various forms over a century or more. It damaged the Tory Party, which was most obviously identified with British or English identity. Above all, it is the driving force behind the reforms which led to the Scottish Parliament. Scotland's new governance has a popular engine, not a party political one.

So what constitutional consequences might one draw from all this? Is the Union threatened by strengthened Scottish identity? Possibly, but not necessarily and not automatically. Is success for the SNP guaranteed? Similarly, not necessarily. What is left of Britishness? The UK government is searching for new answers, without success so far in my view.

First, on the question of the Union, there is no automatic cross-matching between a feeling of Scottish identity and support for Scottish independence. Almost by definition, those who support independence will be basing that view substantially on a sense of Scottish identity. But the reverse is not necessarily true.

As Labour, the Liberal Democrats and the Tories repeatedly point out, a sense of being Scottish does not of itself engender backing for an independent Scotland. People who feel Scottish may want independence, or they may regard their sense of Scottishness as being sufficiently addressed, politically, by devolved self-government. There is no guaranteed causal link from personal identity to political independence. As we shall examine later, that is the core of the quandary facing the SNP.

Second, Britishness. Several commentators, mostly but not exclusively from the Right, have predicted the end of Britain – or allegiance to British identity – as a consequence of devolution. Tony Blair's Ministers have responded by attempting to redefine Britishness. I believe both initiatives are partly based on misconceptions.

It is a commonplace to say that when people south of the border talk about Britain and the British, they really mean England and English. Think of John Major's much-derided sentimentality about warm beer and cycling old maids. His stance on the constitution was a passionate defence of Britain. Yet his imagery is entirely English. Think of the 'cricket test' famously posed by Norman Tebbit to Caribbean and Asian Britons. He was trying to establish their loyalty to Britain by asking whether they supported England at cricket. Frankly, most Scots would cheerfully fail that test. Does that mean they are all rejecting the United Kingdom?

As I say, these are commonplaces. Not universally true, but grounded in fact, grounded in habit. Too little attention, however, has been paid to the mirror image of the question. What do Scots mean when they talk of Britain? If England thinks of warm beer, the White Cliffs and Westminster Abbey, what are the images for Scotland? In decades gone by, the answer would have been relatively easy. The symbols of Britain would have been the Empire, the monarchy, the armed forces, a common stance in time of conflict. Perhaps the created structures of the state such as the National Health Service (NHS) or the welfare system or even the post office. As each of these has declined in status, so too has a sense of Britishness for Scotland. It is important to understand, however, that our Scottish identity never vanished, never at any stage. We were never ineluctably British. Our sense of being Scottish was never entirely subsumed, despite internal and external pressures.

I would argue further that we always viewed the Union in a different light from England. If the English people thought about the Union at all, they saw it as merely a staging post in history. They did not – and do not – view it as an event of huge significance, the merger of two separate peoples. They saw it largely as a point in a long, unbroken history: the history of England. It is that underlying view – that misunderstanding, if you like – which encourages politicians in Westminster to talk sententiously about a thousand years of 'British' history, disregarding the inconvenient fact that the Union only took place some three hundred years ago.

By contrast, Scotland – and I am aware that this is deeply unscientific – has always accorded the Union more historical significance. It was the 'end of ane auld sang'. It was the end of our nation state, a potential challenge to our identity. It was, entirely understandably, not the same for England, which carried on broadly as before.

That historical dichotomy – that twin view of the Union – has two consequences. First, the English seem to me to be rather puzzled by recent developments. They have not had three centuries of agonising over the Union. If they thought of it at all, they took it as a constant. Now they wonder what we are up to, they wonder what is happening to Britain/England, and some are beginning to question what it means to be British/English in the twenty-first century. Second, the Scots may require to reassess their stance towards Britain. For many, being British was always a political rather than a national issue. Scotland offered the identity, Britain the state. With the decline of Britishness and the accompanying rise in Scottishness, that is now more than ever true for more people than ever before.

People in Scotland already seem quite clear as to their identity. They are Scottish. Telling them they are British will not advance support for the political Union one iota. Stressing the practical advantages of Union – while bad-mouthing the alternative – just might. Labour, in Scotland at least, has fully absorbed that lesson.

Equally, telling people – who are already quite clear who they are – that their sense of identity lacks full expression without independence will not work. If they feel that the identity issue is covered by devolution, then – no matter how strident the challenge – they will not budge. However, stressing the practical advantages of independence, while bad-mouthing the alternative, just might. A pragmatic, political choice, either way.

This all leaves the attempts to redefine Britishness undertaken sporadically by Tony Blair and his Ministers. In February 2002, I attended a conference at the Queen Elizabeth II centre in Westminster on the topic 'Devolution and Britishness'. The event was fascinating, although it reminded me, again, that political debate in England is only just beginning to address the identity question after decades, arguably centuries, of comparable debate in Scotland.

One of the principal speakers was Barbara Roche, Minister of State at the Cabinet Office. In truth, it was a poor speech, rather too platitudinous for an audience eager for fresh thinking. However, it did contain some intriguing insights. The Minister noted that 'modern Britishness is defined in significant part through its diversity', which sounds, when you think about it, like exactly the opposite of a definition. A partial description, yes. A definition, no. It is entirely reasonable to observe that modern Britain comprises diverse nations, regions, races and cultures. It is reasonable, further, for government to seek harmony between these various elements. It is not logical, however, to predicate state or national identity purely on the existence of diversity. If Britishness means anything, there must be a common link. The Minister then talked of the shared institutions I have mentioned above – such as the NHS – before reaching the core of her argument: that Britain is bound together by 'shared values'. These were, seemingly, 'democracy, the rule of law, the importance of strong communities and, above all, tolerance and respect'.

This speech, however, does not stand alone. This initiative comes from the top. Two years previously, Tony Blair argued similarly that Britishness depended on 'core values'.[5] The list, admittedly, was a little different – fair play, creativity, tolerance and an outward-looking approach to the world – but the theme was the same.

I understand and appreciate the underlying motivation here. Having created substantial change in the UK constitution, the Prime Minister and his colleagues are keen to stress some sense of continuity, to ensure that the British identity is strengthened rather than eroded, to offer reassurance. However, I believe that the analysis is misplaced. Look at the list of values. Look particularly at the Prime Minister's list. These values are not uniquely or exhaustively British. If anything, they are Blair's own values. If you doubt that, try taking the question the other way round. Suppose Britishness is indeed defined by those values. Does that mean that, in their absence, British identity vanishes? If, for example, you are neither creative nor outward-looking, are you suddenly less British or not British at all?

Look at Barbara Roche's list. Democracy, the rule of law and the rest. Those are values which could be comfortably attached to the USA and to every European Union state. They do not *define* one state or nation. They *describe* attributes common to nations throughout the western world.

For a truer definition of Britishness, I believe we must look at another section of the Prime Minister's speech in which he linked 'shared values' with 'mutual self-interest'. He added: 'We are stronger together, economically and politically, with the nations of the UK able to maximise their collective will and authority. In defence, foreign policy, economic weight, we are better off and stronger together.'

This is, of course, largely an enhanced version of the 'stronger together, weaker apart' mantra regularly deployed by Labour. It does, however, address more precisely the political/economic choice which I identified previously as the true test for the Union. Nations and states are not innate orders, imbued for all time with fixed boundaries and peoples. They are political constructs, brought together by geography and a varying mix of motivations which might include, among others, common security, trade and language. Nations and states change and reform.

I believe the identity issue has provoked the most recent reform, the establishment of devolution within the previously unitary British state. I believe, however, that the attitude of Scotland to that reformed state in future will be predicated more upon political and economic choices.

To repeat, the decline of Britishness does not mean that Scottish independence is in any way inevitable. It does mean, however, that Britishness has to be revisited. The future of the Union can no longer rely upon a simple appeal to patriotism, based on muddled perceptions of identity. That will not work.

The Scots may well be persuaded that continuing membership of the British state is in their economic, social and security interests. Alternatively, they may opt for independence. Either way, the final choice will be based on practical politics as well as identity.

Notes

1. St Andrew's Day lecture by Donald Dewar in St Andrews, Monday, 30 November 1998.
2. Scottish Social Attitudes Survey, presented by the Centre for Scottish Public Policy and the National Centre for Social Research Scotland, City Chambers, Edinburgh, 5 March 2002.
3. Essay by Professor John Curtice, *Scotland on Sunday*, 17 December 2001, based upon *New Scotland, New Society?*, edited by John Curtice, David McCrone, Alison Park and Lindsay Paterson (Edinburgh: Polygon, 2001).
4. Data from the British Election Surveys and Scottish Election Surveys.
5. Speech by the Prime Minister on 'Britishness', London, 28 March 2000.

8 The Scottish Labour Party and Jack McConnell

It was the standard opening pitch, a routine question. The reply, however, was a little out of the ordinary and opened a tiny, corner window into the First Minister's inner thoughts. This was Thursday, 18 April 2002. Jack McConnell was answering questions in the Scottish Parliament as he does each Thursday during the session. As usual, the Conservative leader David McLetchie inquired of the First Minister when he next planned to meet the Prime Minister.

The Tory leader was not desperately keen to learn the First Minister's diary details. Nor was he anxious that Jack McConnell and Tony Blair might be planning a party to which he had not been invited. Rather, David McLetchie wanted to conceal his real target. Opening questions have to be tabled in advance, in writing. Supplementaries, of course, do not. So it is common practice – at Holyrood and Westminster – for Opposition leaders to ask a bland opening question concerning diary engagements, then to follow that up by inquiring whether the Minister will find time within a busy schedule to deal with . . . whatever issue is currently topical or tricky.

Ministers, of course, are well aware of this. So they usually deliver a formulaic answer to the opening inquiry, frequently in a weary voice, as if to say: 'Okay, we both know this is a sham, let's get on with it!' On this particular day, however, Jack McConnell departed slightly from the customary script. Asked by McLetchie when he would meet Tony Blair, the First Minister replied: 'I will meet the Prime Minister the next time I have an available opportunity.' David McLetchie raised his eyebrows and commented: 'Very good of you to squeeze him into your diary.'

It is sometimes said by those keen to fit Scottish politics into a purely Westminster template that Jack McConnell is a 'Blairite'. If he is, then he is a Blairite who seldom speaks to Tony Blair. McConnell's answer to McLetchie reflected the fact that Scotland's First Minister has had absolutely minimal contact with the Prime Minister.

To be fair, I think I can thoroughly understand Blair's 'neglect' of Scotland. For one thing, he has had rather a lot on his plate post-September 11. For another, he might well think that, if Scotland is finally quiescent, then let well alone. For a third, I feel sure he is privately wary of being seen to interfere. In the past few years, Scottish Labour politics seem to have produced a poison of remarkable venom, and Downing Street does not have the antidote. Similarly, Gordon Brown does not feature the telephone number for Bute House in his 'Friends and Family' list. He is not a regular caller, although this is no surprise, given that McConnell and Brown have a history of mutual antagonism, dating back to the period when McConnell was Labour's General Secretary in Scotland. Jack McConnell will never make Tawny Owl in the Brownie Pack.

At first, McConnell felt sore that he was seemingly neglected by Brown and, more significantly, by the Prime Minister. But sources close to him say that he is now reconciled to the situation, that it allows him the freedom to develop his own approach to the governance of Scotland. Plainly, though, it rankles a mite: a sign perhaps that Jack McConnell is a little more personally vulnerable than the customary 'hard man' image would suggest. The image is certainly firmly entrenched. One former Cabinet Minister told me: 'Jack governs from machine not mission. This is Lanarkshire Labour politics – where you fix everything. There is no vision.' Another said: 'Jack only speaks to those who can help him. He disdains those who can't. That brutality may bring him down.'

By definition, of course, those who are commenting are those who are out of favour. The image, however, is diffused more widely than merely among the disaffected. To be brutally frank, the First Minister can *look* on occasion like an archetypal hard man. Smart suit, Crombie coat, fixed countenance, slick hair, aides in attendance, that slight swagger in his gait. The Robert De Niro of Scottish politics, straight off the set of *GoodFellas*. Jack McConnell was born in Irvine in 1960 and grew up on a sheep farm in Arran. He regularly returns to the island – a popular holiday destination for Scotland's middle-class families, especially from the west of Scotland. At Stirling University, he was president of the Students' Association. After graduating, he spent nine years teaching maths, while advancing his political career as a Stirling councillor. He spent two years leading the authority, which had a reputation for innovative service provision, and extremely close Labour/Tory election contests.

In 1992 McConnell became General Secretary of the Labour Party in Scotland after a bizarre contest in which the candidates had to travel to Preston to be interviewed, because key members of the London selection panel were attending a conference in nearby Blackpool. Preston provided the most convenient direct rail connection for both Glasgow and Blackpool. The grim irony of a key Scottish party post being settled by London leaders in an English industrial town would not have been lost on McConnell. He was a prominent founder member of Scottish Labour Action (SLA), the influential and intellectual ginger group formed to agitate for maximum devolution of power – to a Scottish Parliament and to the Scottish Labour Party. Several SLA adherents have gone on to prominence in the party. But back to Jack the Lad. Yes, he is self-serving. Yes, he likes to enhance his own image. I have not yet met a successful politician who does not. Provided that motivation is more than matched by a desire to serve the public – and, more significantly, by competence and integrity – then there is no real problem.

There is a question of trust. McConnell knows that. He knows he had to regain the trust of his family after his affair with a party colleague was disclosed. He knows he had to rebuild trust more widely after he was implicated – but acquitted – in the Lobbygate affair. He knows he has to rebuild trust in the Scottish Parliament – and the office of First Minister – after the turmoil of the opening years.

As noted earlier in this book, I believe that his first reshuffle was unnecessarily brutal. I believe that McConnell may yet have to remedy that by reconsidering at least one or two of the talented individuals who were despatched to the back benches because they were not loyal Jackobites.

So, yes, he is a political fixer. He cannot seem to resist the temptation to swing things his way. But Scottish Parliamentary politics may teach him a lesson – just as devolved politics burned the London coterie around Blair when they attempted to interfere. For example, Jack McConnell blundered badly when he attempted to get Labour's Cathy Peattie MSP elected deputy Presiding Officer. MSPs resented Executive interference in their business. The Tories' Murray Tosh was duly elected and Cathy Peattie – a thoroughly likeable MSP – was left looking lost.

I hear the talk of Lanarkshire Labour 'power politics'. McConnell is MSP for Motherwell and Wishaw in Lanarkshire and does indeed appear to have absorbed some of the manipulative tactics associated with his adopted county. However, I believe there is more, much more to Scotland's First Minister than that. I have encountered thorough-going Labour machine politicians. They are closed to new ideas. Their only – I stress only – interest is power. Privately, they despise the voters who tamely return them to office. Their concept of consensus is squaring the various lobbies so that their own interests are served. By contrast, McConnell is intelligent and thoughtful. He is decidedly a moderniser, with reforming instincts. In government, he is decisive, tracking a path on the basis of the evidence available and then sticking to it.

He is pleasant company, charming and talkative, open to views from others rather than solely projecting himself, as some politicians are prone to do. He is a cultured man, interested in the arts and their place in contemporary Scotland, deriving much of that interest from his wife Bridget, an arts professional. He is a post-devolution First Minister, working with London but by no means in awe of Westminster.

The last element is critical because Labour – even Scottish Labour – has not always been an instinctive party of devolution. By that, I mean that it is not a first principle for the party. Labour has largely followed public opinion on this question, rather than leading it. Let us delve a little into the past before returning to more contemporary challenges.

The history of the Labour Party in Scotland may be traced back to 1888 and Keir Hardie's foundation of a Scottish Labour Party. The modern British Labour movement may properly be sourced to a London meeting on 27 February 1900. Throughout the twentieth century, devolution prompted tension within Labour.

Sporadic conflict is entirely understandable. It arises from the differing perspectives of those devoted to advancing the cause of Labour in Scotland and those attached to the British or international agenda. Indeed, at an earlier stage many socialists – including several in Scotland – were inherently suspicious of Scottish self-government, which they equated with nationalism and the Right. Glasgow or Dundee workers, they would argue, had more in common with workers in Manchester and Liverpool than with the bourgeoisie in Scotland. Others have taken an alternative tack, arguing that social reform could be advanced within Scotland by reform of governance. Occasionally, as during the long years of Conservative rule after 1979, it appeared that the Left in Scotland were partly advocating devolution in frustration at Labour's inability to make progress in British politics.

Many of the earliest advocates of socialist Parliamentary representation in Scotland were sympathetic to the Home Rule cause – either through direct, principled support for self-government or mistrust of the prevailing British state establishment or the belief that socialism could more easily be advanced in a small political arena. Alongside that, however, were always others who felt this ran counter to the movement's internationalist ethos. In practical terms, the Home Rule issue was frequently overshadowed by the efforts of the Labour movement to build and sustain a Westminster Parliamentary majority. For example, the wartime coalition Scottish Secretary Tom Johnston was a Home Ruler, but the Attlee government that won a spectacular victory for Labour in 1945 took no steps to implement devolution, concentrating instead on applying British state solutions to the deep social and industrial problems of the time.

Throughout much of the 1950s and 1960s, Labour in Scotland preferred to stick to issues such as boosting the economy and spreading social provision. The party appeared either hostile to Home Rule or, more accurately, uninterested, although there were thoughtful figures, including a young Donald Dewar, who advocated

Scottish self-government when it was relatively unpopular inside the Labour movement.

Most trace Labour's adoption of devolution to the rise of the SNP in the 1970s when the Nationalists gained first seven and then eleven seats in the two General Elections of 1974. Certainly, the two events are coterminous, although, as I have argued elsewhere, I think it is more strictly accurate to say that Labour was responding to a non-specific mood for a recognition of Scottish identity which the SNP represented. That selfsame mood, in other words, both forged the SNP and threatened the established Labour Party. Had that mood been uniformly and ineluctably for straightforward independence, there would have been little a party like Labour could do, short of overturning its commitment to the Union. Rather, the mood, which was partly expressed through SNP support, was perhaps less clearly defined. It was for significant self-government, for recognition of Scotland's distinct position.

Labour leaders, then, responded – but remained rather reluctant devolvers. Indeed, the Scottish Labour executive voted against devolution in the summer of 1974, although, anecdotally, the balance may have been tilted by a relatively poor attendance caused by a clash with TV coverage of the Scotland–Yugoslavia World Cup tie. Harold Wilson's government persisted with devolution and Scottish Labour's seeming reluctance was overturned at a subsequent party conference.

The tension, however, persisted. In the 1970s, Labour MP Jim Sillars led a breakaway Scottish Labour Party in protest at the British party's alleged lack of genuine commitment to Home Rule. Sillars, of course, later joined the SNP, as did Alex Neil, a leading member of the SLP who went on to become a Nationalist MSP.

In the Scottish and Welsh devolution referendums of 1979, prominent Labour figures like Robin Cook, Neil Kinnock, Brian Wilson and Tam Dalyell voiced strong opposition to the changes proposed by their government. The Welsh plan was heavily defeated while the Scottish scheme – though narrowly carried – was scuppered by the rule obliging 40 per cent of the total electorate to vote yes.

Over succeeding decades, however, support for devolution became steadily entrenched within Scottish Labour. This was partly, as I have argued, in response to the party's inability to gain power at the UK level. MPs and activists, thwarted in the search for Westminster power, sought to redraw the boundaries, to create a legislature which they could command. Perhaps more than that, however, the motivation for the party membership and activists was the developing popular mood of Scotland, the apparently persistent support for a measure of self-government. Scotland was grasping the Saltire, and Scottish Labour could not be seen to be brandishing the Union flag overeagerly.

Labour, in short, followed Scotland, not the other way round. This is not, of course, an ignoble posture for a democratic party but equally not perhaps the image which contemporary Labour likes to present. Political parties – and especially a party like Labour which has maintained substantial support in Scotland – generally like to represent themselves as leading 'their people' or at least as being in synchronisation with popular sentiment. While it is reasonable to analyse Labour's genuine motivation in this field, we should also acknowledge the capacity of the party to detect and reflect a changing popular mood. By contrast, the Conservatives stood against the changing political tide in Scotland and paid the electoral price as a consequence.

The Labour Party in England, of course, could scarcely be expected to pursue this course with the same fervour. Devolution was party policy, but it was not a policy which was much loved in London. MPs from England mostly understood that the Scottish party required to follow the mood of Scotland, or, more commonly, they grasped the raw politics of countering the SNP.

Some, including MPs from the north-east of England, resented and continue to resent the notion of a Scottish Parliament. They fear that Scotland has bigger clout in attracting internationally mobile industrial investment. Others feared that too much attention would be paid to Scotland and Scottish devolution at the cost of more mundane policies likely to be popular in England.

Most, however, tolerated devolution – if they thought about it at all. For these MPs and activists, perhaps understandably, devolution was never a policy of the same nature or calibre as the minimum wage or schools provision or NHS structures, something to be debated and promulgated. Devolution was needed to placate the Scots. It was a tactic, not a policy. Even today, there are senior figures in Labour ranks who question that strategy, who fear the end game. As I have said, it is not instinctive in perhaps the way that support for equality of opportunity is instinctive. Devolution has to be learned and relearned, especially by Labour leaders outside Scotland who still wonder whether the party is conceding ground to an alien concept of nationalism.

In September 1995, I prepared a series of items for BBC Scotland on the detailed consequences of devolution: the big, underlying issues which were sometimes neglected in coverage of the endless cross-party bickering. For one of these items, I interviewed Welsh Labour MP Dr Kim Howells, then the party's constitutional spokesperson in Jack Straw's team. The interview was remarkable, an outpouring of anxiety at his party's constitutional strategy in Wales and Scotland. Howells told me: 'I did not become a Labour MP in order to take part in the Balkanisation of Britain and I am profoundly anti-nationalist.' Nationalism, he added, always contained underlying elements of a sort of fascism. In addition, he questioned the plan for tax-varying powers in Scotland. Howells' statements were disowned by Jack Straw and he was subsequently moved to another remit but he was voicing a strand of Labour thought, undoubtedly more prevalent in Wales and England than in Scotland, but authentic nonetheless and still apparent.

It is not that the party in England or the London-based leadership is overtly hostile to devolution. But the attitude of many MPs when they thought about devolution has been: 'If we must.' There has been a dissonance of approach within the Labour Party across the border between Scotland and England.

No matter how frequently Tony Blair voices his support for decentralisation, the suspicion remains that he falls into the 'if we must' category, at least to some degree. Such remarks, I know, infuriate the Prime Minister. What more, he must ask, does he require to do? He inherited a plan for a Scottish Parliament, subjected it to close scrutiny, steered it almost unchanged through Westminster at the very earliest opportunity – and demanded very little in return. Ah, say the Scots, but are you a true believer?

His exasperation showed in a speech delivered in the Scottish Parliament on 9 March 2000. Blair recalled that the Scottish press endlessly claimed – on each visit he paid to Scotland – that he did not believe in devolution and would never deliver it. It was consequently a little disappointing, he said, to see the same journalists now 'knocking' the new Parliament for which they had apparently yearned.

Blair added: 'Scepticism is healthy. Cynicism is corrosive.' It pains me deeply in my journalistic soul to agree with a politician commenting about the press, but the Prime Minister does have a point. There has indeed occasionally been corrosive criticism of the entire devolved institution, rather than measured, sceptical analysis of daily events. So point taken, but still devolution does not appear to me to be at the core of the Blairite project. Put most simply, Blair did not enter politics or attain the Labour leadership to establish a Scottish Parliament. As leader, he adopted a Scottish policy.

As I have written elsewhere, it is arguably to Blair's credit that he saw the political necessity of legislating for devolution. But it is still an issue of a different calibre for Blairites. Team Blair talk of modernising Labour, of strengthening the economy, of transforming the nature of public service. If they talk of the Scottish Parliament at all, they frequently talk in dismissive terms.

One of the terms used derives from misinterpretation of a previous remark by the Prime Minister, defending the tax powers of a Scottish Parliament. In an interview with *The Scotsman*, Blair had pointed out that the lowliest parish council in England had a certain degree of discretion over finance. Would it not be ridiculous, he argued, to deny financial discretion to the powerful Scottish Parliament?

Blair was, in truth, *contrasting* one with the other, stressing that the Scottish Parliament was an influential and significant body by comparison with the humble parish council. Sections of the Scottish media, however, chose to assert that he had likened the Scottish Parliament to a parish council, that this was an unpardonable slur on Scotland's dignity. Given the sensitivities, his simile might have been more carefully chosen, but the reaction was out of all proportion to the remarks and, indeed, misrepresented them.

Perhaps understandably, Blair's advisers – Team Blair – became deeply suspicious of the Scottish media. Their constant complaint, prior to the establishment of a Scottish Parliament, was that the Scottish media were obsessed with devolution by contrast with the Scottish people. I recall the Prime Minister answering questions from the public in the Glasgow Film Theatre. As the inquiries ranged from employment law to social policy and education, a piece of paper was thrust into my hand. It was a scribbled note passed from Alastair Campbell, the Prime Minister's ever-present aide, which read: 'These are the real concerns of the public.' I glanced towards Campbell and he responded with a cheeky grin.

Most of this tension – between Downing Street and the Scottish media – has evaporated. The Parliament is up and running. The Scottish media happily spend their days in sceptical analysis or corrosive cynicism, according to taste. Downing Street has other things to worry about. The occasional smirking UK Minister will ask me how the 'parish council' is getting on. With the delicacy and tact which is my hallmark, I generally reply succinctly. Quite frequently, two words are enough.

However, Downing Street is no longer the spot to find real vitriol about the Scottish Parliament. For that, you have to turn to Scottish Labour MPs. Most MPs can happily afford to regard Holyrood with benign neglect. Not so the MPs sent to Westminster from Scotland. For one thing, their numbers are to be reduced as a direct consequence of devolution. Scotland has been numerically overrepresented at Westminster, partly to cope with distinctive Scottish legislation being processed there. Such legislation is now handled by Holyrood. So the number of MPs from Scotland is to be cut, partly to reflect that and partly as a sop to English opinion.

There is another aspect to this issue. The Scottish MPs have lost their place in the sun. They see all the media attention devoted to the MSPs, and far less to them, unless they happen to be prominent frontbenchers. This was of course inevitable. The MSPs are closer to home and they are dealing with day-to-day 'newsy' issues like education, health and crime. That inevitability does not make the transition any more pleasant for the MPs concerned. Frankly, the public neglect burns into their soul.

Third, some at Westminster suspect that prospects for career advancement may now be reduced for Scottish MPs. This is not a hard and fast rule, merely a question hanging in the air. Scotland now has its own Parliament: why should the Scots get jobs in the Parliament that sits in England?

It is arguably right to exclude Scottish MPs from Whitehall departments like health, education and even the Home Office. These deal mostly or exclusively with domestic concerns affecting England. However, that was always the case, even before legislative devolution. The existence of a Parliament has simply sharpened the focus.

However, some Scottish MPs suspect that their options may be limited still further by the imprecise feeling that their status has somehow been lessened by the establishment of a Scottish Parliament. For example, some commentators and MPs openly challenged the right of Michael Martin, a Glasgow MP, to be Speaker of the House of Commons, although, to be frank, that was motivated by miserable class snobbery too.

But, privately, the Scots at Westminster mutter to themselves: will there ever be another Scottish Chancellor? Or Foreign Secretary? Or Prime Minister? The answer, I believe, is still, yes – if they are good enough. The problem is that Scots may have to surmount an extra hurdle in the already competitive world of politics. They probably always did. Again, a partially dormant issue has been reawakened.

This suspicion is of course deeply unfair. Westminster remains the Parliament of the United Kingdom. Scotland's MPs are there as full and equal members, not as observers or envoys. They are entitled to compete equally for promotion. However, strict fairness does not always apply in politics, where impressions can count. If the feeling persists that Scotland's influence at Westminster should be curbed to placate English concerns, then that will happen, insidiously, whatever assurances are given to the contrary.

None of which endears the Scottish Parliament to MPs from Scotland. Technically, these issues apply to all MPs from all parties. But Labour dominates Scotland's representation at Westminster. The LibDems gripe a little, but the 2001 election returned only one Tory and the Nationalists spend their days trying to reduce Scotland's representation at Westminster to zero by ending the Union. This is a Labour problem.

To narrow it still further, this is a problem which seems to affect those who are well established in the Commons. The new Labour members seem better able to accept their role, perhaps because they knew the rules when they were adopted as candidates. The older guard were used to being the key figures in the Scottish body politic. They were used to being consulted by the media on every issue. That has gone – and they are taking it hard. I have lost count of the number of times I have been berated by Labour MPs about the 'disproportionate' attention paid to the Scottish Parliament. Mostly, I try to remind them placidly that television news coverage on BBC Scotland is confined to domestic issues – partly at the prompting of Labour Ministers – and that domestic issues affecting Scotland are almost entirely devolved to the Scottish Parliament. It is no surprise, then, that MSPs are on the telly in Scotland more than MPs.

On occasion, though, I lose it. I recall one recent Labour conference at Brighton when the customary harangue was in full flow. The Scottish Parliament was parish pump stuff compared to the big, grown-up version at Westminster. It was all my fault that so-and-so was never on the TV. Finally, in exasperation, I said: 'Look, just what did you think you were doing when you voted for the Third Reading of the Scotland Act?'

The depth of pain and anguish is astonishing to behold. I have heard Scottish Labour MPs talk about devolution as if it were some evil visited upon Scotland by a foreign power, not a keynote Labour promise, delivered by a Labour Prime Minister. I believe, however, that the pain may be receding. First, the sheer novelty of Holyrood meant it attracted huge initial coverage, not all of it by any means positive. I believe there is scope for the fulcrum to tilt a bit back towards Westminster, that Scottish MPs are finding that more media calls come their way. Certainly, from my perspective and that of colleagues from other organisations with whom I have discussed this, there is absolutely no wish to exclude MPs. Westminster remains a critical factor in Scottish politics, not least because Scotland's budget is determined there.

Second, I believe Labour MPs are accustoming themselves more and more to the new politics, building expertise in important reserved matters such as benefits, Europe and the economy. However, it is not possible to disinvent the wheel. Responsibility for Scottish domestic politics – for health, education, criminal law and the rest – has been transferred en bloc to Holyrood. By Labour. Most Scottish Labour MPs will concede – when pressed – that their personal circumstances were bound to change. But it hurts. It still hurts.

However, if palliatives can be applied to that pain, another internal issue for Scottish Labour may be more resistant to soothing balm. That is the question of the party's stand on public services, or, more strictly, how those services are to be delivered.

There is plainly apprehension on the Labour back benches at Holyrood about the involvement of the private sector in service delivery. For a start, they are ideologically and intuitively nervous.

Most of their political lives have been spent vaunting public provision and challenging private profit. Labour previously criticised the Tory strategy of funding public capital projects through the Private Finance Initiative. The system has been reformed, and renamed Public Private Partnerships (PPPs). The reforms have been welcomed, but some fundamental objections still remain.

However, those qualms would undoubtedly ease if it could be shown that private provision is incontestably cheaper and better. Some MSPs frankly doubt that, too. This nervousness manifests itself in two ways. Labour MSPs such as Pauline McNeill have explicitly called for greater attention to be paid to trade union concerns in this area. Alternatively, Labour Ministers may attempt to hint that Scotland is adopting a stance that is avowedly more public sector than that operating in England, particularly with regard to the health service.

The added difficulty for Labour is that this debate does not take place in a vacuum. The party cannot quietly consider the issues, and reach a conclusion. On the one hand, it has the SNP and the Scottish Socialists urging the abandonment of Public Private Partnerships. On the other hand, it has the Tories gleefully pointing out that the UK government is adopting more radical solutions in the health service, for example, and challenging the Executive to follow suit.

As First Minister, Henry McLeish appeared to be sold on pragmatism. What matters is what works, he argued. I do not believe, frankly, that Jack McConnell has altered that perspective significantly. He is still interested in delivery. However, McConnell has altered the tone, most notably when he signed a Memorandum of Understanding with the Scottish TUC on 15 April 2002.

This gave the unions a specific role in consultation over the future of public services in Scotland. It followed a bitter stand-off at Labour's Scottish conference in February that year when union leaders only narrowly failed in an attempt to veto a key policy document in protest at the Executive's stand on PPP. However, even as McConnell signed the concordat, he stressed that private firms would still play a role in the provision of services.

I believe that the Executive does take a different stand from the government at Westminster, to a certain extent. For example, probing written questions submitted by the Tories have disclosed that Scottish Ministers have no plans to follow the English model in health and introduce a star-rating system for hospitals or Foundation hospitals with autonomous decision-making. Equally, it might be argued that the UK government lays greater stress on the use of private health provision to meet gaps in the NHS.

However, I believe the differences are exaggerated by the perceived need for different rhetoric. For an English audience, which voted heavily Tory in recent memory, Tony Blair stresses the sticks that are to be applied to the resistant hide of the public sector. In Scotland, with a political make-up which defaults to the Left, Jack McConnell displays the carrots on offer to the public sector for good service.

Look beneath the rhetoric at the key characteristics in each case, for example with regard to the health service. Do both administrations believe in the provision of universal health care, free at the point of need? Yes. Do both administrations believe that is best delivered by an NHS funded through general taxation? Yes. Are both administrations nevertheless willing to involve the private sector in the construction and provision of hospital services? Yes. Have most recent major hospital projects in Scotland and England been via PPP? Yes. Are both administrations willing to use private health care to fill NHS gaps? Yes.

This issue deserves serious consideration in Scotland – and inside Scottish Labour. Are PPPs more efficient because of private-sector competition? Or do they cost more because profit has to be factored in and the public sector will face substantial longer term repayments? Despite the occasional screeching on either side, this is not a case which can be settled from first principles, from ideology.

Both sides of the argument could take something from an investigation into the private funding of schools, conducted by the financial watchdog, the Accounts Commission.[1] This confirmed that private finance schemes had built or upgraded schools reliably and on time. Councils and schools generally welcomed the results. The financial checks had been rigorous. These conclusions were warmly welcomed by the Executive.

However, the Commission also noted that private finance generally cost more than public borrowing, although they stressed that had been offset by transferring the cost burden of maintaining the schools to the private contractors. They noted further that the present rules were flawed, because they tended to play down the actual gap in costs between the public and private options. These conclusions were pounced upon by the SNP.

The Commission found itself unable to determine, finally, whether private finance schemes were good value for money. However, the report speculates that councils have a considerable incentive to find that private build schemes do indeed meet their financial tests. That is because central government left them with no other realistic funding option. In response, Ministers insisted that private finance had proved its worth, but also stressed that they were looking at giving councils greater flexibility to borrow money themselves.

That report spotlighted the situation in schools. There has been comparable controversy over hospitals. There has been a further, bitter dispute over prisons, with the Executive facing sharp criticism after it announced plans to build up to three new private jails, although that row landed in the in-tray of Jim Wallace, as Justice Minister. Each issue has individual aspects, but there is a central, political core: the trade-off between public and private interests.

Certainly, Labour must consider the conditions of the workforce employed in PPP projects. But producer interests – the demands of Labour-supporting unions – must not be heeded at the expense, for example, of NHS patients. Equally, assertions that private is best and cheapest should be strictly tested, using longer term criteria and, perhaps, casting a more sceptical eye at the claims of independent financial consultants who frequently have a stake in the very private sector they are assessing.

Naturally, this is a huge question for the whole of Scotland. But it is also a defining internal debate for Labour. There are 'New' Labour figures in Scotland who fret that the party is about to lurch back into a producer-driven emphasis on purely 'public services', rather than 'service to the public', however delivered. There are other Labour MSPs who fear that the party's acceptance of private provision will be a vote loser in the longer term.

There are still other voices, arguing for new thinking. On a single day at the Labour conference in Perth in February 2002, two former Cabinet Ministers both set out their ideas in fringe lectures. The conjunction was, I am assured, accidental. Angus Mackay argued that it was 'time to housetrain' PPP projects. Susan Deacon called for a new maturity about the limits – and opportunities – of political power in a global context.

Mackay insisted that PPP had a considerable role where it could be guaranteed that the costs were lower. He stressed that was a pre-condition applied by Ministers in considering such projects. But he argued for reforms such as better conditions for workers transferring from public to private employment and more liberal capital borrow-ing powers for local authorities. Deacon's lecture was an intriguing essay on the sterility of contemporary partisan debate which, she said, was characterised by 'reactivism and crude populism'. She argued that Labour should reassert its core values of public service, and move beyond merely managing the system in response to apparent consumer demand.

Further, I think that Wendy Alexander's decision to resign from the Cabinet was substantially motivated by a wish to engage in this debate from a decidedly 'New' Labour perspective. Yes, I believe she was partly driven by discontent with her own personal circum-stances. I do not believe she would have resigned had Donald Dewar still been First Minister. She might have sought a 'sabbatical', a career break, but I believe she would have been more reluctant to quit.

However, I accept her stress on the need for new, open thinking. She believes that public policy in Scotland requires a fresh approach, and believes she will be better equipped to contribute to that if she is free of the burden of ministerial responsibility.

I noted above that I think rhetoric can occasionally mask the Executive's true strategy in public service provision. Equally, though, I believe that Jack McConnell is acutely attuned to the nature of the debate required in Scotland about the future of public services. In one sense, his concordat with the unions is an effort to win space for that debate to take place. However, he is First Minister, in charge of the Executive, not a detached observer. He knows that voters are crying out for better services, and he has to respond primarily to that call.

McConnell's slogan has been 'do less, better'. This was spelled out explicitly in a Parliamentary speech in which he set out the key priorities for the Executive.[2] He confirmed that his top targets were to improve education, health and transport while fostering job cre-ation and cutting crime. It was a good speech – if slightly hampered by the modern political malaise of substituting platitude for policy.

I prefer the analysis offered by Jack McConnell when he was seeking the support of MSPs for his election as First Minister.[3] In

that speech, he spoke of his own upbringing on Arran before offering a personal creed: to be open and transparent, to enhance rather
than avoid Parliamentary scrutiny, to speak for all the people, to be
decisive but responsive and, finally, 'to have the good sense to say
no – when the time is not right and the money is not there'.
Specifically, on public service, he argued that improvement would
come when power was devolved to community leaders: those
actually working on the ground in hospitals and schools. He said
Scotland had to 'get serious about unleashing all of the talent we
have'.

Tories quickly pointed out that this credo scarcely sat well with
the apparent determination to reverse the autonomous status of
St Mary's school in Dunblane, one of the very few schools which
opted out of local authority control. Setting that aside, I believe this
was a significant speech by Jack McConnell.

The First Minister has instructed his Ministers to make contact
with front-line staff in every sector of Scotland. To speak to nurses
rather than simply the health unions. To speak to teachers rather
than educationalists. To speak to police officers rather than purely
the Police Federation. To speak to council workers rather than
council leaders. McConnell's approach might best be described as
communitarian. Taking what he says at face value, he believes that
people must be given a stake in running their sector of society,
whether it is their school, their health service or their place of work.
This is social democracy from the bottom up, rather than social
control from the top down.

The key exemplar in this field was the insistence on transferring
Glasgow council housing to community ownership. This move –
backed in a ballot – was highly controversial. There were authentic
arguments over basic issues like rent and repairs. But there was also
a fundamental question: is housing best provided and serviced collectively through the elected public authority or is it best delivered
locally through community partnerships? Translate that specific
example into the wider debate about the nature of public service
and you have the fundamental issue underlying Scottish Labour
politics.

As I write in summer 2002, there has been relatively little sign so
far of Jack McConnell putting this communitarian principle into
hard policy practice, beyond that instruction to Ministers to spread

their consultation net more widely. But the intention is on the record and McConnell plainly believes what he says, for there was no need to venture this view at all. An intriguing aspect of Scottish politics will be to watch how this strategy develops.

As things stand, McConnell is plainly in command of the Executive. His status in Scottish politics is unquestioned – at least by comparison with the internal power struggle which characterised the party's campaign for the first Scottish Parliamentary elections in 1999. During the early period, during the preparations for the election, it was very difficult to determine who was in charge of the Scottish Labour Party's campaign. Was it Donald Dewar, as Scottish Secretary? Or Helen Liddell, then his deputy who had previously been asked by Tony Blair to shake up the Scottish operation? Or Henry McLeish, who had helped co-ordinate the 1997 election campaign in Scotland? Or Alex Rowley, who was the General Secretary, installed with the backing of Gordon Brown? Or perhaps Brown himself? The options steadily narrowed as the campaign went on. Rowley was marginalised. McLeish was utilised but was definitely not in charge. Liddell was scarcely evident in the national campaign, but this was understandable, given that she was not a Holyrood candidate. Dewar was the party leader and First Minister in waiting, but Labour media mythology also devised another role for him as a quasi-presidential figure, somehow above squalid politics. He was despatched around the country to woo the voters.

If matters were uncertain at the very beginning of the campaign, by the end there was absolutely no doubt. Gordon Brown took direct personal command of the campaign, with help from key aides like Douglas Alexander, the bright and personable winner of the Paisley South Westminster by-election and now a rising Minister. By all accounts, including those who are not instinctive supporters of the Chancellor, Brown's energy, discipline, motivational skills and sheer talent were critical to the campaign.

However, another figure also entered the scene: John Rafferty, later to become Donald Dewar's Chief of Staff in the office of First Minister. Rafferty took time off from his job running the National Lottery Charities Board in Scotland to assist the Labour campaign. A quintessential fixer, his most prominent Labour role in the past had been to devise and maintain the party's strategy against the poll tax in the 1980s, steering a careful path away from the demand for

Labour to organise an illegal non-payment campaign. Donald Dewar, Shadow Scottish Secretary at the time, was exceptionally grateful for the assistance.

Rafferty is a discreet, smartly-dressed executive type, softly-spoken, with a cultured west of Scotland accent and a speaking style which can veer enticingly between Runyonesque polite precision and subtle menace, according to the taste of the listener. I should add that, personally, I have never found Rafferty anything other than entirely affable. His arrival, however, posed an intrinsic challenge to Alex Rowley, who found that his stewardship of the party came under further question as Rafferty exerted more and more influence. Rowley ended up resigning exactly two weeks after the conclusion of the campaign.

Quite separately, there is said to have been disquiet among those who were despatched on Donald Dewar's campaign battlebus. Departing from Edinburgh's Parliament Square at the start of the campaign, Dewar toured the length and breadth of Scotland evangelising Labour's cause while others managed the campaign from the Glasgow headquarters.

By one interpretation, this was a curious decision, recalling for some the decision to despatch John Prescott around the country in the 1997 General Election. Others, however, insist that Dewar came to revel in his role, meeting voters and addressing genuine concerns. Certainly, Dewar was able to dismiss with confidence any suggestion – in the media or elsewhere – that his place at the core of the campaign had been usurped.

Apparently, others in the bus party were less contented. The squad included, at various points, Westminster MPs, Dewar's adviser Murray Elder and Lorraine Davidson, the party's director of communication. Some members of the battlebus team, it is claimed, felt rather left out of events. They felt they were traipsing round the country when the strategic campaign decisions were being taken back in Delta House, the party's Glasgow HQ, by acolytes of the Chancellor and by relatively new arrivals like John Rafferty.

One source even suggested to me that the battlebus featured alongside its high-tech equipment a puppet or doll nicknamed 'Rafferty', which was 'no doubt kicked from one end of the bus to the other'. In addition, Lorraine Davidson, who had been assuring everyone that the battlebus was the most splendid fun, resigned from

her post shortly after the election. There had previously been
rumours that she was discontented.

On his departure, Alex Rowley raised another issue: the question
of Scottish Labour autonomy. He made plain his belief that the
party in Scotland must be given more discretion to run its own
affairs. To be fair, that has steadily happened. The party's conference
in Scotland determines Scottish policy. As an aside, it might be
noted that such a focus tends to alter the nature of the conference,
somewhat sidelining the debates on 'reserved' issues such as defence
and foreign affairs, which were such a feature of Scottish Labour
gatherings in the past.

Also in the past, however, the notion of Scottish Labour policy
autonomy was regarded with horror by some. Writing in *The
Guardian* in 1999, Matthew Taylor of the Institute for Public Policy
Research, a former assistant General Secretary of the Labour Party,
offered his views.[4] He argued that the emergence of distinct Scottish
Labour policies would jeopardise the presentation of a single British
Labour 'brand'. He added: 'Devolution gave the people of Scotland
and Wales the right to elect their own government, not to redesign
the political platform of each party.'

Further, he said: 'To suggest that devolution to the Scottish
Parliament means that Scottish Labour politicians have free rein to
redesign the party's values and core policies is to deny the very
definition of a political party.' A cynical observer might paraphrase
that as 'you can have your own Parliament if you insist but you must
not dare to do anything different with it'. I would not want to suggest that this is the established London Labour perspective. Equally,
I do not believe that it is a maverick standpoint. Scratch a nib across
the Westminster Cabinet list and you will be underlining the names
of several individuals who also feel that the Scottish Parliament must
not be allowed to diverge from British policy.

However, the Prime Minister has laid down the devolved law.
Addressing MSPs, he said that cross-border policy differences were
'not an accident, but the intention'.[5] Quite. There is simply no point
in a Scottish Parliament with 129 MSPs elected on a Scottish
mandate if policy is directed by the party machines in London. But
the Parliament should also guard against setting Scotland apart from
English policy simply for the joy of it.

As an aside, I believe Labour Ministers – and the Parliament more generally – should look at the increasing use of the so-called Sewel Convention, which allows Westminster to legislate in areas that are devolved to Scotland. I am not alone in voicing concern about this. The SNP has drawn attention to it. Significantly, Lord Sewel himself – a former Scottish Office Minister – is also believed to harbour considerable doubts about the way the convention which bears his name is being deployed.

As first outlined by Lord Sewel,[6] the convention was intended to deal with a potential quandary: that domestic power had been devolved but that Westminster – as a sovereign Parliament – formally retained the ability to legislate in any area it chose, including Scottish domestic issues. Lord Sewel promulgated a convention that Westminster 'would not normally legislate with regard to devolved matters in Scotland without the consent of the Scottish Parliament'. To be absolutely clear, this was designed to forestall unwarranted interference by Westminster in devolved matters. Further, it was specifically envisaged by Donald Dewar as Secretary of State that the convention would only be deployed sparingly.

In practice, the convention has been somewhat turned on its head. It is now deployed almost on a routine basis to allow Westminster to legislate for the whole of the UK. Such a procedure may often be sheer common sense, but overuse brings problems. For one thing, Scotland's elected MSPs are denied the opportunity to scrutinise proposed legislation as it develops. For another – and this is potentially serious – legislation which finally emerges from Westminster after the Commons and Lords have had their say may be nothing like the draft Bill which began the process. By using the Sewel Convention, the Scottish Parliament is handing a blank cheque to Westminster. MSPs may not like the final outcome in individual cases but, having handed power away, there will be little they can do in practice.

Labour, in particular, may be tempted to concede that legislation should be taken on a UK-wide basis in partnership with their Westminster colleagues. They should be wary, however, of establishing a precedent that may pose immediate problems, and store up additional trouble for the future.

I believe, though, that the logic of Labour's position is that the Scottish party's autonomy will strengthen, although I do not remotely envisage anything in the form of a break from London. Labour's

instincts and interests point to strong and continuing cross-border
co-operation. It will simply be practical politics – particularly when
confronted by the Nationalists – to determine Scottish Parliamentary
Labour policy in Scotland. This trend will increase as, steadily,
Labour candidates and MSPs owe their allegiance solely to Holyrood
politics, as those with a Westminster background step down.

Finally, I come to one more contentious aspect of Labour in the
Scottish Parliament. The calibre of the party's MSPs. In addressing this
sensitive issue, let me begin by stressing that all parties are blessed
with a mixed bag of Parliamentarians. All parties have highly talented
members alongside others who, to be polite, are unlikely to command
places on the front bench. I shall look in the next chapter at the
problems which have confronted the SNP over candidate selection.
However, Labour is the largest party, and does appear to have featured the most internal disquiet about its initial group membership.

Most critics look to the original Labour selection procedure,
when potential candidates were interviewed and assessed for their
suitability. Only if you passed that test, could you go forward to
individual constituencies to be adopted or hope to add your name
to regional Labour lists. One senior MSP told me the party would
'never forgive Rosemary McKenna', the MP who chaired that
process of sifting applicants.

Rosemary McKenna is acutely aware of this criticism. She
defends the procedure on the grounds that it had to be 'legally
water-tight'. The timing of the selection process prior to the 1999
elections coincided with a separate, formal challenge to Labour
over the legitimacy of women-only shortlists. There was widespread
anxiety about the whole question of choosing candidates. Partly as
a consequence, the Scottish selection proceeded according to rigid
rules in an effort to forestall any subsequent challenge in the courts.

There were twenty-five members in total on the vetting panel,
drawn from Labour's National Executive, the Scottish party Executive,
the wider party and professional advisers who had experience of
employment law. Commonly, one from each sector took part in
each interview session. Eleven hundred hopefuls put their names
forward. The panel interviewed between 300 and 400.

The interviewees were given marks for a range of aptitudes such as
knowledge of Labour policy and media awareness. The professional
advisers tallied up the total score for each interviewee. If you did not

make the pass mark, you were out. This selection procedure sounds fair, if a little inflexible. The snag was the outcome. As one Minister, looking at the result, told me: 'How did we end up with so many numpties?' I stress again this is not my opinion but a view commonly – if strictly privately – expressed within Labour ranks. Look at the names who failed to make it through this exhaustive and supposedly fair procedure.

Jeane Freeman – now senior policy adviser to the First Minister. Esther Roberton – a key figure in the cross-party Convention who has had to console herself with helping run Scotland through the indirect route of a place on several key quangos. Murray Elder – former party General Secretary and senior adviser to Donald Dewar, now a peer. Susan Deacon – rejected by the panel, only to get through on appeal and straight into Donald Dewar's Cabinet. Mark Lazarowicz – a former council leader and lawyer, now MP for Edinburgh North and Leith. Kaliani Lyle – chief executive of Citizens Advice Scotland. Mary Picken of the Scottish TUC. For many, the episode has left a sour taste. Looking at some of the women who made it and the women who did not, one feminist insider observed to me, as a bitter joke, that the process 'seemed designed to prove that women were not meant to be in the Scottish Parliament'. Another retorted: 'That might be one answer – but how do you explain the men?'

Then there were the MPs kept out. Most attention was directed at Ian Davidson and Dennis Canavan who appealed against their exclusion from the list. Canavan, of course, subsequently stood as an independent and won. However, insiders insist that Donald Dewar discouraged others from applying in the first place, presumably to give the Parliament a fresh start. Some feel that was sensible, others that Scottish Labour could have used a leavening of experience from the outset.

The system has since been adapted. There is more pre-training of interviewees so that they are not artificially stumped by questions which, in practice, say little about their capacity to serve the people or the party as MSPs. Labour has moved to open up its system of ranking candidates for the top-up lists to one member, one vote. That is a significant reform, although counter-balanced in importance by the fact that so few Labour MSPs are likely to come from the regional lists.

I am aware of the danger of overstating this problem. To stress again, there is a range of talent in all the parties. Even some of the Labour backbenchers who visibly struggled at first have grown in confidence. Several were sharp from the outset and are developing into astute Parliamentarians. However, there are still too many pedestrian speeches, still too many who find the concept of debate foreign, still too many who seem incapable of offering a comment without reading it out, still too many who seem to have forgotten that they are making the law of Scotland, not trying to remit a motion at Labour conference.

To recap, I feel confident that this problem will ease as the Parliament and the Labour group mature. In the longer term, too, I feel certain that Scottish Labour will develop still greater autonomy. By no means neglecting Westminster but thinking first and foremost of the legislative and governmental challenges presented by the Scottish Parliament.

That is natural territory for Jack McConnell, the former Scottish Labour Action campaigner. At the same time, though, McConnell did not become First Minister without exercising caution where merited. He is aware that Labour has to steer carefully in stressing its Scottish credentials.

For one thing, while policy autonomy is integral to devolution, McConnell – the Labour politician – will not want to shift ground too far from London. He has no interest in token defiance nor in picking fights unnecessarily with colleagues at Westminster. When merited, the Executive under McConnell will go its own way, but only when merited.

Second, McConnell, the former party General Secretary, is well aware that there are strict limits to such policy autonomy. Even post-devolution, Labour remains a British party. In the recent past, Labour leaders in Scotland tried, understandably, to trumpet their Scottish credentials. There was an outbreak of tartan, and staunch claims that Labour was truly the national party of Scotland.

It was fascinating stuff – and a source of entertainment to one and all – but it was not a sustainable strategy. A British party, even the devolved, semi-autonomous Scottish wing of a British party, cannot 'out-Nat the Nats' on Scottish credentials. The Nationalists can always trump their British UK rivals on this aspect of politics, perhaps by pointing to some policy which has apparently been tweaked to meet London concerns – or, more simply, by arguing that, by definition, the SNP is the only party which pays no attention to London whatsoever. Jack McConnell knows that – as do Scottish Labour's bright party strategists. So, under McConnell, look out for policies made in Scotland, but look too for a continuing recognition of the British dimension in Labour politics.

Notes

1. *Taking the Initiative*, Report by the Accounts Commission, 12 June 2002.
2. Speech by the First Minister, Jack McConnell, in the Scottish Parliament, 9 January 2002.
3. Speech by Jack McConnell, Scottish Parliamentary election of First Minister, 22 November 2001.
4. Article by Matthew Taylor, *The Guardian*, 11 May 1999.
5. Speech by the Prime Minister in the Scottish Parliament, 9 March 2000.
6. Speech by Lord Sewel, House of Lords, 21 July 1999.

9 The Scottish National Party and John Swinney

If the very phrase Scottish Labour can be said to represent inherent tension, then Scottish Nationalism has historically combined a series of dichotomies. Is it a movement or a party? Do its voters all believe in independence? Should it adopt a political platform tailored to the existing political structures or focus almost exclusively on overturning these political structures? Is it left, right or centre or none of these? Does it believe in achieving independence at one jump or gradually?

As the Scottish National Party has matured, these questions have steadily been answered, or have declined in relevance. Like all parties, the SNP is a salty amalgam of cool politics and obsession. However, there is an added tang to the Nationalists. Go to an SNP conference and you will still find more of a sense of mission than is commonly present at comparable events in rival parties.

Still, to get back to the questions listed above, the SNP *is* a political party with a broadly centre-left outlook. Not all its voters believe in independence, but then there are supporters of other parties who do. The SNP has a dual policy approach. Think of a TV remote-control handset where, from the comfort of your sofa, you can switch from terrestrial telly to satellite or cable. The SNP has a policy programme for a devolved Scotland, but press a button and they can offer you a much wider menu to suit independence.

The big question, though, is the last one. Just what is the strategy for achieving independence? Is there a 'big bang' which will produce independence in a single stride? Or must it be achieved step by step? Under John Swinney – and previous SNP leaders – that issue has been earnestly discussed by the party.

There are related topics, however, which are less commonly discussed. In an interdependent Europe, how would we recognise independence, how do we define independence? Is France 'independent' now that its currency rates are set in Frankfurt? Is Belgium 'independent', given its willingness to share power over defence and foreign affairs? In the nineteenth-century sense of national sovereignty, no. Is there then a new definition of independence to which the SNP aspires? More subtly still, is it conceivable that the party – and Scotland – might rest at a point on the path to independence and choose to stay there?

John Swinney is a Nationalist to his core. He joined the SNP in his mid-teens. However, he is acutely aware of the potential internal dilemmas confronting the SNP over its core aim, if, frankly, some activists are not. Swinney knows that it is not enough to yell

Scotland's Shadow First Minister? John Swinney and the Saltire.

'freedom', and expect an answering cry from the Scottish people. A political party must define its objectives and its strategy.

Swinney took over the leadership from Alex Salmond on Saturday, 23 September 2000. In a ballot declared at the party conference in Inverness, the new leader had defeated his MSP colleague Alex Neil by 67 per cent to 33. Significantly, the contest had hinged almost entirely on the party's strategic attitude to the devolved Scottish Parliament. This confirmed – if confirmation were needed – that virtually the entire political focus of the SNP is now upon the Scottish Parliament, rather than Westminster. For the SNP, the road to independence – however defined, however understood – lies through Holyrood.

In the leadership contest, Neil sought to criticise the new devolution settlement as inadequate. He wanted the SNP to campaign much more frequently and assertively beyond the confines of the Scottish Parliamentary chamber. While acknowledging the merits of country-wide campaigning, Swinney believed the SNP should work hard within devolution to win the trust of the Scottish people for the next steps towards independence.

For ease of description, Swinney was seen then as the 'gradualist' and Neil as the 'fundamentalist'. Those descriptions are fairly loose: Swinney was more impatient for independence than the label would imply, Neil more assiduous within the devolved structure than his occasionally dismissive rhetoric would suggest. Since his victory, John Swinney has gradually sharpened the focus upon the SNP's fundamental aim of independence. However, he still faces disquiet from those who want to go further, faster.

Privately, Nationalist insiders accept that there was a 'basic flaw' at the core of their campaign for the first elections to the Scottish Parliament in 1999. That flaw was whether they wanted to govern under devolution or to transform devolution into independence. The answer, of course, was that they wanted both, and the campaign was, arguably, confused and undermined as a consequence.

Independence was placed tenth on the party's list of priorities for that election – behind social and economic concerns which could largely be addressed under devolution. It was a tactical blunder, despite the unconvincing efforts of party officials to argue that independence should be seen as the 'culmination' of the SNP's programme.

Further, the campaign was dogged by problems, largely caused by lack of money and staff. One senior insider told me the Nationalists were 'out-resourced, out-gunned and driven into the ground' by their Labour rivals. It was left to a tiny core team to direct the party's strategy – with that same team then broadly expected to implement that strategy on the ground. According to insiders, that accounted for a lack of readiness, a lack of sharpness in the campaign. Take a tiny but instructive example. One particular day, the Nationalists volunteered a policy for enhancing the teaching of modern languages in primary schools. At the news conference, I inquired: 'Which languages would you propose to teach to primary children?' Nicola Sturgeon, as education spokesperson, was unable to specify although she did indicate a comforting preference for European tongues. She was rescued by Mike Russell, the chief executive, who suggested, as I recall, French and Italian. This was their main policy announcement for the day, and yet they had not worked through the elementary details.

There were more serious problems. The party failed to prepare the ground properly for its 'Penny for Scotland' plan to use the Scottish Parliament's Tartan Tax power to fund additional spending in Scotland. Arguably, the first focus should have been upon the productive use of such expenditure – not the downside cost.

Then there was the impact of the broadcast by the party leader Alex Salmond in March 1999 when he condemned the NATO bombing of Yugoslavia in the Kosovo campaign as 'unpardonable folly'. SNP insiders back Salmond's judgement on the issue itself, but concede that it was damaging, politically, to appear to be condemning a continuing Allied action in which Britain was involved.

Finally, there was the attempt – in April 1999, late in the campaign – to analyse the economic impact of independence.[1] After considerable media pressure at the news conference which launched the document, the Nationalists eventually conceded that Scotland might face an initial deficit under certain circumstances. These circumstances were broadly an insistence by the rest of the UK in the negotiations leading to independence that Scotland must bear a share of the UK national debt.

Under this 'worst case' scenario – incorporating that debt cost – the Nationalists finally acknowledged that Scotland might face a deficit of around £1.5 billion in 2000/1, but it would steadily shrink, they argued, and turn into a surplus.

However, in the 'worst case' section of their published document, the SNP neglected to mention that deficit. They chose instead to publish only the rosier end of the picture: the forecast for 2002/3 showing Scotland virtually in balance, and for 2003/4, showing a projected surplus of £1 billion. Their justification was that they felt it right to publish the full picture for the anticipated point of entry to the Euro. Further, they discounted the prospect of this 'worst case' scenario coming to pass, arguing that Scotland had already contributed its share of the UK debt through North Sea oil in the 1980s.

The Nationalists also argued that any such 'worst case' deficit would be less than for the UK, and would still be easily low enough to enable Scotland to meet the Maastricht criteria for membership of the Euro zone. They argued – in the main document – that their 'base case' showed a surplus for Scotland of £869 million in 2000/1, rising to £3.3 billion in 2003/4. These figures excluded the UK debt share estimate.

The exercise should perhaps be praised for its relative detail and political courage so close to an election, but the Nationalists would have helped their case substantially if they had been prepared to be frank and to include all the deficit estimates in the main document. Journalists, myself included, were obliged to pursue the issue with the party's (then) Treasury team of John Swinney and Andrew Wilson outside the news conference.

As Swinney stood on the banks of the Clyde outside the Moat House Hotel in Glasgow, he attempted to answer our persistent queries with the use of a calculator borrowed from the *Financial Times* reporter. Eventually, Wilson produced a document with the figures listed. This was not the SNP's finest moment. One insider told me that the entire exercise was 'a disaster'.

Since then, the party has refined its economic approach. Instead of attempting to produce a zero-sum balance sheet, the SNP builds in an estimate for growth in the Scottish economy, arguing that independence itself would be a revitalising factor. This approach has been spelled out in a briefing for business devised by Jim Mather, the party's Treasurer, and Andrew Wilson.

Mather apparently relies heavily upon the work of Dr Eli Goldratt, an Israeli thinker, who has posed a 'theory of constraints' whereby a business or organisation proceeds by steadily identifying the core obstacles standing in the path of advancement. You will not be surprised to learn that Mather and Wilson conclude that Scotland's key constraint is a lack of political power.

The presentation itself is punchy and impressive – reflecting Mather's background as a successful businessman. The core message, which has now been transmitted to the wider party, is that economic growth must take precedence over spending aims in political priorities. This reflects John Swinney's long-held view that the SNP must be firmly pro-enterprise and that this approach must flavour all its policies.

Essentially, the Mather exercise is aimed at minimising the fear of independence in the business community. Mather believes that, by inviting business to make a link between independence and growth, he can at least begin to counter the more common concerns. Privately, it is hoped that by pitching for a win, the party may achieve a score draw, that they may neutralise some of the more damaging disquiet over breaking the Union which exists in corporate and economic Scotland.

I believe there is a fundamental flaw in the exercise which is that very linkage of independence and free enterprise. The two are not causally connected. One does not lead inevitably to the other. It is conceivable, for example, that an independent Scotland in certain circumstances might pursue a command economy, that you would have a Scottish Albania rather than a Scottish Luxembourg.

The process of independence does not dictate the economic strategy to be pursued when independence has been attained. Mather and Wilson acknowledge that problem but argue, with some justice, that they see the SNP itself as the conduit to independence, and that the SNP as presently constituted is firmly pro-enterprise and pro-growth. This strategy of factoring in an estimate for growth is, of course, open to challenge by rival parties, who are free to assert that independence would have a detrimental effect. At the very least, however, the SNP's economic planning seems more sophisticated. There should be no more scenes of calculators by the Clyde.

Similarly, the years of Scottish Parliamentary work – the close scrutiny in committee and chamber – seem to have helped to sharpen the SNP as a political machine. Party documents seem more carefully crafted, the research more thorough. However, the core problem still remains. How is independence to be achieved?

John Swinney has made three contributions to that debate. First, prompted by Alex Salmond, he set out the mechanics. An SNP administration in the Scottish Parliament would hold a consultative referendum among people in Scotland to gain a mandate for independence in advance of a detailed settlement ending the Union. That approach deliberately replicates the road to devolution whereby the Labour government held a referendum *before* legislating for change. Second, as with the economic campaign, Swinney has attempted to still Scotland's fears about independence. He tries to answer the questions raised on the doorstep, the substantive and the slight. Will my pension be safe? Will I still be able to watch *EastEnders*? (Yes and yes, according to the SNP.) Third, he has attempted to define independence in pragmatic terms; a lot less *Braveheart*, a lot more economic and social policy.

Most of these initiatives were begun by Salmond, who calculated that the SNP must offer much more than simply the Holy Grail of independence. It must brush aside the practical obstacles in the way, and offer a vision of what independence might mean in Scotland's housing schemes and rural areas. This stance meant adopting a clear policy stance to the Left of centre in line with the SNP's instincts and the Scottish consensus. He summed this up by arguing that the SNP 'must take sides within Scotland as well as taking Scotland's side'. Salmond faced two problems. First, he was distrusted by the 'fundamentalists', who felt that he was obscuring the simplicity of the independence message. Some even grumbled privately that he had abandoned independence, or refined it to such an extent that it had lost its bite. Second, the latter stage of Salmond's leadership coincided with the referendum campaign to achieve a devolved Scottish Parliament, where the SNP worked alongside Labour and the Liberal Democrats. The SNP message was inevitably blurred as a consequence.

In the early phase of Swinney's leadership, there was similar blurring, and similar mistrust. However, John Swinney has since set out a strategy, *Talking Independence*,[2] which attempts to end that confusion. Launched in spring 2002, the campaign returns the party to its basic objective of breaking the Union and securing an independent Scotland within the European Union.

On the face of it, the strategy appears puzzling. Private polling confirms that voters already link the SNP quite clearly with independence. Indeed, most link it solely with independence, and still have very little concept of where the party stands on economic and social issues. The fundamental issues which worry voters, in other words. The issues which swing elections.

A marketing guru would probably tell the SNP: 'Enough independence. Everyone knows you want that. You've got all the votes from that you're going to get. You need to tell people what you're going to do for *them* – what you're going to do on jobs, schools and hospitals.' Privately, party strategists acknowledge that my notional guru might have a point. There are other reasons, however, why John Swinney insists on *Talking Independence*. First, he needs to keep his own party activists – and MSPs – contented. Like true believers everywhere, they are permanently on the look-out for backsliding or heresy. They want incessant stress upon independence and tend to mistrust leaders who fail to deliver that. Second, the strategy is intended to anticipate and, if possible, neutralise Labour attacks. The SNP knows that Labour's anti-independence message – 'divorce is an expensive business' – was hugely successful in swaying voters in 1999. Swinney's aim is to retaliate first, to hype the issue of independence at a time of his choosing.

The objective has been to provoke political rivals to join in, to launch their attacks on independence. The hope is that the SNP's counter-attacks – their soothing answers – will then have time to become firmly lodged in the public mind. Swinney had intended to launch his campaign even earlier, in autumn 2001, but cancelled his plans after the September 11 terrorist attacks, calculating that voters would not be in a mood to receive sophisticated political persuasion.

Third, a more obvious point. The SNP campaigns on independence because it *believes* in independence. It assumes that voters would find anything else baffling. However, party strategists know they have to move beyond independence, to get on to the issues which worry voters rather than their own activists. They have my notional marketing guru barking in their ears. So Swinney's aim is to talk independence, but, increasingly, to link that fundamental message with issues like jobs and services. He wants to convince voters that independence would empower Scotland to boost the economy, to make schools and hospitals better. That is why Swinney took the lead, personally, in the SNP's campaign against the private financing of schools and hospitals. He wants voters to equate him with public services, not just independence.

The *Talking Independence* document begins by stating: 'Independence is what the SNP stands for and it is our core belief.' It may seem remarkable that such a statement has to be made – after seventy years of political agitation – but the confusion surrounding the transition to devolution made it necessary. The document largely proceeds by attempting to assuage common concerns about independence. Will my job be safe? Will my pension or my mortgage or my taxes be affected? What about transport? What about other public services? Can Scotland stand on its own two feet, without London subsidy? What about the Queen?

Most of these issues have arisen at various times in the past. Equally, most are a question of trust – not precise definition. In particular, do you believe the SNP when they say that an independent Scotland would prosper economically, or do you believe rival parties who say, variously, that the very process of ending the Union would be damaging or that Scotland requires subsidy from Westminster to thrive?

I am more intrigued by the definition of independence adopted by the SNP, by the clear focus upon finance rather than the trappings of statehood or the alleged attractions of national freedom. The *Talking Independence* document states at the outset that 'independence is full control by the people of Scotland over all their own affairs apart from control in any areas where they have freely agreed to share power with others'. This then is to be a political doctrine, with caveats, not a rallying cry.

The justification for independence – for moving beyond devolved powers – is largely expressed in economic terms. The 'urgent priority', we are told, is to obtain 'full financial independence', the ability to control all taxation and to disburse funds solely in line with Scottish priorities. In listing the claimed downside of Westminster control, the document lists three financial aspects: first, taxation, Scottish spending and welfare; next comes broadcasting, which is reserved to Westminster; and, finally, Scotland's relations with the European Union and the rest of the world, plus defence.

I believe this list confirms a process, again begun under Salmond, of narrowing the scope of independence to meet contemporary realities. For SNP strategists, independence no longer implies a nineteenth-century concept of undiluted national sovereignty. By Scottish independence, SNP leaders mean maximum financial control and full membership of the European Union.

Look, for example, at the issue of defence. The SNP has long faced awkward questions on this. Yes, the party seemed pretty sound on retaining the historic Scottish regiments, but how would Scotland be defended, globally, when the SNP envisaged an independent Scotland leaving NATO? How many aircraft carriers or submarines would an independent Scotland require?

To be fair, as the party's defence spokesperson, Colin Campbell has battled hard on this topic. But, mostly, party activists have been decidedly reluctant to engage in this wider defence debate, pre- ferring to concentrate upon the objective of removing Britain's nuclear deterrent from Scottish territory, banishing Trident from the Clyde.

When the agenda was published for the 2001 party conference on 27 August of that year, the schedule contained a motion from the party's Brussels branch advocating that the SNP end its opposi- tion to NATO membership. John Swinney confirmed that day in a BBC interview that he welcomed this debate and, further, that he hoped the party 'moves in that direction to strengthen our co- operation with other countries in conventional defence but reit- erating our determination to remove nuclear weapons from nuclear soil'.

It was clear to me that this initiative, this discussion was being driven by the leadership. SNP leaders saw that the party's defence strategy was incomplete and open to criticism. They hoped to settle this issue – indeed, to park it – by reversing the stand on NATO membership. An independent Scotland would shelter beneath the NATO umbrella, but would not contribute to the western alliance's nuclear force.

It has since been suggested to me that the leadership played the role of Switzerland in this debate: neutral but keen to foster discus- sion. I hear and acknowledge that argument. I have to say it was very far from my impression at the time the conference agenda was published. By the time of the conference in Dundee, the whole world was in turmoil as a consequence of the September 11 attacks.

In keeping with all other democratic parties, the SNP focused upon that, and agreed to sideline its discussion on NATO membership. The issue was handed to a review group to be chaired by the deputy leader, Roseanna Cunningham. Privately, it was said that the presence of the Left-wing deputy would reassure those who suspected a Swinney stitch-up.

The Cunningham committee duly deliberated, but the outcome was the status quo. The SNP retained 'an implacable opposition to nuclear weapons', according to that report. That opposition spilled over into the attitude to NATO. The party, it seemed, found the NATO umbrella uncongenial as long as it remained a nuclear organisation.

So was this outcome propagated in a straightforward fashion by the 'neutral' leadership? Not quite. The report was slipped round the Scottish Parliamentary press rooms at 5 p.m. on a busy news day, the day when one of those accused of the Lockerbie bombing had lost his appeal and was despatched to Barlinnie Prison in Glasgow.

Roseanna Cunningham was unavailable to speak owing to a family illness, and no-one else from the party would comment in her absence. Opposition critics accused the SNP of 'doing a Jo Moore', sneaking out a difficult announcement on a day when media attention was elsewhere in the manner of the former Department of Transport aide who suggested that the September 11 atrocity offered a good day to bury bad news. One internal party critic was more dismissive, telling me: 'Strategy? They couldnae spell strategy.'

It was obvious that the party simply was not ready to shift on defence. That much became clear from the Cunningham review, if not before. Arguably, the leadership then had little option but to play down the exercise. It does not alter the fact that – Trident aside – defence policy stands low in the list of SNP priorities. The leadership's private hope is that the European Union will make further progress in establishing a common security and foreign affairs strategy. The SNP could then shelter beneath that umbrella, reverting to its core concerns: finance and parity with other small European nations.

John Swinney further refined the SNP strategy with a key speech in May 2002.[3] In this, he attempted to tackle the blame culture in Scottish politics. The stereotypical Scot has a balanced view of the world: a chip on both shoulders. As P. G. Wodehouse said: 'It is never difficult to distinguish between a Scotsman with a grievance and a ray of sunshine.' Swinney apparently wanted to end Scotland's endemic habit of griping.

I recall opening my televised report of this speech by playing a clip from Rikki Fulton's magnificent BBC Scotland character, the Rev. I. M. Jolly – with his customarily miserable view of life. I am told that, when Swinney saw this report, he roared with laughter. Behind the fun, of course, the SNP leader had a serious message to impart.

First, he was rephrasing a common SNP theme; that independence will only be possible once Scotland has dispensed with the notion of depending on others for support. More significantly, though, Swinney intended to encompass both the devolved Parliament and his own party within the scope of his remarks.

The difficulty for the SNP is that they are twice tempted to criticise, even to condemn, the practical consequences of devolution. They want, understandably, to attack the governing Labour and LibDem Executive, but also to go further and to argue that independence would offer a much greater opportunity to address Scotland's problems. The snag is that the public do not necessarily follow the Nationalists in making such a sharp distinction between devolution and independence. Voters are inclined to equate the SNP with self-government more generally. They see the Scottish Parliament as being, to some extent, an SNP project.

This perception means it is difficult for the SNP to attack the limitations of devolution. Unless subtly handled, it can lead to confusion. Voters will feel that the SNP are disowning a structure which they played a part in building. Never mind that the SNP stayed out of the constitutional convention. Never mind that they wanted – and want – an independent Scotland. Voters may say to the SNP: you asked us to support devolution in the referendum. Now you tell us it's useless, but you want to go further and create independence. How can we trust you? Swinney's 'blame culture' speech was deliberately designed to address that quandary. In it, he says explicitly to his own party that it is fruitless to attempt to condemn devolution. He notes: 'If the Parliament has made mistakes, then we are all responsible. And if Scotland has failed to flourish, then that is our collective fault too.' He adds later: 'The politics of grievance will not deliver the kind of Scotland we all want.'

Instead of saying 'devolution bad, independence good', which meets consumer resistance, Swinney has developed another formula. 'Devolution better, independence best'. This is an attempt, a clever attempt, to finesse the quandary identified above: that the voters equate the SNP with self-government in the broadest sense and consequently, to a large extent, with devolution.

From now on, the SNP will argue that devolution is undoubtedly better than undiluted control from London, that it allows more decisions affecting Scotland to be taken in Scotland under a Scottish democratic mandate. They will also argue that independence would be best, allowing maximum control over those Scottish issues.

The problem for the SNP is that, once you get past the simple slogan, this is a relatively complex political message to present. Think back to the image of the TV remote control, with options to enter the terrestrial and satellite menus. SNP leaders effectively want us to view a split screen, with both menus on offer, simultaneously. Some days, they will want us to tune into their policies for devolution. Other days, they will want to wow us by trailing future attractions on the independence channel. During election campaigns, there is a significant danger of confusion.

However, that risk is nothing new for the SNP, and experience may have taught them how to cope with it. The SNP came into existence on 7 April 1934 following the merger of two predecessor parties. There had been a number of pro-independence organisations, often founded on cultural concerns, from the early years of the twentieth century.

The Scots National League was founded in 1921 on a platform of Highland land reform and Gaelic revivalism. The Scottish National Movement grew out of the Scottish literary renaissance. In 1927, John MacCormick – a key figure in Home Rule politics – formed the Glasgow University Scottish Nationalist Association. These groups came together in January 1928 to form the National Party of Scotland. A separate organisation, the Scottish Party, was founded in 1932. Eventually, these two merged in 1934.

The early years of the party were spectacularly unsuccessful on the fringe of Scottish politics. From foundation to the early 1960s, it hovered around 1 per cent in overall support, partly because limited resources meant it presented relatively few candidates: only two, for example, in each of the general elections of 1951 and 1955.

The Nationalists took their first Westminster seat in 1945 when Dr Robert McIntyre won a wartime by-election in Motherwell, only to lose again a few months later in the face of Labour's General Election triumph. In the debate between romantic Nationalist and political pragmatism, McIntyre was very firmly on the pragmatic wing. He was known in his early days as a party hard man who laid down the law against a background of factional conflict. I recall interviewing him in his tidy home in Stirling, not long before his death in February 1998. He argued that it was critically important to present the Scottish people with a practical, political answer to their unfulfilled sense of national identity. Indeed, he informed me in a quiet, unassertive way that he believed it was only the existence of the SNP as an organised political force which had prevented the wider nationalist movement from descending into sporadic violence. The wilder forces, he said, had been contained. This argument, presented entirely without sentiment or exaggeration, somewhat startled me, but of course we tend to take for granted the virtual absence of violence or indeed disruptive protest from the Home Rule movement in Scotland. It is a curious presumption when one has only to look over the water to the island of Ireland to find an example of a self-government cause which has been immersed in violence.

There have been sporadic incidents of course, the occasional letter bomb, and no doubt the security authorities are vigilant. But the Scottish National Party remains a resolutely democratic and civic organisation. In a Scottish context, such a remark seems trite, almost unnecessary and unwarranted. However, nationalism elsewhere has not been so benign and it is perhaps worth while to examine the nature of the Scottish manifestation. One occasionally hears it said, from both Left and Right, that Scottish Nationalism is inherently wrong, inherently misplaced. Both appear to argue that the phenomenon is disruptive and almost counter-intuitive. From the Left, one sometimes hears it said that nationalism as a creed runs counter to international co-operation, that there is something inherently fascistic about it. From the Right, one quite frequently hears the argument that nationalism within the British Isles is destructive of the common Unionist heritage, that it further weakens Britain's role in Europe and the wider world. Both also occasionally argue that the Scottish manifestation of nationalism gives succour to disruptive substate movements elsewhere.

I would not regard such an absolutist stance as justified. I believe, rather, that it is up to rival parties to issue and argue their specific objections to Scottish independence and the SNP. It is then up to the Nationalists to respond, again in precise terms. I do not believe that such a contest can be fought from first principles.

First, unless there is to be a world government, there must be governmental organisations which are commonly, easily and under-standably based on national allegiance or on combinations of national allegiance. These allegiances have historically been shown to shift. They must ultimately be based on popular acceptance. Otherwise what is in play is not national self-identification but colonialism.

Those on the Right who condemn Scottish Nationalism as disruptive are, ironically, often the same individuals who resent what they regard as European Union interference in the governance of the United Kingdom. They appear to feel – in the manner of Voltaire's Pangloss – that all is for the best in the best of all possible worlds, that the UK has reached a state of absolute constitutional perfection which must not be jeopardised by any questioning from within or without.

Those on the Left who question the elemental nature of nation-alism have, I feel, had more substance to their concern in the past. I recall conducting picture research for an item on the SNP and feeling distinctly uncomfortable as I surveyed scenes from a party conference long past when a 'colour party' marched to the front of the hall with banners aloft on commands from the platform.

However, that mock-militaristic element is absent from the mainstream of the modern SNP. Further, Swinney and the broader leadership have taken pains to offer a civic and inclusive nationalism which completely eschews ethnic origin as an issue. They stress that Scottish citizenship under independence would be automatically open to those living in Scotland, born in Scotland or with a parent born in Scotland. All others would be free to apply.

There are, it should be said, occasional anti-English sentiments raised within the confines of Scottish Nationalism. But the prepon-derant appeal remains inclusive, and the party has made deliberate efforts to recruit support among Scottish residents of varied origin. This is an issue to watch, an issue for the media to monitor but it is not, I would argue, an incontestable ground for rejecting Scottish Nationalism.

Then there is the question of fostering nationalist movements elsewhere. For the thinkers within the SNP, this is perhaps a more significant challenge. They comfortably summon up comparison with Scandinavia, where Norway and Sweden separated or with the 'velvet divorce' which transformed a single state into the Czech Republic and Slovakia. They tend to turn their thoughts away, however, from the Balkans and ethnic, religious and political division.

This is undoubtedly a challenge for the SNP to surmount on two counts: first, the basic question of whether Scottish independence would foster any such divisive elements in the British Isles and, second, the question of whether the assertion of Scottish independence might be said to represent an added destabilising challenge to an already shaky global political order.

It is a talking point but, again, not an issue which is clearly settled from first principles. It is reasonable to argue politically against Scottish independence but not to argue that there is something inherently and unarguably destructive about the entire notion of Scottish nationalism, of Scottish independence.

Further, it does not seem to me reasonable to argue – from first principles – that Scotland must abandon all notion of independent self-government for fear of encouraging disruptive protest elsewhere or unbalancing geopolitics. To argue that Scotland *should not* be independent is an entirely valid political point of view. To argue, however, that Scotland *cannot and must not* be independent is of a different order and is, again, reminiscent of the colonial perspective which argued that Indian or, before that, American independence was inherently wrong. For the avoidance of any doubt, let me stress two things. First, I do not attribute the above views to the mainstream opponents of the SNP. Almost without exception, senior politicians including successive UK Prime Ministers have freely conceded that Scotland could be independent, and have been content to argue their case against such an initiative. They have argued from pragmatism, not generally from spurious first principles. Occasionally, however, the other form of reasoning has been allowed to muddy the waters. Second, to examine the counter-standpoint, I am not for a moment stating that the case for Scottish independence can be asserted positively from first principles. Rather, I believe that nations are political and constitutional arrangements, generally derived from geographical and historical motivation with a continuing existence dependent on internal popular acceptance and the tolerance of other states.

In short, there is no reason, inherently, why Scotland *should not* be a nation state. Equally, there is no reason, inherently, why Scotland *should* be a nation state. The same, incidentally, applies to the United Kingdom or France or Germany. Under their current boundaries, each is a political and popular construct.

The SNP's contention is that Scotland naturally forms a national governmental unit. Other parties contend that Scotland's future prospects rest more securely on shared sovereignty within the United Kingdom. These contentions represent a political choice. Neither can be said to be either inherently right or inherently wrong.

In its earliest days, the Nationalist movement in Scotland largely pursued efforts to build a consensus with supporters of various forms of Home Rule in established parties. Frustration in that field led the SNP to follow the path of seeking partisan electoral support. The modern party is generally traced to Winnie Ewing's by-election defeat of the Labour Party in Hamilton in 1967. There have been other by-election successes: Margo MacDonald in Glasgow Govan in 1973; Jim Sillars, again in Govan, in 1988; Roseanna Cunningham in Perth and Kinross in 1995.

The party's period of greatest apparent promise in Westminster politics occurred in the 1970s. In the February 1974 election, the Nationalists took 21.9 per cent of the popular vote in Scotland along with seven seats. In the October contest the same year, they increased that to 30.4 per cent and eleven seats. The objective at that time was to secure a majority of the Westminster seats in Scotland – and to petition for repeal of the Act of Union.

Without renouncing it formally, it is clear now that the Westminster route is unrealistic. The distribution of Nationalist support, relatively thinly spread, certainly militates against success in a first-past-the-post system. Even with nearly a third of the popular vote in the later election of 1974, the Nationalists gained less than a sixth of the seats in the Commons from Scotland. Other performances, of course, have fallen far short of that peak. In any case, the advent of a Scottish Parliament has changed the rules. The Nationalists will now concentrate their endeavours on winning success in a purely Scottish political arena. The mandate for independence is now defined in terms of support within the Edinburgh Parliament: a mandate that, of course, was denied in the 1999 contest.

During that campaign, there was a substantial media focus upon Alex Salmond. It was claimed that he appeared out of sorts. There was vague talk of problems at the core of the SNP. For myself, I thought then and think now that the party problems were mainly lack of resources, physical and mental exhaustion, allied to the unresolved contradiction of an independence party fighting the first elections to a devolved Parliament.

There was, however, additional strain upon the leader. He was facing persistent pressure from gossip that was circulating privately among politicians and the media. The smear was seen to be without foundation. Not a line was published in any newspaper, despite intensive investigation. However, it destabilised his efforts during the campaign.

Let us recall Salmond's reputation. He is among the outstanding political performers of his generation, sharp, witty and focused. On a platform, he is a powerful orator. In debate, particularly broadcast debate, he can be coruscating, destroying opponents with barbed and biting comment. With a grounding on the Left of politics, he is authentically concerned about the condition of his fellow human beings. For other parties, that adds up to a potentially powerful rival.

Track back to that 1999 election campaign. On the day the SNP manifesto was launched – Thursday, 8 April – Alex Salmond was not at his best. It is difficult to be precise. His opening presentation seemed low key. He seemed unnecessarily irritated by some of the questions. Certainly, they ranged far beyond the scope of the manifesto itself but that is part of the election process. The sharp leader – and Salmond is incontestably sharp – tackles and rebuts questions, the penetrating and the vacuous, the distinct and the repetitious. That particular day, he seemed to me to be wearying of the task.

After the manifesto launch, a photo-call was held at the old Royal High School in Edinburgh. I took the chance to suggest, solicitously, to Salmond that he looked and sounded a little tired. I wondered whether a previous problem with back pain had resurfaced. Never, he insisted, had he felt better. He did not seem, however, on top form. Insiders concede that the entire leadership team, relatively small in number, began the formal campaign somewhat fatigued after the extensive and lengthy preparations of the build-up period. I believe, however, that the leader was facing an additional problem.

Alex Salmond is keen on horse-racing, and decidedly knowledge-able about the sport. He acts as a newspaper pundit – and, seemingly, a rather successful one. He likes a bet. The smear circulating at the time of the 1999 campaign was that he had indulged his interest overenthusiastically, that he had run into debt. The gossip was given added colour by claims that he owed a substantial sum to an Irish bookmaker. Salmond believes, privately, that the smear was spread by political rivals.

The problem was that he had no opportunity to rebut the gossip. One newspaper after another investigated the claims and found no substance whatsoever to stand up the story. Not a word was printed, and so no rebuttal could sensibly be issued. Privately, Salmond insisted repeatedly that he had never placed a credit bet in his life, that he was not in debt to a bookie from Ireland or anywhere else. He had no opportunity, however, to put that on the record. The accusations were never made openly.

I am aware that, by telling this story, I may be thought guilty of repeating the smear. However, this story is well known in political and media circles. It has been referred to in passing in at least one newspaper diary. I thought it right, on balance, to explain to the voters for the first time the problem that Alex Salmond faced in that 1999 campaign.

I recall one particularly febrile weekend – at the mid-point of the campaign – when the Sunday newspapers appeared convinced that one of their number was about to break the story. Salmond and party officials were besieged by phone calls from journalists. Eventually, Salmond broke from campaigning to phone the editor of the paper concerned. He was told that the claims had been investigated some time back, and completely dismissed. For Salmond, this was the worst dilemma possible. He was not facing an enemy he could challenge directly, a political or personal claim he could counter. He was facing insubstantial rumour, wild gossip without foundation. Little wonder he was under strain. Further, this episode added to the distrust felt by Salmond and the SNP for sections of the press. Late in the campaign, the party published its own newspaper: a somewhat mishandled project which was probably inspired by that continuing mistrust.

Salmond is a complex character who blends intensely private thoughts and emotions with an occasionally jovial outward appearance. Perhaps it is his own nature, perhaps it is the essence of Nationalist politics, the perpetual challenge of overturning the established constitutional structure, but Salmond seems, more than most, a driven politician. He can seem sometimes possessed by politics.

In company, particularly private company, Salmond can be charming, intelligent, diverting and intriguing. He is without doubt one of the closest and most thoughtful observers of the political scene, acutely aware of potential problems and opportunities for his own party and his rivals.

Despite the problems, despite the private strain, Salmond performed well at subsequent points throughout the 1999 campaign. He argued his case vigorously and with conviction in the various broadcast debates. If there were internal party problems – and there were – then Salmond and the wider SNP rallied to give a good account of themselves as the election contest progressed.

I should stress that I believe the Salmond strategy of offering to work with the grain of devolution was inevitable – and correct. The voting public, who often blur the distinction between devolution and independence, would have found an SNP 'No' campaign in the referendum incomprehensible. Similarly, the voters would not take kindly to a party which then immediately implied that it was out to undermine the devolved Parliament before it had even opened.

The SNP had to contest the Parliament on offer: the devolved Parliament. They could not fight the election purely on independence. An independent Parliament did not – and does not – exist. They had to work with devolution, to project their policies on public services and other issues within the framework of devolved powers. While working with devolution, they could not and did not wish to ignore entirely their core objective of independence. The outcome was inevitable: a mixed message, blending policies for devolution with that aim of independence.

Inevitable, but, at the time, confusing and electorally awkward. The Nationalists, I believe, faced a fundamental mismatch then, which they have yet to resolve entirely satisfactorily. I believe John Swinney's strategy of 'devolution better, independence best' is astute, but it may require to be road-tested over an extended period before it is pronounced a success. In 1999, they struggled, in the face of Labour attacks, to transform independence into a choice deferred, into an issue to be settled by a subsequent referendum.

Strictly speaking, the SNP were only seeking to match tactics deployed by Labour at the 1997 General Election. Labour argued then that a vote for Tony Blair was not inherently a vote for devolution, that there would be a subsequent referendum, that the election hinged rather on issues like jobs, health and education. However, independence is more than a policy for the SNP: it is their defining characteristic. In the 1999 Scottish campaign – by dint of persistent repetition – Labour managed to equate a vote for the SNP in a devolved Parliament with a vote for independence. They thus contrived to depict the SNP as potential 'wreckers' of the new and hard-won constitutional settlement.

I am aware that I am in danger of overemphasising the negative side of that campaign for the SNP. There were successes. The party produced some effective hits against Labour, for example on the use of private finance for public projects. This particular issue has repeatedly surfaced as a problem for Labour while the SNP pursues its policy of not-for-profit trusts to provide public services.

There was also a change of emphasis when Salmond took the campaign out on to the streets, declaring that it was time for SNP leaders to 'get the jaickets off and get stuck in'. This switch was prompted by internal party anger at the nature of newspaper coverage but it did seem, psychologically, to energise the wider Nationalist campaign, to convince supporters that the party was ready to fight.

The Sean Connery rally in Edinburgh on 26 April was memorable, if not, perhaps, a seminal moment in Scottish politics as some Nationalists appeared to think at the time. Most newspaper coverage spotlighted Connery's condemnation of the 'control freaks', presumably inside the Labour Party, who had overturned the collaborative spirit of the referendum. My own personal recollection is of Connery's forecast that the devolved Parliament would 'evolve with dignity' into full-scale independence.

This all brings us back to the core question: how? How will devolution 'evolve' into independence when only one major party backs that option? Are the SNP's rivals right to say that the majority of people in Scotland do not want independence – and never will? This is the question that confronted Alex Salmond and now confronts John Swinney.

Salmond's resignation from the SNP leadership on Tuesday, 17 July 2000 was a shock to the political system. However, although Salmond kept his specific plans secret, he had given earlier indications that he intended to stand down. When first elected leader in 1990, defeating Margaret Ewing, he had openly set himself a ten-year target. If the cause of independence had not advanced substantially in a decade, he would step aside.

Salmond could reasonably argue that there had been progress: a devolved Parliament with a significant SNP presence. But that ten-year political target had turned into a personal deadline. Leading the SNP is a demanding job. This is a party with a mission. Visionary political activists can be hard to handle, and hard to discipline. Further, the very vision of independence marks the SNP out as a special target for those parties which favour the Union. Salmond's predecessors had tended to serve ten years at the top of the SNP. Privately, it seemed to Salmond that his time was up.

The inevitable weariness associated with leadership had been exacerbated by the enervating campaign in 1999, followed by the challenge of heading the main Opposition party in the new Parliament. He had performed well in the first year of the Scottish Parliament, but, by his own very high standards, he was not quite at the top of his form.

Some observers point out that he seldom discomfited Donald Dewar in the chamber. I factor that into my own assessment, but I am also inclined to lodge caveats. It is exceptionally difficult for an Opposition party leader to land persistently telling blows. The First Minister has the last word, has the government machine providing factual information and, by definition, has more voices raised in his support than an Opposition leader can muster. Then there is another point. Dewar was good: intelligent, hard-working and sharp on his feet. But still, Salmond seemed a fraction below par. According to insiders, he had to be dissuaded by senior colleagues from standing down on three previous occasions. The first time was just before the party's conference in September 1999. Sources in the SNP believe that Salmond saw nothing but dissent ahead as the so-called 'fundamentalists' continued to suggest that he was underplaying the main aim of independence.

There was even talk of challenging Salmond for the leadership. That came to nothing, and Salmond would have won comfortably. But it added to the disquiet felt at the top. In the event, Salmond stood down at the last moment to meet his ten-year deadline. He resigned just in time to allow nominations for a formal contest at the September 2000 party conference. John Swinney's leadership has not been without its problems, as we shall discuss. But there were early successes too. He improved the party's finances. He made changes at party headquarters where, he felt, there had been some evidence of slackness. For example, the SNP failed to meet the deadline for submitting financial and statistical details to the Electoral Commission about the party's handling of the 2001 UK General Election. This is a legal requirement, designed to assist the Commission in ensuring that elections are run fairly. The SNP details should have been returned to the Commission on 24 December 2001. But its accounts were not sent to auditors until Christmas Eve, and were not sent to the Commission until 11 January 2002. Swinney, who is a meticulous man himself, was privately angry.

Swinney made changes in personnel and organisation which were designed to ensure that headquarters had a clear political role as well as its important administrative functions. There is now an enhanced research and policy team at party headquarters, working on 'greenfield' ideas rather than the day-to-day challenges presented by Parliament. Peter Murrell – a bright and dedicated tactician, who had been working on presentation – was appointed chief executive; the first person to occupy such a post since Mike Russell moved out of party headquarters to become an MSP in May 1999.

Equally, Swinney has defined – and refined – the party's strategy, mainly through the *Talking Independence* process. There are, however, still significant problems. First, Swinney does not lead a united party, or, more accurately, a united Parliamentary group. Neither, of course, does Jack McConnell, David McLetchie or Jim Wallace. In-fighting is endemic in politics. All parties strive to suppress such internal tensions. By contrast, the SNP inadvertently provided the combatants with weapons and a well-lit public arena. This gladiatorial contest was formally known as the candidate selection process. There were warm-up fights as the party selected candidates for the first-past-the-post constituency seats. The championship bout, however, was on 18 June 2002 with the ranking of candidates for the eight regional top-up lists. The SNP relies on these lists for most of its MSPs. The names near the top are guaranteed election. The names closer to the bottom are destined for oblivion.

The particular problem for the SNP was that the party persisted with its system of allowing delegates – rather than the membership as a whole – to rank the candidates in order. It should be said that this is in keeping with the party's long-established structure which gives precedence to the branches. The snag was it meant that the contenders – existing MSPs and hopefuls – were being judged by a relatively small number of other activists. This meant the customary motivations of local activist politics were brought into play. These are, of course, envy, small-minded spite, personal hatred, misplaced loyalty and arm-twisting. In vain did one search for a pattern from the outcome. Margo MacDonald slumped from first place to fifth in the Lothian list. So was that punishment for criticising the leadership – or a reflection of regional rivalries and shifting personal loyalties?

By contrast, what about Mike Russell and Andrew Wilson, who both slipped down their lists? Was that a blow for John Swinney, that two of his most prominent colleagues had lost support? Or did Wilson suffer for advocating that Scots support the England football team, and Russell for . . . who knows what, being too clever perhaps. John Swinney topped his own list, but then so did Alex Neil, who stood against him for the leadership.

I am not sure that Swinney was entirely wise to declare his doubts about the selection system while the process was under way. I understand his motivation: he wanted to contain the row, to refocus his party as quickly as possible upon external rivals, as opposed to internal conflict. However, if he harboured doubts, he should perhaps have attempted to change the system in advance, rather than voice disquiet during the selection itself. To be fair, the SNP branches are notoriously resistant to any innovations from the leadership which appear to reduce their status.

To be fair a second time, conflict over candidates is definitely not confined to the SNP. On this occasion, the other parties were able to look on with an attitude of smug virtue. In ranking their lists, Labour, the LibDems and the Conservatives have all adopted a system of one member, one vote. The Conservatives had only arrived at such a system a fortnight previously after a special party meeting overruled their own party executive. However, they still joined in the criticism of the SNP with enthusiasm. There was much clicking of Tory tongues and shaking of heads.

As political rivals voiced their comments, senior SNP strategists toured the Lawnmarket building where the journalists covering the Scottish Parliament are based. They pointed out that the vast majority of those on the lists who were now potential MSPs had voted for John Swinney in the leadership contest. They argued that the selection – however difficult – was now concluded and that the party was again free to contest its opponents, rather than itself. Reasonable points, cogently delivered. However, the very fact that this exercise in persuasion was undertaken is perhaps also a reflection of the permanent internal anxiety which is a function of party life. I stress again, the life of all parties, without exception.

However, in the SNP, the intrinsic squabbling perhaps has an added edge, related again to the issue of strategy and the nature of Nationalist politics. The SNP does not merely want power under the existing structure. It wants to transform that structure, to achieve independence. The 'fundamentalists' – or however you care to style them – are driven by permanent suspicion, a little like the traditional Left in the Labour Party. They are endlessly on the look-out for signs that the movement's main aim, independence, is being diluted or betrayed. One senior 'fundie' even suggested to me that those around the leadership of the SNP were a bit like New Labour activists. They had boundless enthusiasm, but little real grounding in Nationalism, little respect for the soul of the party.

When MSP Dorothy-Grace Elder resigned from the party, she blamed a 'small clique of cronies' clustered around the leader for trying to force her off the Parliament's health committee. In a quite splendid fifteen-page rant, Ms Elder used her skill as a journalist to lampoon her colleagues mercilessly. She depicted a ludicrous 'officer class' at the top of the party, 'prancing about like Hyacinth Bucket', the insufferably bourgeois star of the BBC series *Keeping Up Appearances*. The behaviour of the leadership, she said, was 'stupid, arrogant and bullying'.

Frankly, this episode was miserably badly handled by Swinney's team. Dorothy-Grace Elder had already signalled she was standing down from Parliament. Smart politics would have left her where she was on the health committee, where she was doing no discernible harm and, according to colleagues, considerable good with her campaigns on issues like chronic pain. She is also a character – and characters should be preserved in these dull days. One of her earliest Parliamentary speeches was on the topic of witchcraft in Scotland. Dorothy-Grace, as I recall, was against it.

But she was generally out of line, a maverick, thought to be sympathetic to the Scottish Socialist Party. (She confirmed later she had had talks with Tommy Sheridan, but absolutely no intention of defecting.) She did not fit into the grid, the minute tactical planning which eventually obsesses most political leaders. I doorstepped John Swinney in the Royal Mile and sought his response to the resignation. He said her removal from the health committee had been widely endorsed by the group. If Ms Elder did not like that, then 'tough'. It was a snappy, rehearsed soundbite, but it was the polished prose of his former colleague's resignation statement which lingered.

John Swinney, however, can afford to ignore one maverick resignation. As for every political leader, the more significant pressure comes from those inside the upper reaches of the party who might potentially replace him. At various points, Alex Neil, Kenny MacAskill, Mike Russell and Roseanna Cunningham have been suggested as possible rivals or replacements. It has even been said that Alex Salmond will return. It is all fairly innocent fun; the sort of thing endured by Donald Dewar, Henry McLeish and others. It is scarcely pleasant, however, for John Swinney and scarcely helpful to the SNP. In May 2002, a fresh outbreak of gossip allowed Jack McConnell to describe Swinney as 'the temporary leader of a permanent opposition'.

Alex Neil, naturally, would prefer to be leader. He stood against Swinney for the top job and commands respect as a talented speaker and able committee convener. He still represents the strand of opinion he represented during the leadership contest, the feeling that the SNP must be more of a vanguard for dissent, driving Scotland beyond the devolutionary settlement. I do not believe, however, that he leads a clearly defined faction with followers. There are few 'Neilites' in the way that there were Bennites in the Labour Party.

Similarly, MacAskill, Russell, Cunningham and the others. I am sure that, at various points, they feel they could do better than the leader on individual issues. Their objective, however, is to secure advancement for the SNP. They are committed Nationalists who know that the party tends to dislike personal betrayal, just as it suspects betrayal of principle. Loyalty – to cause and leader – is a big issue in the SNP.

At John Swinney's request, Alex Salmond returned to Westminster to give added bite to the SNP team in the Commons. But Salmond has repeatedly indicated that he regards his second sojourn there as a 'sabbatical', that he intends to return to the Scottish Parliament, perhaps in 2007, probably via the top-up list.

Salmond would scarcely be human if he did not hope, privately, that the party in Scotland missed his presence. One or two eyebrows were raised when he turned up at the sitting of the Scottish Parliament in Aberdeen in May 2002. He was leading a team of petitioners protesting at the closure of Peterhead Prison in his constituency. Cynics from the sidelines noted that prisons policy is devolved to Holyrood, not reserved to Westminster MPs like Salmond. They felt further that the former leader perhaps lingered in Aberdeen a little longer than was strictly necessary on a day when John Swinney was under fire for a poor Parliamentary performance.

Alex Salmond vigorously denies that he was grandstanding as the former leader while his successor struggled. He chided me gently for the 'tone' of my report, which, he thought, suggested that his presence contained significance beyond the prisons petition. More generally, he also ridicules the notion that he envisages a comeback as leader.

However, Swinney *has* occasionally struggled. He seldom landed a significant political blow on Henry McLeish, while complaining privately that it was impossible to debate with McLeish because he would wander off the topic at will, completely ignoring the question posed. He has had good days against Jack McConnell, most notably when he pursued the First Minister over the apparent manipulation of hospital waiting lists by health boards seeking to meet government targets. McConnell was so enraged that he confronted his own health officials and ordered an immediate investigation.

More generally, though, Swinney faces the problems of opposition outlined above. You can say, but you cannot do. You can challenge, but you cannot act. Government can always sideline you from the news agenda by a significant announcement. Swinney has added to this problem with one or two relatively poor performances.

The worst was on Thursday, 30 May 2002 in Aberdeen. The Parliament had moved to the Granite City to let the Kirk back into its Edinburgh premises for the General Assembly in the Queen's Golden Jubilee year. Earlier that week, on the Tuesday, the Queen had addressed Parliament in Aberdeen; it was a significant speech in which the Sovereign stressed that devolution was working, that the UK could demonstrate 'unity through diversity'. She argued that the new institution must be given more time to thrive.

Thursday's session was designed to debate the Executive programme for the final year of the Parliament's four-year term. In all honesty, the First Minister's speech was not all that wonderful, a rather tedious list of objectives met and challenges to be delivered, but, in response, John Swinney was simply woeful.

He tried to satirise the Liberal Democrats for failing to resurrect their party's grand tradition of 'eloquence'. Instead, he accused them of displaying 'elegance'. Jim Wallace may be many things, but he is scarcely the Beau Brummel of Holyrood. The Executive benches roared with laughter. He said that 'one in three children live in Scotland', when he meant to say 'poverty'. They roared still more loudly, slapping their collective, governmental thigh. And there was no-one on the Nationalist benches to roar back. Half the MSPs were missing from this debate, which kicked off at half past nine in the morning. Was this a protest against Swinney? Was a plot afoot? As the speculation reached ludicrous levels, one senior Nationalist offered me a more prosaic explanation: 'They were probably too pissed from the night before to turn up.' Well, perhaps. But the party whips should have had the numbers there – and they know it.

More to the point, I have looked back at the text John Swinney was meant to deliver that day. Those oratorical lapses apart, it is simply not a very good Parliamentary speech. It is ponderously written. There are virtually no genuine funnies. There are no wow moments, soliciting applause from the leader's supporters.

Swinney knows it was a poor performance. He confessed as much to an SNP group meeting soon after the Aberdeen debate. But he also ordered his party colleagues to buck up in offering him consistent support. Then he repaired much of the damage with a fighting performance at the very next session of questions to the

First Minister when he pinned Jack McConnell down over the issue of youth crime. It was Swinney's best display in Parliament to date.

More generally, John Swinney is a talented politician. He is bright, capable, self-possessed. Beyond that, he is open, pleasant and chatty with a droll sense of humour. He can look and sound a little like a stereotypical Scottish bank manager. The downside is that he has a slightly dull image; unfair, perhaps, but there it is. The upside is that he has a reputation for integrity, a reputation that the SNP intends to play for all it is worth.

Despite that sober, almost sombre image, Swinney is decidedly sharp. He can be remarkably acerbic and pointed, when necessary, giving little quarter to those who stand in his way. Indeed, he declared in a speech in Perth, the week after his Aberdeen disaster, that he would treat internal opponents with the same vigour as external rivals.

I recall identifying John Swinney as a star in the making when he was still in his early twenties. He joined the SNP in his mid-teens and has worked hard at every challenge which has come his way within the party. He was so dedicated to the cause that an aspiring Edinburgh punk band with Nationalist sympathies titled one of their seminal numbers: 'John Swinney, we salute you.' An Edinburgh lad himself, Swinney made his career in the world of finance before entering the Commons in 1997 as MP for Tayside North, the constituency he now represents in the Scottish Parliament.

More to the point, though, Swinney is a key Nationalist reformer, both of policy and strategy. It is a role he occupied long before becoming leader. He saw that the SNP needed to modernise its approach and its appeal. So he has laid great stress on working with business, on building policies which are pro-enterprise. He has also updated party strategy, offering the best solution so far to the conundrum of how an independence party should treat devolution. As we have already discussed, his slogan of 'devolution better, independence best' is neat and intelligent.

Yet major challenges loom. The voters may never turn to independence, however positively the SNP present themselves in a devolved Scottish Parliament. If *Talking Independence* does not work, might the party end up tolerating devolution? Privately, Swinney is acutely aware of that potential hazard, although he ultimately dismisses its potency.

The prospect is not that the Scottish National Party actively turns against independence. It is rather that key Nationalists among the group in the Scottish Parliament and among their supporters may become inured to devolution. They may become institutionalised by the devolved settlement rather like fervent Euro-sceptics who are elected Members of the European Parliament and are then steadily entranced by the apparent power and importance of Brussels and Strasbourg.

Gradualism may become so much a part of their psyche that independence is increasingly marginalised. If they come to believe that all-out independence is hard to sell, then it may become tempting to play down that aspect in pursuit of political power or cross-party accommodations within the Scottish Parliament.

One parallel is with Catalonia, one of the semi-autonomous provinces of Spain with its capital in the beautiful and wealthy city of Barcelona. The Catalans have a clear cultural identity, their own language, which they propagate enthusiastically, and a history, admittedly relatively distant, of self-government distinct from Spain. During his years as leader of the Catalan Nationalists, Jordi Pujol has contrived to maintain relatively firm control of the region's government by vigorously pursuing sectoral interests for Catalonia and by exerting political pressure on Madrid.

He is a politician for whom the adjective 'wily' might have been invented. Pujol, however, has come to disdain any notion of break-ing away from Spain. Indeed, he became notably irritated when I asked him about this prospect during an interview. Pujol's powerbase lies in playing Catalan provincial interests against Spanish federal interests. Equally, he is able to exert a degree of influence at the European level – maintaining a Catalan presence in Brussels, for example – without over-reaching himself and usurping, or appearing to usurp, Madrid's role in representing the interests of the Spanish member state. In short, he knows his political place.

The parallel, of course, is not exact. Catalonia's relationship with Spain is decidedly more subordinate than that between Scotland and England. There are fewer overt signs of nationhood, such as the separate legal system, separate church and separate national sporting teams that mark out Scotland. In addition, Catalonia is only one of a series of provincial governments which cover the whole of Spain, with powers which vary according to each area's demands.

However, senior Scottish Nationalists are aware of the Catalan model. The thinkers among the SNP leadership privately acknowledge that it is at least theoretically possible that Scottish Nationalism might go the same way, accommodating itself to the devolved settlement. Again, I stress that I do not remotely envisage that the SNP would abandon the objective of independence. Rather the potential scenario is that the emphasis falls ever more strongly upon making devolution work, upon perhaps extending the powers of the devolved Parliament into new domestic areas such as the party suggested during the passage of the Scotland Act. Gradualism becomes semi-permanent.

In a curious way, the globalisation of politics may militate both for and against this scenario. On the one hand, it is entirely possible to envisage Nationalists – or at least ardent Home Rulers – who would not necessarily agitate permanently for the establishment of separate Scottish armed forces or a separate diplomatic network. Such individuals may well be content to extend Scotland's domestic potency and leave the historic trappings of statehood to wider, international collective organisations.

However, I believe that the European Union dimension may provide pressure the other way. Since adopting a pro-European policy, the SNP has made much of the demand for a 'seat at the European top table'. It is difficult to see that demand lessening in the immediate future unless the UK government handles particularly sensitively the accommodation of Scottish interests within the new collective arrangements for relations with Europe. The familiar answer to Nationalist demands for Scotland to become a distinct member of the EU is that Scotland has access to greater influence through adherence to the UK, one of the most powerful members of the club with considerable voting and diplomatic clout. The UK's punch, it is argued, can be exercised in Scotland's interests, while small member states gaze on impotently from the sidelines. However, as we shall examine in Chapter 14, if that were incontestably true and if it superseded all other interests, then Vienna would seek to have its opinions within the EU advanced by Berlin and Dublin would defer to London.

There is, undoubtedly, merit in the argument that a bigger nation can exert greater influence. There can, however, be a counterargument: that a small member nation can occasionally extract a concession on an issue of vital interest to its own citizens in return for supporting a larger voting bloc on wider matters. Such leverage may, of course, diminish with expansion of the EU, especially if the Union's internal voting system is reformed to narrow still further the scope for individual nations to exert a veto.

For now, the demand for European representation is likely to exert considerable sway within the SNP, perhaps helping to keep them targeted on the wider aim of independence. Equally, however, as I have outlined above, there may be pressures the other way. What if it could be demonstrated that the Scottish people had become satisfied or relatively satisfied with the degree of self-government tendered by devolution or by some further enhancement of devolved powers? What if they were not interested in talking independence? The gradualists in the SNP might come to feel that the only obstacle to gaining power in the available, devolved Parliament was their adherence to independence, to a radical transformation of the Parliament's nature. Even subconsciously, as they become more and more accustomed to the new Parliament, to its devolved dynamic, they may find themselves trying to play and win the game by the existing rules, rather than devoting all or most of their efforts to changing the rules.

When I interviewed Gordon Wilson,[4] the former leader of the party, he was alert to this prospect. He told me: 'There are temptations in following the Catalan model because they can settle for regional status and it has a certain logic, it has merit in itself.' Wilson, of course, was speaking as a so-called 'fundamentalist' who has tended to regard devolution as a trap to placate the Scots. He would be utterly opposed to succumbing to the temptations of the Catalan model.

Wilson offered his view that the Nationalists were far safer in opposition in a devolved Parliament, that they would be less inclined to fall under the spell of devolved ministerial power. Finally, he envisaged that the Scottish National Party might – I stress might – diverge or even split under the new Scottish political settlement, that it might be impossible to sustain the gradualists and the fundamentalists under the same political banner. Wilson's scenario is that the party might well be pulled in two directions: one motivation being to work with the grain of devolution, the other to press relentlessly for independence.

Politics is dynamic. All parties represent an assembled coalition of interests, sometimes more or less united, sometimes frankly uneasy. When an emerging divisive issue becomes more important than the motivation which initially forged the coalition, then the party realigns or splits. This happened with the Liberals over Irish Home Rule and, more recently, it has regularly loomed as a possibility for the Conservatives over Europe.

Constant unity is far from guaranteed. It is not intrinsic in Scottish politics that there must be one party and only one party advocating autonomous Scottish government. It is at least theoretically possible that there might be a divergence between the gradualists and the fundamental supporters of independence.

It is instructive to reflect that just as there is no single definition of devolved power, so there may be no single goal shared by those who would commonly call themselves Nationalists. Certain earlier advocates of nationalism, indeed, were occasionally pressing for reform which might now be characterised as devolution.

Rather, Scotland's constitutional options may be represented as a spectrum, ranging from full incorporation within the United Kingdom through various forms of devolution, to virtual domestic autonomy, or to independence inside or outside the European Union.

To emphasise, I am by no means firmly forecasting a rift within the SNP. The more likely scenario remains that the gradualists and the fundamentalists will continue to find ways of accommodating their differing positions, their different emphases within a common party structure. If anything, that has been reinforced by the passage of time – and by Swinney's determination to reassert the primacy of the party's core aim.

One of the main internal motivations for his *Talking Independence* campaign is an attempt to square the circle of working within devolution while simultaneously striving for independence. However, longer term, the tensions may return. Just as for Labour, the new Scotland may bring pressures as well as potential for the SNP.

Notes

1. *Taking Scotland into the Twenty-first Century: An Economic Strategy for Independence*, published by the Scottish National Party, April 1999.
2. *Talking Independence*, published by the Scottish National Party, 28 February 2002.
3. Speech by John Swinney, Edinburgh, Wednesday, 1 May 2002.
4. Interview with Gordon Wilson, 28 November 1998.

10 The Scottish Conservative Party and David McLetchie

The rain was horizontal, seeping into his cynical soul. Edinburgh was the capital city of rain. Davie Boy Blue shrugged, hoisted his tattered coat collar a little higher – and stepped outside. The rain slithered down his neck and he shivered. Then he thought. He thought about what he was going to do to the Big Mac. And he grinned: a long, slow, dangerous smirk . . . Enough. My one and only venture into detective fiction. I have inflicted this upon you simply to illustrate a tiny point with regard to David McLetchie, the leader of the Scottish Conservatives. Davie Boy Blue is a big fan of crime thrillers.

He is never happier than when coiled up with a novel from the Chicago school, or, better still, one of the *Rebus* series by Ian Rankin, or perhaps one of Christopher Brookmyre's works. Actually, when it comes to making McLetchie happy, a pint of lager and a sirloin steak probably have the edge, but I am sure you will permit me a little literary licence. I share McLetchie's admiration for those who craft the real thing, rather than the feeble pastiche which opened this chapter. I confess I race to the shops each time Rankin gives us the latest instalment in the tragic but somehow elevating lifestory of his Edinburgh detective. I thoroughly enjoy Brookmyre's brutal, biting satire. The sleeve note to one of his novels,[1] inspired by devolution reads: 'New century. New parliament. New Scotland. Aye, right.'

So I should have spotted the reference when David McLetchie rounded upon the former First Minister Henry McLeish and ridiculed his efforts to explain his Westminster office expenses. As described in Chapter 3, McLetchie caricatured the First Minister grubbing round for an excuse and complaining: 'It wisnae me. A big boy did it and ran away.' This was, of course, street parlance. McLetchie was subtly confirming that he, for one, was not an ultra-posh Tory, remote from popular concerns. However, still more subtly, he was deliberately quoting one of his favourite authors. 'A big boy did it and ran away' is the title of a novel by Christopher Brookmyre.

There is then a subtlety, a sense of intrigue to David McLetchie, despite the self-image as a blunt, no-nonsense Scottish Tory from a working-class Edinburgh background. That self-image is by no means entirely a front. McLetchie *is* outspokenly Conservative. Mention social outreach groups or community inter-action to him and he'll snort 'bollocks' before reaching for his pint.

He is a cigar-smoking Hearts supporter. Take me as you find me. What you see is what you get. Old Tory to the core. Except. Except that his speeches are witty and tricky rather than bluff and uncompromising. Except that he turns down invitations to join shooting parties because he feels personally queasy at the prospect, while supporting the freedom to pursue country sports.

In the absence of a silver spoon, McLetchie has had to rely on talent to make his way as an Edinburgh lawyer. As he explained in a speech,[2] he was a lone parent for three years after his first wife died. I doubt he endured abject poverty during this period, but his point was made. By contrast with the common Conservative image, he likes to feel he is in touch with popular concerns.

To address those concerns, political parties are permanently in search of the fabled 'big idea'. This can be a policy initiative like the Tory endorsement of the sale of council houses to sitting tenants. It can be an ear-grabbing slogan like Tony Blair's determination to remain 'tough on crime and tough on the causes of crime'.

It must catch the imagination, scramble for attention. There is apparently little room for complexity in the modern political world. Most politicians now follow the doctrine: say what you intend to say, say it, then sum up what you've just said.

The message must be simple – with a punch. It must summarise, preferably with a real-life metaphor, the party's core appeal. In this regard, I am reminded of a splendid parody of political campaigning which I first heard at a Liberal Review, that scurrilous amalgam of sketches and songs which was such a feature of Liberal conferences in the past. This particular sketch portrayed a team of earnest Liberal campaigners, beards and sandals at the ready, rehearsing their chant in the manner of Left-wing protesters at a jobs rally or outside the US Embassy. 'What do we want?', the lead chanter demanded. Back came the reply: 'The single transferable vote in multi-member constituencies!' The prompter pursued: 'When do we want it?' Answer: 'In due course.' You get the point. Vision – but no punch. Not long after he was elected leader of the Scottish Conservatives, David McLetchie was asked by *The Sun* to outline *his* vision for Scotland.[3] 'We stand,' he replied, 'for the folk that take their turn at cleaning the stair.'

Perhaps not quite the intellectual ferment of Hayek's *The Road to Serfdom*. Not quite the call to political revolution of *The Communist Manifesto*. Yet for Scotland's Conservatives, a worthy and indeed noteworthy aim. McLetchie, of course, was referring to the arduous task of scrubbing the common stone staircase in a Scottish tenement. Perhaps it is my intrinsic sense of mischief, but I imagine his statement baffled quite a few Tories for whom stairs are internal, replete with thick carpet or polished wood. Such cleaning as is required is best left to the daily help.

Andy Nicoll – the paper's Scottish Political Correspondent and an estimable Dundonian with a droll sense of humour – drew upon his own origins to remark that McLetchie's objective appeared to owe more to *The Broons*, Scotland's couthy family of *Sunday Post* fame, than to contemporary politics.

McLetchie was, however, reflecting a fairly obvious fact. For a range of reasons, the Scottish Tories appeared to lose touch with the everyday concerns of the Scottish people. They came to be seen as the posh party, as quintessentially an English party, remote and distant. Unfairly or not, their crusade for the Union, coupled with fervently expressed opposition to devolution, conspired to place them outside the Scottish body politic. While not actively anti-Scottish, they appeared to some extent to be something other than Scottish. Their loyalties appeared to lie elsewhere.

A pensive David McLetchie considers his party's prospects.

This was bluntly admitted on the very first page of the Tories' manifesto for the first elections to the Scottish Parliament which acknowledged that the Scottish people had come to believe that Conservative policies had 'London stamped all over them'. The people of Scotland, it confessed, had told the Tories what they thought. The verdict was: 'We got it wrong.' At the 1997 General Election in Scotland, the Tories had lost every remaining Westminster seat. The obliteration which had been predicted for the 1992 contest finally worked through. From that moment, the Scottish Tories set out on a long transitional road to change, a process which mirrored the party's previous internal transformations.

According to the party's historian Gerald Warner,[4] the predecessors of the modern Scottish Conservatives were 'the only party consistently and unanimously opposed to the Union' between the Scottish and English Parliaments in 1707. Warner traces the Tories back to the Jacobites of the late seventeenth and early eighteenth centuries.

In sharp contrast, for much of the twentieth century, Conservative adherents north of the border were known as the Scottish Unionists, founding their appeal firmly upon the preservation of the United Kingdom and adopting the nomenclature of Northern

Ireland politics in the process. In addition to their customary middle and upper class support, the Tories were able to garner working-class Protestant votes as a consequence. In short, they pitched for the Orange vote.

Tory fortunes have long vacillated in Scotland. They quailed before the all-powerful Liberal Party in the nineteenth century. They thrived in the early 1930s, partly as a consequence of internal problems besetting the emerging Labour Party. Finally they peaked in 1955, gaining a majority of Scotland's seats, 36, and more significantly an overall majority of votes cast: attracting 50.1 per cent of the popular vote in Scotland. To date, they are the only party to achieve this feat in Scotland since the arrival of universal suffrage.

From that point, the history of the party in Scotland up to the arrival of the Scottish Parliament was one of slow, persistent decline, punctuated by occasional brief revivals. The low point was the UK General Election of 1997, which gave them 17.5 per cent of the popular vote and left them at that time with no Westminster MPs, no members of the European Parliament and no Scottish councils under their control.

The Scottish election of May 1999 returned them to Parliamentary politics. They gained 18 seats in the new Scottish legislature, one more than the Liberal Democrats, who ended up joining the governing coalition with Labour. Yet the Conservative share of the vote – midway between 15 and 16 per cent in both the constituency and list sections – was still a very poor performance, worse even than the 1997 result, which was widely and rightly described as a catastrophe for the Tories.

The Scottish Conservatives did not win a single constituency seat in those elections although they came very close in Ayr – and subsequently took that seat at a by-election on 16 March 2000. That victory did a lot to improve Tory morale. It showed they could win something after a history of semi-permanent defeat.

But back to those 1999 Scottish elections. Scotland had got used to the Tories as a marginal party. They had become accustomed – unlike their counterparts in England – to deploying a particular species of self-deprecating, black humour in describing their own prospects. When they won seats in 1999 – albeit through a PR system which they had deplored – it seemed like a triumph, particularly when they came ahead of the LibDems. Consequently, they smiled and smiled, but, privately, their sharper strategists knew that the result confirmed that the Tories still faced a substantial fight to regain their status in Scotland.

The decline of the Tories has been attributed to various factors: the steadily entrenched, seeming dominance of the Labour Party, the rise of a new powerbase in the shape of the SNP, individual constituency targeting by the Liberal Democrats, and Scottish hostility to Margaret Thatcher.

Many Tories, however, would concede that there has been an underlying cause, a core problem. Across Europe, parties of the Right like the Gaullists and the German CDU have tended to represent themselves as the patriotic parties. It is certainly a card which the Tories play strongly in England. The trouble for the Tories in Scotland is that they came to be identified with the 'wrong' patriotism. Wrong, at least, for their hopes of Scottish electoral success.

They regarded themselves as British patriots. The voters in Scotland, however, steadily came to see matters in a different light. Particularly under Margaret Thatcher, the Tories became identified in the popular mind with England – even with English nationalism – at a time when Scottish identity was apparently becoming more important to Scottish voters. The Tories were brandishing the Union flag while Scotland was tentatively, then confidently, grasping the Saltire. For a party seeking electoral support, this was a disastrous combination.

An earlier indication of this trend was perhaps the evaporation of the working-class Orange vote. A few Tories still regret the decision to disavow any appeal to such sentiments when, in 1965, the party formally changed its name. The Scottish Unionists became the Scottish Conservative and Unionist Party. From that moment on, the Conservative element was more prominent than the Unionist, although the second strain was never entirely neglected. Indeed, it was frequently stressed.

The west of Scotland in particular remains sadly sectarian, even today. Indeed, it is one of the more depressing aspects of Scotland that even supposedly intelligent individuals in business or public life can occasionally find it funny or faintly daring to refer to the supposed icons of Scottish sectarianism, to prate of Parkhead and Ibrox in terms remote from football. Sectarianism is of course insular, small-minded, sapping and tedious.

In reality, however, any serious prospect of appealing to an Orange vote had vanished for the Tories by the time of their name change. The vote no longer existed; at least in a form which could be targeted and gathered. The Scottish working and middle classes steadily came to base their electoral choices on matters other than religion, on financial motivation or class loyalty or, increasingly, Scottish identity.

If Warner is right in tracing the origins of the Scottish Tories, then politics had come full circle. The party which began as the inheritors of Jacobite sentiment, implacably opposed to the Union of 1707, had arrived close to the point of obliteration partly as a consequence of their apparently unquestioning support for that Union.

I discussed this phenomenon with Sir Malcolm Rifkind,[5] who became President of the Scottish Conservatives after losing his seat and his Cabinet place in the General Election of 1997. Rifkind endorsed the analysis that the Conservatives had lost out partly as a consequence of their popular identification as an English party at a time of growing Scottish identity. That, he said, had been particularly evident in the Scottish reaction to Margaret Thatcher, Prime Minister from 1979 until 1990. Assuming an ironic grin, he told me: 'She was three things for the Scots: she was a woman, she was English and she was a Tory. They could forgive one or maybe two of these things. But they could not forgive all three.'

Rifkind, however, drew comfort from a sense of history when he pointed out that the Tories had been down before in Scotland, subsequently to thrive. He confirmed that the Tories in government, during his tenure as Scottish Secretary and at other points, had regularly considered the question of Scottish governance, had looked indeed at various points at the issue of an elected Scottish legislature or assembly.

They concluded, as they always had done in the past, that they could not easily find a way to resolve the apparent contradictions – the English question, the question of money – which we shall look at later. At the same time, they feared for the Union. Further, few Tories had much appetite for the notion in any case. Rifkind's team opted – as in the past – to focus upon the structure of administrative devolution to Scotland.

The recent history of the Conservative Party – the history of the

British State over the past century or so – is dotted with efforts to appease the seemingly restless Scots with administrative reform, rather than directly elected self-government. While the present Parliament was instigated by Labour, and planned with the Liberal Democrats, many if not most of those previous administrative efforts came from Conservative administrations anxious to offer an answer which fell short of legislative power.

When a feeling grew towards the end of the nineteenth century that legislation affecting Scotland was receiving insufficient attention, Westminster responded. A Scotch Education Department, as it was called, was formed in 1872. A Secretary for Scotland, with an office in Dover House in Whitehall, was appointed, although the first incumbent reportedly thought the measure 'quite unnecessary'.

That post was occupied by a full Secretary of State from 1926. The Scottish Office progressively developed, opening headquarters in Edinburgh and steadily taking over the powers of the Boards (or quangos) that had administered Scotland since the Union. Immediately before the establishment of the new Parliament, the Scottish Office was responsible for virtually the full range of Scottish domestic issues, including health, education and the rest.

None of these (mostly Conservative) initiatives placated the Scots. This is, I believe, because the core argument could not be addressed by administrative changes, however inherently worthy or valuable. The core argument has been that Scottish governance should not be dependent on political control created by a Commons majority in which Scotland – with a numerically small presence at Westminster – inevitably could play only a minor role. It is not enough, this argument runs, that Scotland's priorities may coincide for a time with those of England, meriting similar or identical treatment. Scotland's political structure should be capable of responding to changes in Scottish voters' priorities, quite distinct from developments in England.

The Tories could privately acknowledge this analysis, without endorsing the related demand for legislative devolution. Instead, they resorted repeatedly to administrative change. From the honestly held Conservative perspective – that is, apprehension over the Union – such change, while strictly contained, was relatively substantial. John Major's government attempted – in a process popularly known as Taking Stock – to reform the handling of Scottish business, including more imaginative use of the Scottish Grand Committee of MPs.

The party, however, has often appeared simultaneously alert to the limitations of this approach. At various points in the past the Tories have gone further and have issued statements of support for some form of elected devolution, most obviously through Edward Heath's Declaration of Perth at the Scottish Tory conference in 1968. In the 1979 referendum, the former Conservative Prime Minister Lord Home advised Scots to vote No, so that a better devolution Bill could be subsequently introduced. To no-one's surprise, this freelance offer later came to nothing when the Tories regained Westminster power.

Such initiatives reflected political pragmatism, political fear. The Scottish Tories could see that Scotland apparently wanted some imprecise form of self-government, some governmental recognition of Scottish identity. In the circumstances, they occasionally attempted to go with that flow. Indeed, many contemporary Scottish Conservatives have form as past advocates of devolution, a legacy of their party's vacillation on the topic. Occasionally, entertaining little pamphlets from the past, scribbled by youthful enthusiasts, have turned up to bring a bashful glow to the faces of their now-mature authors.

The big change in Tory attitudes to devolution came when Margaret Thatcher became leader of the Conservatives in 1975. After a very brief period sustaining the Tories' Declaration of Perth tolerance of the policy, she came out firmly against elected devolution. In Opposition, she condemned the Labour government's 1970s attempts to devolve power to Scotland so severely and with so little quarter that key members of her Scottish front bench, including Alick Buchanan-Smith and Malcolm Rifkind, felt obliged to resign their posts.

In truth, her principled, even dogmatic stance was more in tune with the underlying attitudes of the party. Customarily polite and docile towards the leadership, the Scottish Tories had broadly opted to live with Heath's Declaration. They were, however, happier with the Thatcherite approach. They were – and are – Unionists. They did not trust devolution, and in many respects still feel exactly the same way.

Their approach was more in keeping with the appeal issued by

Michael Forsyth in a speech to west of Scotland Tories in January 1996. Speaking of devolution in terms that make it sound like a rabies scare, he urged the party: 'I implore you, for the sake of all our people, to do everything humanly within your power to alert your friends, your neighbours, your communities to the dangers of what is being planned for them.'

Forsyth duly implored, the Tories duly alerted their friends, the people duly voted overwhelmingly for devolution and the party duly turned around and endorsed the change which they had reviled for years. In reality, they had little option – either now or in the past. They had little option but to endorse a Parliament which had been backed so heavily in a referendum. Also, historically, they had little option but (mostly) to oppose devolution.

The bulk of their members were simply against the notion of a Scottish Parliament. There would have been intolerable internal strain from attempting to support Labour's devolution plans. It might have bought passing popularity from the Scottish voters – although that is questionable, it might have looked like a ruse – but it would have fractured the coalition of interests that comprised Scottish Tory activists: outraging the staunch Unionists and baffling the undifferentiated middle while probably stopping short of satis- fying the generally unstated demands of the devolutionists, closet and self-confessed, within Tory ranks.

Seen in that light, then, the 1997 General Election result and the subsequent establishment of a Scottish Parliament cleared the decks for the Tories, although it was of course a thoroughly painful way to achieve such an aim. Their objective now is to neutralise the Scottish question, to convince Scots that the Tories are again at least worthy of consideration on the basis of economic and social policies, free from the taint of being a party whose roots lie outside Scotland.

What has happened is a bit like the scenario that one or two Tories privately envisage with regard to the party's disputes over European integration. Quietly, a few senior Tories are praying that Tony Blair will manage to take Britain into the Single European Currency, that the issue will be settled, that it will no longer be available as the standard around which Euro-sceptics can cluster.

Similarly, the Tories knew that their stance on devolution was electorally damaging, but they could not see a way out of the bind. Now that devolution has arrived, the correct strategy – frankly, the only strategy – is to accept change, to strive to be supportive, to make the best of it. For the Scottish Tories, the early changes after that 1997 electoral collapse in Scotland were overtly substantial. First, a commission chaired by Lord Strathclyde produced a new structure for the party, sweeping away the old division between the formal, professional party and the voluntary Scottish Conservative and Unionist Association. The title of the Strathclyde report, 'Made in Scotland', signalled the new direction.

Then Sir Malcolm Rifkind chaired a policy commission which outlined the party's direction, subsequently reflected in the Scottish Parliamentary manifesto. At the launch of the commission report in Edinburgh, Rifkind reflected that a new, more open politics now appeared possible. He spoke of a 'golden age' returning to Scotland, a throwback to the Enlightenment and Edinburgh's reign as the Athens of the North.

The age was not sufficiently golden, however, to tempt Sir Malcolm and other senior party figures like the chairman Raymond Robertson to put their names forward for the Scottish Parliament. They preferred to retain the possibility of returning to Westminster. It was left consequently to David McLetchie to head the party's pitch for the Scottish Parliamentary campaign after he defeated ex-MP Phil Gallie in a leadership contest.

McLetchie was a student associate and long-standing friend of Michael Forsyth, which led him in early newspaper portraits to be categorised as a rabid, unthinking right-wing zealot. First, Forsyth himself is considerably more thoughtful and open to ideas than some caricatures would represent. Second, McLetchie has not borrowed his every waking thought from his colleague. His economic thinking is free market: he is, in short, a self-confessed Conservative. However, he has demonstrated the potential to be open to a range of ideas on the social policy front.

As leader of the party in the run-up to the 1999 elections, McLetchie signalled the new road ahead for the Scottish Tories. They were to remain 'staunchly Conservative', but to put the inter-ests of Scotland first. He delivered this verdict in a speech[6] to party candidates at Hampden Park in Glasgow, the national home of Scottish football. In a conference suite admittedly, rather than on the field of play, but an emotively chosen venue for all that.

To follow New Labour, McLetchie was offering New Unionism.

He said Conservatives could no longer resist the mood swing which was evident in Scotland, the 'stronger cultural nationalism' which had become evident. The Tories' failure had been to miss that mood. He said: 'When the crowds at Murrayfield and Hampden sang "Flower of Scotland" so lustily, it became more than just an expression of pride in our rugby and football teams, it was an assertion of a national identity across the whole of Scottish society.'

McLetchie added later in this speech that the Tories had contrived to lose a generation of potential supporters. He said:

> This lost generation sees itself as Scottish and British, not British and Scottish, and we must see it that way too. From now on, in Scotland's first and oldest political party, we will be putting Scotland first.
>
> That will be at the heart of new Unionism. Labour tries to label the SNP as Tartan Tories as a badge of shame. But we must claim it as a badge of pride. We *are* the Tartan Tories – Scotland's other national party.

In the early days, many Tories harboured doubts about David McLetchie. He had relatively little experience, and none as an elected politician. Some questioned his leadership skills. It is fair to say that he has, mostly, confounded those critics. One or two still privately wonder whether he exercises sufficient discipline within his group. Against that, McLetchie has been a definite success in the Scottish Parliament.

He is a star in the chamber. A star, admittedly, in a fairly sparse constellation, but a star nevertheless. His witticisms are genuinely funny, genuinely clever and generally well received. He frequently contrives to give rivals a hard time by sticking to authentic popular concerns and matching his rhetoric with evidence. His 'prosecution' of Henry McLeish was relentless and controlled.

Consider McLetchie's speech on Wednesday, 8 May 2002, the day Jack McConnell's reshuffled team of Ministers was endorsed by Parliament after Wendy Alexander's resignation. On that day, John Swinney for the SNP ploughed through a harsh condemnation of Team McConnell. It was reasonably well drafted but missed the mood. By contrast, McLetchie caught the mood exactly. He satirised the Executive remorselessly. By that Wednesday, there had been five days' intense coverage of the story. We knew the personnel involved, the farce and the furore. There was scarcely a detail of Wendy Alexander's relatively young life that had not been explored. McLetchie brushed aside the numbing detail and went for the droll throat.

He caricatured the Executive as 'an equal opportunities employer – everyone gets a shot and everyone gets fired'. After three years, he said, there were just eight backbenchers who had not had a go at something, a ministerial post or a role convening a committee. He urged the 'awful eight' (listed only by their initials 'to protect the innocent') to persevere. Nobody, he argued, was too useless in the new Labour Scotland. Ability was no barrier, and there were '358 reshuffling days to go before the next election'.

The Tories roared their approval. The LibDems grinned. Labour MSPs stifled guffaws and privately congratulated McLetchie afterwards. The SNP benches sat, mostly, in glum silence, knowing McLetchie had outshone their man.

Now you will tell me these things do not matter, that it is only Parliamentary rhetoric. In the short term – and externally – that is true. I doubt if a single vote was swayed by David McLetchie's performance that day. However, there is another consideration. It is important for political leaders to build and sustain the respect of their party. Parliamentary performance plays a large part in that – either positively or negatively.

McLetchie's good displays in the chamber help Tory morale and, eventually, over an extended period, might help his party. They certainly help his own standing. Look at the alternative. Look at the consequences of a poor performance. Look at the damage done to Neil Kinnock by his Commons speeches, which were seen to be lengthy and lacklustre. Look, in Scotland, at the problems John Swinney faced over a poor speech when the Scottish Parliament met in Aberdeen. Speech-making is not everything, but it matters.

It matters, personally, to David McLetchie. Privately, he felt decidedly unsure when he took over the leadership of his party in Scotland. He was uncertain about his role, uncertain about his standing in the party. Perhaps insidiously conscious of his own 'humble' background, he doubted whether he could impress the Tories in Scotland and, perhaps more significantly, among the London party leadership. Again, privately, insiders say that all changed after McLetchie brought down McLeish.

He is now demonstrably more confident. However, he can still slip up. In November 2001, on the BBC Radio Scotland programme, *Eye to Eye*, he was reminded about the Tories' past opposition to devolution. The presenter, Ruth Wishart, asked whether McLetchie would now vote yes to a Scottish Parliament, if given the chance in a referendum.

McLetchie hesitated, then replied: 'Er, no, I wouldn't but then we are not going to have a rerun of the referendum.' He went on to acknowledge that he was still 'largely unpersuaded' as to the merits of devolution. Opponents who recorded the programme say they will ensure these comments get an airing in future.

On the surface, the remarks are relatively tame, but this was still a mistake by the Tory leader. His party's strategy must be to endorse devolution, to offer a Tory perspective within that new devolved Scotland. There is no point in fighting the battles of the past. To be fair to McLetchie, he believed he was simply saying that he would not pretend to rewrite the history of Tory attitudes from the time of the referendum. He believed, further, that he was clearly blaming the Executive for the failings of devolution. It sounded, however, as if he was not reconciled to contemporary politics – and that was a slip.

The Tories have an unlikely ally in their attempt to rehabilitate themselves in Scotland. The Labour Party would very much like to see a Tory recovery – as long as it was principally at the expense of the Nationalists and did not go too far. Labour would privately prefer to see the Tories installed as the Opposition in Scotland.

For Labour, it would be a cleaner, purer, neater politics. They could trade insults and statistics with the Tories, just as they do at Westminster. The ground would be economic, social and criminal policy – just as at Westminster – without the addition of the shifting swamp that is constitutional politics. Having established a Scottish Parliament, Labour would dearly love to marginalise the SNP and their agenda of independence.

Both Labour and the Conservatives would like to revert to the politics of money, the politics of class, if you like, and to sideline the politics of Scottish identity, which played such a large role in the decline of the Tories and Labour's decision to create a Scottish Parliament. Labour, the Tories and the LibDems all fear identity politics to varying degrees. They fear they can always be trumped by the SNP at that game.

So there is common ground between Labour and the Conservatives in Scotland – or, more accurately, a common enemy. In an early conference speech, David McLetchie confirmed that – in the final analysis, in a confidence vote – his party would sustain Labour in power rather than give succour to the Nationalists with their policy of breaking the Union. The snag with this theory of a Tory revival is that the party remains internally divided and does not appear, yet, to be rebuilding the support which has been lost. To be fair, that support was lost over decades and it may be still too soon to judge Scottish Conservative prospects. But the early signs for the party, post-devolution, have not been particularly encouraging. There are tensions within the Scottish Parliamentary group. Broadly, those tensions reflect a left versus right argument, but there is also a strategic dispute between those who believe that the Tories will thrive by working consensually with other parties and those who insist they must offer their own distinctive agenda, in sharp contrast with rival programmes. In essence, this is a rerun of the 1980s argument as to whether the Scottish Tories are required to be more or less Thatcherite than their English counterparts.

Within the group, key figures on the 'Left' include Annabel Goldie, the deputy leader, plus Murray Tosh, who became deputy Presiding Officer, and David Mundell. The leading players on the 'Right' are Brian Monteith and Murdo Fraser. McLetchie tries to referee in the interests of party peace.

There are regular outbursts of internal manipulation. For example, in May 2000, ten MSPs signed nomination papers for Kim Donald as party deputy chairman in an effort to keep out the right-wing former MP Bill Walker. The row was bitter, but, for the party, mercifully short. Walker won the ballot a month later.

In November 2001, shortly after Jack McConnell became First Minister, there was a fierce row over the post of deputy Presiding Officer in Parliament. McConnell had wanted to install Labour MSP Cathy Peattie. Many in the Labour group wanted another of their members, Tricia Godman. There were bitter complaints about Executive interference in a purely Parliamentary post.

At the same time, the Tory Right was plotting. Exploiting Labour's internal division, they hoped to persuade David McLetchie to nominate Annabel Goldie for the post. She would have been, by common consent, an excellent deputy Presiding Officer, but she would also have been neutralised, politically, by this manoeuvre to get her into the Parliamentary chair. She would have been, mostly, unable to intervene in partisan affairs, either within her party or in Parliament.

The Right had it all worked out. Murray Tosh had already said he was standing down from Parliament. Goldie could be given the job as the deputy Presiding Officer, with a serious subsequent prospect of the number-one job as Presiding Officer. The Tory 'Left' could be marginalised. Game, set and match to the forces of libertarian Toryism.

However, things went a little awry. McLetchie – and Goldie – declined to play ball. Murray Tosh was nominated for the post and duly won as MSPs exacted revenge upon McConnell for seeking to influence the outcome. Tosh has performed splendidly, as if born for the job. Reborn indeed. Suitably revitalised, he has now changed his mind about quitting Parliament. There are other tensions. Several active Tories – including several MSPs – distrust party central office in Edinburgh. They do not find there the drive and determination which they believe is necessary to revive the party. This was exemplified by a sharp controversy over the method for ranking Parliamentary list candidates in which the party executive took a different stance from the MSPs, including the party leader.

I must not exaggerate this. All parties routinely squabble internally. The true fun in politics lies in stitching up your chums. However, the Scottish Tories do seem to have absorbed Machiavelli's teachings just a fraction too avidly. Equally, the active core of Tory support is now so small that internal disputes swifly become all consuming.

Go to local Tory gatherings in Scotland. They are entertaining, even cheery affairs: a blend of black humour from those who realise what has happened to this once great force and staunch defiance from those who do not. They seem to me a little like Jacobites, toasting the king over the water, pining for a bygone age. Alternatively, they can seem like expatriates in their own land, puzzled and disquieted by the new order in which their party has so little place. Longer term, I do not believe that such a situation will continue in a mature

European democracy like Scotland. I believe there is room for a relatively significant presence on the centre-right. There is a gap in Scottish politics, created by the historic decline of the Tories. In simple terms, it is open to the 'new' Tories to fill that gap.

However, the gap is not all that wide, and it is by no means guaranteed that, without significant effort, the Tories will easily benefit. For one thing, rival parties – Labour, the LibDems, the SNP – have crowded into the centre ground where most of the votes are to be found. If anything, they have contrived to blend characteristics of the centre-right into their policy mix. As the Tories justifiably point out, many Conservative policies – on housing tenure, on business growth, on crime and punishment – have been lifted by these other parties. It must be frequently tempting for the Scottish Conservatives to abandon that crowded centre ground, to move discernibly to the Right, to stand out from the herd with policies which their rivals would then undoubtedly label 'extreme'. They have, mostly, resisted that temptation. However, this only increases their search for a big idea which attracts attention, which enables them to be heard at all. David McLetchie has offered two. First, he has suggested that the Scottish Parliament might be 'cut down to size', that the number of MSPs should be reduced, that there should be fewer Ministers. The Tories believe this is in keeping with public scepticism about politics in general and devolution in particular.

To make this strategy work, I believe they will also have to sound more convincing when they say they now favour devolution. They will have to suggest ways in which this shrunken Parliament might work in the interests of Scotland. If all they are suggesting is a cut to save money, then voters might reasonably ask why they do not go the whole way and abolish the Parliament, cutting the number of salaried politicians from 129 to zero.

Second, David McLetchie has followed his London leader, Iain Duncan Smith, in seeking to relate modern Conservativism to the needs of the vulnerable in society. IDS – as he is familiarly known – seemingly developed this strategy after a visit to the Easterhouse scheme in Glasgow in February 2002.

The visit, of course, was specifically designed to coincide with the announcement of the new Tory strategy. IDS did not tour the mean, redeveloped streets of Easterhouse and proclaim: 'That's it, we must do something for the poor and disadvantaged.' He knew in advance what he intended to say – and used Easterhouse as the launch platform.

To be fair, this was a serious attempt by IDS to advance his agenda of modern, caring Conservativism. In the teeming rain, he toured Easterhouse, chatting to those who are the grateful beneficiaries of modern, caring municipalism. He then held talks in a local church. The visit, however, was not without its moments of entertainment for the ever-vigilant, ever-wicked media pack.

At a news conference inside the church, I took the opportunity to raise the issue of the moment with David McLetchie. Was he a Freemason? There had been a passing ferment in the Scottish Parliament over whether MSPs should declare 'non-pecuniary interests' which might influence them, such as whether they were members of the Masons. Four Tories had volunteered their membership. These courageous Brothers were Keith Harding, Phil Gallie, Jamie McGrigor and Brian Monteith. To varying degrees, they stressed that their active involvement in the craft was minimal.

I am afraid I could not resist asking David McLetchie whether he, too, was a Brother. I know, I know. Trivial matter compared with urban poverty. In my defence, I might say that my televised coverage concentrated mostly upon the new Tory strategy. Subsequently, I filed other reports dealing with the issue of deprivation and the various political responses. That particular day, however, the question of 'Masons on the Mound' was topical. I simply could not resist.

David McLetchie smiled, and said that, no, he was not a Mason. Fired by a spirit of investigation, I asked how many in his party group were Freemasons. Neatly deflecting the issue, he replied: 'I haven't the foggiest clue. I'm told it's a secret!' Laughing, McLetchie and IDS then tried to 'out' the press, inviting the media Masons to roll up their trouser legs. It subsequently transpired I had asked the wrong question. I should have taken a tip from Senator McCarthy and inquired of the Tory leader: 'Are you now – or have you ever been – a member of the Freemasons?' Two days after these Easterhouse exchanges – and following further inquiries by the diligent press – David McLetchie was obliged to concede that he had been a Mason 'over ten years ago' but had neither paid subscriptions nor attended meetings since. There were one or two mutterings about 'once in, always in', but the issue largely fizzled out.

David McLetchie returned to the Easterhouse theme of poverty, and the Tory response, in a significant speech[7] in Edinburgh in May 2002. In this, he linked the 'new' Tory interest in the fate of the powerless with an older Tory enthusiasm for family values. He tied together the 'new fragility of family, public order and failing public services'.

Scotland, he said, could not afford to be 'neutral on the family'. Tackling family breakdown was at the core of tackling the social problems besetting the vulnerable in our poorest communities. This was not, he repeatedly stressed, to condemn the lone parent, but rather to understand that the most elementary safety net in society was the wider family. This particular speech, frankly, was a little short on detail, which prompted criticism, particularly from lone-parent groups. However, McLetchie promised that detail on the Tory package to restabilise the family in society would subsequently emerge and it was at least possible to discern a new philosophical underpinning for Toryism in this speech. Or, more accurately, an ancient underpinning to contemporary Tory thinking.

In the speech, McLetchie listed five key objectives: economic security, safe streets, strong families, welfare reform and other measures to provide a real safety net for the vulnerable, plus, finally, first-class public services for all, delivered with help from the private sector. It was the underlying approach, however, which I found intriguing. McLetchie castigated the 'bureaucratic and politically correct' arrangements which denied support to local, voluntary groups and yet backed 'a professional poverty industry' with 'close connections to the Labour establishment'.

Specifically, he signalled support for churches and other faith-based initiatives. Remember this was a speech in a church to a Tory Christian organisation. Iain Duncan Smith had launched the entire initiative in an Easterhouse church. McLetchie announced that Murdo Fraser MSP would follow this through in talks with Scotland's churches. At their Perth conference in May 2002, Fraser and Brian Monteith signalled their warm support for small, new, independent schools, linked to particular churches or denominations.

Iain Duncan Smith is a keen student of American politics. It is hard to escape the conclusion that his thinking derives much from the faith-based politics that is common on the American Right and heavily influences the Republican Party. When asked, senior Tories repeatedly stress that they are not about to become an overtly faith-based party. They stress further that any religious contacts will be with all faiths. They stress that the principal aim is to build a new, Conservative response to the problems of deprivation, problems which the present social structure is patently failing to tackle. They stress that they want to energise genuine communities, not purely churches. They are offering one nation Toryism.

I accept that the Tories are not seeking to turn themselves into the Christian Democrats of Scotland. I acknowledge that they want to broaden their appeal, not confine it to the religious Right. However, it is intriguing to note the extent to which they are relying upon a bedrock of long-established belief in building their new model Toryism.

As to the future, the Tory hope must be that the residue of hostility towards them over the identity/devolution issue will sub-side, that voters will again choose them or disdain them purely on the basis of their economic and social policies.

Ironically, as one or two Tories privately recognise, such a process might be assisted if the powers of the Scottish Parliament were to be strengthened. Specifically, the logic of the Conservative position is to argue, ultimately, that the devolved Parliament in Edinburgh should have full taxation powers. Within such an extensive fiscal system, the Tories could credibly argue for spending constraints and a tax-cutting strategy. It is difficult to argue for such tactics in Scotland, where the budget is largely determined by Westminster and the power to vary income tax is very strictly limited.

I should stress that 'fiscal freedom' – as the Nationalists formerly styled this approach – is very far from being Conservative policy at present. I am simply noting that it would be easier to act as a Tory on a broader economic stage. But, of course, Scottish Conservative fortunes are dependent on a range of other factors.

First, despite their reaffirmed semi-autonomous status, they are inevitably affected by the performance of the party throughout Britain. If the Westminster Tories bicker over Europe or fail to advance their party's standing, then the Scottish Tories will suffer. Perhaps more directly, they are affected by the Westminster Tories' standpoint on Scotland's new Parliament and its place in the wider British constitutional settlement. The party in Scotland is fully alert to the need to accept devolution, to work with it. Iain Duncan

Smith is similarly on board. He endorses the line, advanced by his predecessor William Hague, that the Tories must not fall into the trap of becoming an English nationalist party, simply because they have only one MP from Scotland after the 2001 UK General Election. Iain Duncan Smith knows that such a move would be counter-intuitive and politically catastrophic for the self-styled defenders of the Union.

However, the wider party at Westminster and throughout England has not yet got the message to the same degree. Every time a Westminster Tory spokesperson challenges devolution or talks slightingly about subsidies to Scotland, the party in Scotland utters a collective groan. This is not the same as questioning the implications of Scottish devolution for England, either in terms of finance or the balance of power at Westminster. As I shall examine later, these are completely legitimate areas for debate.

Rather, it is a question of tone. If the Conservative Party at Westminster talks with a sneer about Scotland or the Scottish Parliament, then the Scottish electorate may feel entitled to think twice about the Scottish Tories' commitment to the new settlement. It may be unfair to the self-styled 'new Unionism' in Scotland but that is how it is.

The Scottish Tories are, presently, a secondary opposition party. That may seem a trite statement of the obvious but it has taken a considerable period of time for the Scottish party to adjust to its true status. For decades, the Scottish Tories were a substantial party in their own right. For years, they governed on the basis of a British mandate. Scots Tories became used to being in government or on the verge of government. Now the challenge facing them is to act like a party which has to clamour to be heard. The voters will decide whether to pay attention.

Notes

1. Christopher Brookmyre (2000), *Boiling a Frog*, London: Little, Brown and Co.
2. Speech by David McLetchie to the Conservative Christian Fellowship, Edinburgh, 10 May 2002.
3. *The Scottish Sun*, 28 January 1999.
4. Gerald Warner (1988), *The Scottish Tory Party – A History*, London: Weidenfeld & Nicolson, p. 12.
5. Interview with Sir Malcolm Rifkind, February 1999.

6. Speech by David McLetchie, Glasgow, 29 January 1999.
7. Speech by David McLetchie to the Conservative Christian Fellowship, Edinburgh, 10 May 2002.

11   The Scottish Liberal Democrats and Jim Wallace

They are a sliver of permanence in a slough of Labour transience. Still in the jobs they took when the coalition was formed. Jim Wallace and Ross Finnie. Ever present and even, occasionally, correct. Among Labour Ministers, only Jack McConnell is still in Cabinet from the original team, and he is on his third job. Jim Wallace has been at Justice and Ross Finnie at Rural Affairs from the outset.

Yes, Wallace's role goes well beyond his departmental responsibility. As Liberal Democrat leader, he is deputy First Minister and has stood in at Question Time for the First Minister more than once. Yes, Finnie has added the environment and, famously, water to his workload (when Wendy Alexander refused that remit.) But, table a Parliamentary question about prisons – and Jim Wallace will reply, just as he has done from day one. Ask about barley or pigs and up will pop Ross Finnie to set rural minds at rest. Just as he has done from day one. For MSPs, beset by the perpetual turmoil of the Scottish Parliament's opening spell, there must be something curiously soothing about Wallace and Finnie. They are like family GPs, always there, always reliable. Dr Cameron and Dr Finlay, back from their rounds and settling down for a comforting dram and a blether about Archie's troublesome kidney. Still, rousing themselves from the torpor of familiarity, some MSPs – including some LibDems – can end up questioning the value of such permanence. Is there complacency creeping in? Do Wallace and Finnie challenge the establishment enough? Are they in thrall to their civil servants?

Certainly, Jim Wallace has proved a capable Parliamentary performer, especially when he has been obliged to fill the number-one post in the absence of the First Minister. For example, on Thursday, 7 March 2002, Jack McConnell felt unwell, and took himself off to hospital for tests (which proved all clear). Immediately, civil servants tried to reach Wallace to tell him that he would have to deputise in the chamber at Questions. Wallace could not be reached because he was already in the air, flying up from a London meeting.

On arrival at Edinburgh Airport, he was greeted by frantic officials who briefed him hurriedly in the car about likely lines of attack from the Opposition, including the latest breaking controversy surrounding 'Officegate'. Anxious advisers reminded him that he had less than an hour to prepare. The reply was: 'Well, that means there's less time to get worried!' Finnie, similarly, is adept in the Parliamentary chamber: dry, witty and sharp. He is known to one and all as Captain Mainwaring because of his visual and vocal resemblance to the splendidly pompous commanding officer from *Dad's Army*. I once agreed to portray Finnie as his television alter-ego in a review sketch – on the strict understanding that the target was overseas on Executive business. On the night, he was sitting in the front row of the audience, chuckling mightily.

The Scottish farming sector is famously suspicious of outsiders. So, when Finnie was first handed the rural remit, he faced an intrinsic challenge. Had he ever plunged up to his welly tops in glaur? Could he tell a neep from a nowt? I recall being present when Finnie first faced the combined expertise of the Scottish agricultural media. He entered, beamed at one and all and declared: 'I hope to bring to Scottish farming all the skills I have obtained – as a Greenock accountant!' The subsequent interrogation was still tough, but he had disarmed his potential accusers.

While I believe Ross Finnie has been a successful Rural Minister, I confess that verdict is based upon an urban perspective. Growing up in Dundee, my concept of the countryside was a Sunday outing to Glen Clova or berry-picking in Blairgowrie. One or two sources say that Finnie's reputation is less secure among those immersed in rural affairs or rural politics.

I hear what they say. However, my own impression is of a capable Minister. Even faced with the horror of the foot and mouth outbreak, he appeared assured, and, more to the point, reassuring. At the time, it was felt that Scotland handled the disaster better than the comparable department in Whitehall. Equally, Finnie has coped with the various additions to his remit without complaint.

It is perhaps fitting that the Liberal Democrat pair contrive to act as the glue in the coalition, occasionally, in the past, making peace between Labour colleagues. The party has a keenly developed sense of its own central role, often well beyond its actual influence.

The Liberal Democrats – or more accurately the Liberals – are much possessed by history. If a speaker at a party conference is seeking a burst of fervent applause, that speaker has only to evoke – preferably in sonorous tones – 'this great Liberal movement of ours'. Self-evidently, the modern organisation is not remotely the same as the amalgam of Whigs, Peelites and Radicals which forged the Liberal Party on 6 June 1859 in opposition to the Conservatives. However, that sense of sustaining a proud tradition matters, and can have a direct impact on contemporary politics. Modern LibDems can never quite forget that their predecessor party utterly dominated late nineteenth and early twentieth-century Scottish politics, to an extent that left them far more strongly entrenched than the Labour Party of recent history.

Liberal Democrat activists regularly claim ownership of the devolution movement. If our party conference speaker wants a second round of similarly fervent applause, a guaranteed route is to remind supporters that 'for more than a century this great movement of ours stood for Scottish Home Rule'. The subtle speaker will then remind the audience, with a defiant frown, that others had not shown such noble adherence to the cause.

I have long thought that this is decidedly a sword with two edges. On the one hand, it can be said to show political consistency. On the other hand, it is a reminder that for 100 years the Liberals and their successors were either unwilling or unable to do anything to implement Home Rule. It is an illustration of a party which has shivered on the excluded doorstep of politics, shorn of power.

However, that very contrast between self-image and harsh reality sums up the challenge which confronted the modern Liberal Democrats over their initial coalition decision in the Scottish

Parliament. Some adhered to the first element: that the Liberal Democrats were the true believers, the pure flame of Scottish Home Rule. They argued, in essence although not in such terms, that their purity could only be corrupted by an arrangement with the Labour Party. History, that all-consuming sense of history, had taught them to mistrust Labour as late, unconvincing converts to devolution.

Others, including Jim Wallace, laid stress on the second element of the Home Rule duality: that it would be perverse for the party to neglect an opportunity to join Scotland's devolved government after a century of agitation for reform. Years of experience in government have, mostly, won the internal critics round to Jim Wallace's way of thinking.

There is an essential core to Scottish Parliamentary politics, a zone where MSPs and media combine to assess underlying developments. Not the chamber. Not the office block where the MSPs squat. Not the Lawnmarket media centre, where we poor hacks huddle. But the pubs surrounding the Parliament's temporary home.

This is the 'amber triangle'. The Jolly Judge for the Nationalists, if they want to plot privately. The Bow Bar and the Grassmarket for Labour, similarly. But, at the apex, Deacon Brodie's Tavern for pretty well everyone. The fire alarm once sounded in the Lawnmarket while my colleagues were preparing an edition of *Politics Tonight*. They were obliged to take refuge in Deacon Brodie's, across the Royal Mile. By the time they got the all-clear to return, they had picked up two new stories for the programme.

In the early days of devolution, the LibDem gossip in Deacon Brodie's was of tension in the coalition. Could Labour be trusted? Sip the drink, crunch the peanuts, incline the head sorrowfully. Not sure, Brian, just not sure. But, as time moved on, the gossip was of hard policy bargains, of pressure upon Ministers – often Liberal Democrat Ministers as well as Labour. Like the whisky on sale, the LibDems matured with age.

That was most sharply in evidence at the Scottish Liberal Democrat conference in April 2002. Held in Perth, the event was remarkable for one particular sight: a trades union lobby, by the Scottish Prison Officers' Association, eagerly striving to get their message across to arriving delegates, touchingly grateful when their pamphlets were accepted.

This, mind you, was a LibDem conference – the also-rans, the neglected party. In the past, such conferences were renowned for worthy tedium and endless nit-picking challenges to the chair. Admittedly, I once saw a Scottish Liberal conference really roused, but that was in Rothesay, in stormy weather, after Russell Johnston announced from the platform that the last ferry was about to leave.

By contrast, the anxiety at Perth 2002 was over policy. Jim Wallace was the Minister responsible for the hugely controversial review of the prisons' estate, including plans to close Peterhead and build up to three new private prisons. The prison officers, who opposed this strategy, wanted a word in his ear. Plus they wanted to influence party delegates to put pressure on their leader, the Minister.

Inside the conference, there was a heated debate, with many delegates also sceptical about private prisons. But, more than that, there were prolonged offstage negotiations about the motion under consideration which resulted in a form of words giving Wallace room to manoeuvre. Senior delegates privately acknowledged that stark opposition to their own Minister's stance would be counter-productive, particularly as he was plainly struggling to reach a solution with the prison officers and other parties.

At the same event, Ross Finnie faced substantial criticism for continuing to authorise genetically modified crop trials. Finnie insisted he had no option but to let the trials continue. The party – with its much-vaunted green credentials – ended up demanding a halt. But this was not done without fully considering the Executive standpoint, and the likely external impact.

This was not rebellion for the hell of it, as so often in the past, but hard-edged politics. They wanted the Minister to change his stance. This was not a debate about vague generalities but an open negotiation about practical options affecting a real and present decision. All around the hall, in both the prisons and GM debates, you could hear the penny dropping. Government. The party of permanent protest is in government.

Of course, as I noted earlier, the groundwork for co-operation between Labour and the LibDems goes back years. However, there was still no absolute guarantee that the LibDems would end up in government after the 1999 Scottish election campaign. Jim Wallace had a bad day on 28 April during that campaign. The news agenda was dominated by claims in a biography[1] of Peter Mandelson that Tony Blair and Paddy Ashdown had paved the way for a Scottish coalition over claret at Lord Irvine's West Hampstead home. The talks, involving other senior Labour and LibDem figures, were said to have taken place perhaps early in 1996. At a Labour news conference that day, 28 April, Donald Dewar stumbled a little over the nature of the talks, but firmly denied that they had involved any pact with regard to a Scottish Parliament. That was subsequently confirmed to me by Liberal Democrat sources who acknowledged that, in other respects, the account in the Mandelson biography was broadly correct, including the assertion that Labour and Liberal Democrat leaders had outlined ways to narrow the scope of the overt conflict between the two parties.

It was made clear by Labour that any talks which had taken place, and they declined to confirm either the venue or the refreshment served, had been based upon the emerging possibility of Westminster co-operation between the two parties in areas of mutual interest. This, it was said, paralleled the formal discussions on the constitution led by Robin Cook for Labour and Robert Maclennan for the Liberal Democrats. Labour sources pointed out that the party did not at that stage anticipate the Commons majority of 179 which the 1997 General Election subsequently provided.

From an awkward start, the Labour spin gained momentum. Definitely no deal covering Scotland, merely a convivial chat among politicians who might need to be friends, within strictly defined limits of amicability, at Westminster.

If anything, the Scottish Liberal Democrat response was more hesitant. Party headquarters in Edinburgh appeared slightly bemused at first. Jim Wallace was on an election tour of the north-east and his immediate advisers seemed initially reluctant to facilitate a response from the leader. When a response did emerge, via a doorstep interview in Aberdeen, Wallace described the speculation about a pre-arranged pact as 'total rubbish'. He rather spoiled the effect of this comprehensive dismissal by disclosing that he had checked with Paddy Ashdown first.

I can accept that there was no formal Treaty of Hampstead which affected Scottish politics, eased by claret or any other libation. Both parties – eventually – pointed out that their Scottish spokespersons would have had to be on the guest list for any such conclusion to be reached. In any event, it was stressed that, in 1996, a Scottish Parliamentary election was a decidedly distant prospect, that there was the small matter of a UK General Election first. Yet, still, the claim gained credibility because the dynamic between the two parties at the highest level was all in the direction of the conclusion which ultimately emerged: a partnership government between Labour and the Liberal Democrats in Scotland.

Now that the partnership has survived years, one might argue that there has been a change of gear in the drive for Lib/Lab co-operation, and a change of locus. Beyond the boundaries of Hampstead, it is now canvassed less as an issue in London. By contrast, pragmatism and policy compromise have produced a relatively solid coalition in Scotland.

Interviewed by *The Guardian* in 2002, Charles Kennedy, who succeeded Ashdown as federal LibDem leader, attacked Labour robustly over civil liberties, the environment, public services, Europe and a lack of leadership.[2] He then added: 'I don't see a future in co-operation with Labour if all we achieve is the perception that we are bit players in someone else's show.' Kennedy's objective, plainly, was to confirm that the days of the Blair–Ashdown 'project' were over, that he felt the Liberal Democrats were sufficiently strong to advance their own brand of politics to the people.

The snag, of course, was that the statement did not sit very well with the fact of the coalition in Scotland. Scottish rivals pounced, saying that Kennedy in 'a rare moment of political honesty' had disclosed the true nature of the LibDem relationship with Labour. A little tetchily, the LibDems stressed that their amiable and highly articulate federal leader – a Scottish MP – had been talking purely about Westminster, with no reference to the Scottish Parliament, where the arrangement between the two parties was legitimised by PR voting. It is not the only time LibDems from the Scottish Parliament have had to depart from the line taken by their Westminster colleagues. Indeed, the Liberal Democrats pride themselves upon their federal structure, pointing out that Jim Wallace is the Scottish leader, and takes the Scottish decisions in consultation with his Scottish colleagues and party.

At a social event during the Scottish LibDem conference in Perth in 2002, I listened as Jim Wallace gently chided his MP colleague Michael Moore over the future attitude to Labour. Moore had suggested that the classic LibDem position of studied neutrality towards possible coalition partners would be sustained. Wallace reminded him that he had spent several years in government with Jack McConnell, and was not about to imply that those years had been wasted by suggesting that he could easily and comfortably start from scratch in another arrangement. Wallace appeared to feel that the serious alternatives were coalition with Labour, or returning to the Opposition benches. I found this mild dispute intriguing. To me, both were right. Michael Moore was understandably influenced by a Westminster perspective which requires formal distance to be maintained between the Liberal Democrats and other parties. At Westminster, the third party has to shout to be heard, sidelined as it is by Commons rules and speaking arrangements, which give virtually complete precedence to the government and the Conservative Opposition.

Even as an MP from Scotland, Moore had not absorbed the daily experience of coalition which had influenced LibDem MSPs. Wallace was pointing out that, by vaunting the existing coalition, he was not defending Labour. He was defending his own government, his own record.

This was not mere social chat. Michael Moore has a key role at the core of LibDem tactics and planning, both at Westminster and in Scotland. As the party's campaign co-ordinator in 1999, he devised a tightly-worded strategy document which was endorsed by the executive of the Scottish party on 30 January that year at a meeting in Glasgow.

Moore has blossomed – from victory in his Borders seat in 1997 as the constituency successor to David Steel – into an influential figure in the party. Good-humoured, disciplined and alert, he played a key role in the initial coalition talks, although not a Scottish Parliamentarian. That 1999 strategy paper had two main aims: to convince troubled party activists that the LibDems would not enter a coalition simply for the sake of power and to head off persistent media questions about the party's possible partners. Each time we asked subsequently, we were advised to reread the strategy paper.

This paper began by stressing that the Liberal Democrats were determined to win as many seats as possible and deliver as many of their policies as possible. Moving fairly swiftly on, it acknowledged the remote possibility that the Liberal Democrats might not sweep to total power with the absolute approbation of the Scottish voters. According to Moore's paper, the LibDems would then talk first to the party with the largest number of seats in the Scottish Parliament, and would deal exhaustively with them, only moving to an alternative party if those initial talks failed. It was a simple but effective arithmetical formula which returned power to the electorate and allowed the LibDems, consistently, to deny that they had a preferred partner in mind.

To emphasise the point, Moore built informal contacts with the Nationalists to supplement the links with Labour that already existed through the convention and other avenues. Moore was seen boldly lunching with John Swinney, then the SNP's deputy leader and key strategist. The LibDem scheme certainly slackened the fervour of media questioning on the issue of coalitions or, more accurately, gave the LibDem leadership a consistent line to peddle in response. The exchanges became almost formulaic. At news conferences during the 1999 election campaign, there would occasionally be journalistic visitors, new blood in the media ranks, eager to demonstrate their incisiveness. 'Who', they would demand of the LibDems in tones that brooked no vacillation, 'are you going to work with in coalition?' Smugly, they would sit back implying that they had instantly grasped the very core of the contest, the nub of the matter which had eluded the resident Scottish hacks.

Back would come the reply: 'We want to win as many seats for Liberal Democracy as possible. If no party has a majority, we are prepared to work with the largest party. We are happy to leave this to the voters.' By the end of the campaign, we were able to chant it along with them, like a nursery rhyme.

There was, of course, a flaw in this mantra. This was that the Liberal Democrat leadership did not – and do not – seriously envisage working with the Scottish National Party. Within the Scottish Liberal Democrats, there are individuals who would tolerate or even favour the idea of an accommodation with the SNP. Their liberal consciences glow at the thought of a popular plebiscite on independence, on letting the people decide. Others, if forced to choose, narrowly prefer the broad Scottish patriotism of the SNP to the hard, focused pragmatism of Labour. The vast majority, in their souls, simply want the world to be other than it is, to remove such a troublesome choice from them.

But, frankly, most LibDem MSPs have found coalition with Labour more palatable than they perhaps expected. They have got their way on key issues like tuition fees and free personal care. They rather like the thought that their views and their votes matter. Individually, there is always the prospect – remote, admittedly, for some – of a telephone call enticing them into government. The ministerial car may be parked just round the corner.

There is another aspect to this issue, more directly connected to Jim Wallace. The leader of the Scottish Liberal Democrats is a thoroughly likeable individual: pleasant, well-mannered, bright and hard-working. He can also prove considerably tougher than his commonly smiling exterior would suggest. Wallace can be resolute and determined. To be blunt, stubborn. During the run-up to the 1999 Scottish elections, he made perfectly clear that he would not endorse a referendum on independence. He took considerable care to ensure that this position was thoroughly understood – and endorsed – by the key decision-making centres within the Scottish party, including the executive. He got everyone on side.

Wallace could not have been plainer on the topic of a referendum. The people of Scotland could have independence if they voted for the SNP. If they did not vote for the SNP in sufficient numbers, the Liberal Democrats would not facilitate independence by the back door through the device of a referendum. Scotland, according to Wallace, had endured enough constitutional navel-gazing. A little rich, perhaps, coming from the party of proportional representation and a century of agitation for Home Rule. Still, let that pass. Wallace made it abundantly clear. The Liberal Democrats would not endorse a coalition if it involved a referendum on independence. His stance on that question has not materially altered. If anything, it has been stiffened by his experience in devolved government.

It is a facet of Wallace's character that he is – in his own quiet way – as staunch a Unionist as one would find in the Labour Party or even within the reformed Unionism of the Scottish Conservative Party. He believes strongly in the link with England. It is a belief that goes beyond the pragmatism one finds elsewhere on the centre-left in Scotland, the vague feeling that independence would be costly or that the process would be too much trouble. Wallace authentically backs the partnership with England.

He wants Scotland to remain, along with England, a member of the British family. Not a fellow member of an association of British states. Not a co-partner in the European union. Wallace positively wants firm ties with England in a United Kingdom. However, he is a reformer. Ultimately, he would wish a federal structure for Britain. It is, he says, up to the people of England whether the English components of this federation are the entire nation as a unit or distinct regions. Put most simply, the Scottish Liberal Democrats suspended their federal ambitions in order to work with Labour, to advance the cause of devolution, the policy of another party.

Wallace, however, still believes in substantial autonomy for the Scottish Parliament; greater, he imagines, than Labour is presently prepared to concede. He told me some time back that he believed Tony Blair's undoubted support for devolution was based on a pragmatic assessment of what Scotland required to sustain the Union.[3] Wallace said: 'I think Blair understands that devolution is right. I think still in his guts he just can't quite let go. Perhaps it's like the father of a son who's moving from adolescence to his twenties. He still wants to keep the tie there. I say: let's grow up. Let's grow up and still remain a member of the family.'

Jim Wallace has not changed that opinion, although, to be frank, there is minimal sign of agitation from the LibDem leadership to extend the scope of devolution. They seem demonstrably content to exercise Executive power, to work within the present boundaries. To be fair, those boundaries were negotiated with the LibDems in the convention, but they were ultimately set by the UK Labour government.

I would not want to carp too much about this. Wallace is in government, dealing directly with deeply serious issues like criminal justice and prisons, and indirectly with the entire gamut of Executive powers. It would, arguably, be irresponsible to neglect that task in favour of an internal campaign for further constitutional change.

It is, however, reasonable to inquire what the Liberal Democrats are for – beyond maintaining their foothold in government. Arguably, they now place a cautious caveat on every one of their supposedly cherished objectives, including the constitutional aim of a federal UK. It is entertaining to recall that tuition fees became an issue in the 1999 coalition talks precisely because the LibDems had not surrounded their stance with a hedge of compromise. In their manifesto for the 1999 elections, the Liberal Democrats had made a precise pledge: they would scrap tuition fees for students. Tuition fees were an abhorrence, an abomination to be rejected by all right-thinking people.

Scottish Labour supported tuition fees. Few Labour activists were prepared to agitate for their abolition – as long as there was continuing provision to assist lower income families who did not pay fees. Inevitably, during an election campaign, parties will attempt to stress their areas of distinctive appeal to the electorate. From a Liberal Democrat perspective, the stance on tuition fees clearly differentiated their party from Labour.

It appeared to Labour strategists that the prospects for a coalition were being narrowed by an issue – tuition fees – to which their own activists attached little importance. According to one source, Labour let it be known informally to the Liberal Democrats that they would welcome a slackening of the LibDem line on student fees. Labour apparently questioned why the Liberal Democrats felt the need to be quite so firm on a relatively minor matter: minor, that is, in the context of the multi-billion-pound budget available to the Scottish Executive. It is impossible to say whether this approach had high-level sanction or was simply a freelance effort by a Labour strategist over an obstacle which appeared to be standing in the path of one route to power for his party.

There was, however, a follow-up. On BBC Scotland's *Campaign 99* programme, Jim Wallace had caused a stir by indicating that the question of tuition fees might be 'on the table' for negotiation if there were to be talks with Labour. Wallace, it appeared from this remark, was also privately aware of the potential for conflict with Labour over this single issue. The LibDem leader, however, came under subsequent pressure both from his own candidates who craved a simple, unvarnished line, and from Tory and Nationalist opponents who wanted to pin the LibDems down.

On Tuesday, 4 May – two days before the 1999 election – Wallace appeared on another BBC Scotland programme, *From Here to Holyrood*, alongside rival party leaders. Repeatedly pressed, Wallace now declared that the people of Scotland had made the issue of tuition fees 'non-negotiable'.

According to my source, the Labour strategist, who had originally urged the LibDems to play down the issue of fees, was watching the programme from the wings and immediately commented sourly:

'That's the coalition buggered, then.' As it turned out, that prognosis was inaccurate, although the coalition talks were made much more difficult as a consequence. I think it fair to say that Wallace will be anxious not to repeat this episode. I am convinced that each policy will be subjected to three clear tests in future. Is this a good idea? Will it win votes for the Liberal Democrats? Finally, is it coalition friendly?

All of which leaves some Liberal Democrat activists nervous about their own party's autonomy in coalition. They suspect that every liberal dream will run up against the hard reality of coalition politics. They wonder if there is some truth in the jibes from rival parties that the Scottish LibDems have become a wholly owned subsidiary of Labour. I understand the motivation underlying that anxiety, and it is an entirely reasonable challenge for rival parties to pose. However, I do not believe it stands up to scrutiny. If anything, there may be more substance to the alternative Labour complaint that the LibDems have obtained more than their voting strength would warrant.

To reiterate, they got their way (almost entirely) on tuition fees when Scottish Labour would have left the issue well alone and Labour in London found comparisons between the English and Scottish systems of student finance decidedly uncomfortable. Intriguingly, there have been suggestions that the system for England might end up facing reform as a consequence. They got their way on free personal care, when Henry McLeish was virtually the only Labour Minister who enthusiastically backed the idea. (It helped, of course, that he was *First* Minister at the time.) Their presence in Cabinet – and Finnie's remit – arguably places a much greater emphasis on rural affairs than would happen under Labour alone, with its predominantly urban base.

It will, however, be important for Jim Wallace to demonstrate that he can continue to gain practical advantages for his voters, for his party's own priorities, from the Scottish coalition. There were decidedly embarrassing moments for the Liberal Democrats in some of the early sessions of the new Parliament. Labour MSPs were challenged by rivals, principally the Scottish Nationalists, to state what their party had *conceded* in the coalition negotiations. There ensued silence – followed by bluster.

Since then, the LibDems have been careful to publish regular updates on their 'successes' inside the coalition, trumpeting for example the Freedom of Information legislation for Scotland, which is more liberal than the regime applying in England.

Frankly, the LibDems may find it difficult to continue devising policies that meet all three tests outlined above, that are populist, distinctly liberal but capable of implementation by a coalition with, in practice, Labour. In reality, they hope to carry on broadly as before, promising to improve education, health and other services. But such promises – while the core of 'real' politics – can sound like tepid generalisations when tested in the heat of an election campaign.

To be fair, this applies also to Labour, although, psychologically, it is less of a problem for the majority party. Labour, as the dominant partner, can tend to blur the distinction between party and Executive, proclaiming past achievements and future plans without worrying too much as to their provenance.

However, senior sources acknowledge that both parties are aware of the need to think about tailoring their policies to the prospect of continuing coalition. One Minister even suggested to me with a grin that Labour leaders might privately favour a particular policy which would be difficult to sell to their activists. In which case, it could be inserted in the LibDem manifesto, and Labour could subsequently concede the issue in coalition talks. This was, I am sure, a joke. Tongue firmly in cheek.

All in all, the LibDems have thrived reasonably well under coalition. There remain, however, one or two question marks over the performance of their Ministers in Cabinet. Perhaps it is envy, perhaps it is partisan rivalry, but a standing accusation is that both Jim Wallace and Ross Finnie pay too much heed to their civil servants. These claims come mostly from the Labour side but are not unknown in LibDem quarters.

For example, one environmental campaigner in the LibDems told me that Finnie had now become 'far too grand and was a prisoner of his civil service'. Referring to Wallace, another LibDem insider argued privately that the Justice Minister had not been sufficiently robust in tackling vested interests in his department, including within the prison service. Deploying a colourful metaphor, this insider told me: 'If the prison service think they're going to get this scheme for umpteen new private prisons past us, then they can think again. They're going to get two fingers right up the rectum on this one.'

So *are* Wallace and Finnie tantalised by their paid-up membership of the Scottish establishment? I believe three factors are at play here. First, Labour critics may be contrasting the LibDem attitude with their own permanently prickly relationship with the civil service. Second, LibDem activists may be displaying their own intuitive resistance to established authority. Third, there may be something in it.

Wallace and Finnie naturally insist that they are innocent as charged. They say there is nothing inherently wicked about occasionally conceding that, just once in a while, the civil service might have a point, that official advice might be right. They have chosen broadly to work with the machine – rather than engage the civil service in civil war. But both stress their personal and political aims are clear – and clearly understood.

I think it is at least arguable that both Finnie and Wallace have found the structures of power beguiling. Perhaps the smiles on stepping into the ministerial cars have been a fraction too broad. However, the LibDem pair must find life wearing on occasion: if they are not lampooned as Labour lapdogs, then they are condemned as prisoners of the civil service. In their defence, one might note that they are demonstrably able Ministers, confident in the Chamber and in public liaison. They have doggedly pursued certain key LibDem aims in coalition to the occasional frustration of Labour colleagues. Plus of course they have a splendid opportunity to expunge any lingering lapdog whiff by insisting on reform of local government.

At various points, those observing Scottish politics have speculated about issues that might break the coalition. Tuition fees? Yes, that would have done it: the LibDems had boxed themselves in. Free personal care? Not initially, but it turned into a breaker. The fishing vote? No. It was an important issue – critical to certain communities – but the future of the Executive did not hang in the balance. Proportional representation for local government? Definitely.

For the LibDems, reform is the core. Partly, it is an instinct dating back to Whig roots; that all-embracing sense of history again. Partly, they see the present system of council elections as a gross misuse of ill-founded power by one party, the Labour Party. Partly, they believe that their own team would stand to gain from altering the system.

For all these reasons, the LibDems genuinely believe that Scotland must change the system of electing local councils from the present first-past-the-post method to a system of proportional representation. Specifically, they advocate the Single Transferable Vote (STV). You would have one ballot paper. But, instead of marking a cross against just one name, you would rank your chosen candidates 1, 2, 3 and so on. Each ward would be larger – and would contain several councillors. Overall, seats gained would match party voting share more closely.

The advocates of STV – including the Executive-appointed review committee under Richard Kerley – say it maintains a modified link between ward councillor and voter while introducing a 'fairer' political outcome. They argue it would increase public interest in the elections as every vote would count towards the final result.

The main alternative reformed method of voting is the Additional Member System deployed in the Scottish Parliament itself. Applying this to local authorities would mean there would be ward members plus top-up councillors from party lists. This would be proportional but would fracture the ward link, introducing list councillors with no local basis. Kerley[4] also looked briefly at a system known as the Alternative Vote but dismissed this fairly swiftly in that it would not provide a proportional outcome.

Those who oppose PR for councils say it would risk jeopardising that ward link and, more, that it would produce a tyranny of the tiny, obliging major parties to strike a bargain with minor players in order to produce a stable administration. Critically, those who oppose PR include many Labour councillors who fear that their own party's powerbase – and consequently their own power would be diluted.

I believe the ward link case has merit, and requires answers. A councillor – even more than a Parliamentarian – must be a trouble-shooter for local issues in precise local areas. People must know that they have a real link to their elected representative, that they can call upon the combination of advice and amateur social work which ward work so often entails. Arguably, councillors have already become sufficiently detached from the people they represent without accelerating that deterioration through weakening the ward links. Besides, political manipulation is not entirely unknown in Scottish local government. Party lists would undoubtedly be subject to the same suspicion. I can see the argument that any reformed system must maintain the ward link.

I am less impressed by the argument as to 'stable' administration. That can so easily mean permanent rule or misrule by a single party unfairly entrenched by the voting system. Are we seriously saying that it is better to allow a minority to exercise sole power than to reflect the political balance that actually emerged in the democratic ballot?

Think of it this way. Suppose we were starting from scratch in a Scottish city. Suppose we knew in advance from comprehensive opinion polling that no one party had majority support among the voters. Would we then fashion an electoral system which nevertheless allowed the largest of those minority parties to wield complete power, taking the leadership of the council and the convenership of every committee?

It might be said such autocratic stability is preferable to endless horse-trading between two rivals in a coalition. There is something to be said for that. In such circumstances, the minor partner can end up wielding disproportionate power by repeated threats to end the bargain. However, to counter that, it might be said such an open argument is preferable to the private disputes which already exist within controlling council groups. In these private arguments, the balance of opinion may have been relatively close inside the controlling group. But, in open council, the group will exercise discipline and vote en bloc. By such methods, a policy which has *majority* support within the controlling group but only *minority* support in the council as a whole can get through.

So there are tricky choices to be made. Inherent virtue does not rest with any particular voting system. It would be heartening to think that such balanced considerations would dominate the debate over the future of Scotland's councils. Such was certainly the agenda of the Kerley Committee and of earlier scrutinies of Scottish local government.

However, this is raw politics. Several of Labour's council groups rely on first-past-the-post voting to enhance or even create their powerbase. PR reform would threaten that powerbase. So they oppose such a reform. Externally, they rely upon the intellectual arguments against PR: not entirely cynically, many genuinely believe PR has fundamental flaws. Internally, within Labour, they tend to appeal more to gut instinct. Why should Labour throw away power?

Indeed, this is very far from being a purely constitutional argument, to be settled by inquiry and intelligent discussion. This is about power, entrenched power. In practice, entrenched Labour power in central Scotland. All of which leaves the Liberal Democrats looking on – and waiting. The LibDems know that endless smart comments from them about the joys of PR will simply exasperate Labour still further. This is not a case to be won by argument. This is a case to be won, silently and patiently.

If it were simply up to the Labour Ministers, this case might already be settled. Jack McConnell is an instinctive reformer, as his period as council leader in Stirling displayed. Despite his reputation as a political fixer, he has little patience with unthinking Labour council power where reasoned, internal criticism is equated with treachery and external views are scorned and ignored. Privately, McConnell knows that such attitudes may preserve local powerbases in specific areas but that they damage the party's wider reputation in Scotland. However, this is not simply down to the First Minister. This is not a deal Jack McConnell and Jim Wallace can strike between them. Both have to take their parties with them. If there is to be change, McConnell has to give Labour – particularly local authority Labour – time to adjust. Wallace has to urge his Parliamentary group to display continuing patience: not, perhaps, their innate attribute, but one they have steadily acquired.

In a sense, all the studies, all the consultation, all the endless agonised discussion amount to a mask for those simple facts. They are a way of spinning out the debate while the ground shifts beneath Labour and while the LibDems accustom themselves to the notion that they are not going to get precisely what they demand, precisely when they demand it. In practice, the essential choice is fairly straightforward. Not remotely easy, but straightforward.

As things stand, the Executive is quietly drafting clauses for a possible Bill to change the voting system for local government – alongside other changes which might include a salary system for councillors. That does not mean instant change, by any means. The council elections in 2003 will go ahead with the first-past-the-post voting system.

However, the firm expectation within the LibDems is that the council elections in 2007 will be held under a revised system. As SNP rivals frequently point out, the LibDems have given ground.

They have moderated the tone of their demands, not over principle but over timescale. They have learned to appreciate the depth of Labour's difficulty, and to give their partners some space.

Not, however, endless space. Ultimately, they will have to demand action. For one, they believe in the principle of council voting reform. For another, their rivals are watching closely for any sign of a climbdown. For the LibDems, this one really is 'non-negotiable', to import a phrase from the earlier row over tuition fees.

As I write, it does indeed seem likely that the 2003 council elections will be the last to be held under the present system. Of the options, the Single Transferable Vote has at least the attraction of maintaining a form of ward link. Here's a mischievous thought, suggested to me by a Labour Minister. Wouldn't STV have been better for the Scottish Parliament too, getting round the problem of all those 'added members', which many Labour members seem to find so irritating?

If such gossip gets to the ears of the LibDems, they might well be tempted to point out gently that it was Labour leaders who insisted upon the top-up list system in the first place. Or they might maintain a diplomatic silence. Diplomacy, tact and political maturity. Not labels frequently attached to the Liberals in the recent past. I feel sure a healthy outburst of ludicrous posturing over some minor issue cannot be long deferred. But they are learning. They are definitely learning.

Notes

1. Donald Macintyre (1999), *Mandelson: The Biography*, London: HarperCollins, pp. 342–3.
2. Interview with Charles Kennedy by Jackie Ashley, *The Guardian*, 21 January 2002.
3. Interview with Jim Wallace, 7 December 1998.
4. Kerley Committee Report to the Scottish Executive, 27 March 2002.

12 Three Amigos?
Sheridan, Harper and Canavan

Throughout the first devolved Parliament, they have presented a band of colours. Tommy Sheridan, Robin Harper, Dennis Canavan. Red, Green and indignant purple. From day one, they sat together in the chamber in a little block with only three seats, one row behind the front bench. The three amigos, a rainbow reminder of increasing diversity in Scottish politics. Never a composite group, more a convenient huddle, sheltering against the frowns and stares of bigger party politics.

Their first tiny triumph was geographical. They bagged those three seats, and declined to shift, leaving Jim Wallace, the deputy First Minister, to sit in front of them, somewhat detached from his own Liberal Democrat group. Wallace endured months of televised coverage showing three sceptical faces behind him – before he shifted to the other side of the chamber, taking his LibDem troops with him.

However, they have done rather more than that. Each in his own way has contributed to legislation, debate and controversy in Parliament. The major parties still seem unsure how to handle the amigos. Ignore them? Patronise them? Confront them?

It is feasible, in future, that there might be a 'minor parties' Parliamentary group. Perhaps red/green, a political bloc which is relatively common in some European Union nations. Perhaps predominantly socialist. Such a group, if it had at least five members, would be entitled to membership of the Parliamentary Bureau which agrees the programme of business to be debated by MSPs. Throughout the first Parliament, however, the amigos have co-operated loosely while still pursuing their individual perspectives.

The three are very different. Dennis Canavan was first elected as a Labour MP in 1974. Always on the Left of the party, he had a reputation for rebellion, for distrusting the misuse of authority. He had a reputation, too, for well-aimed wit and barbed comment, alongside his evident concern for the disadvantaged.

Canavan can switch from dry, intelligent drollery to stinging fury – and back again – with scarcely a pause. He generally chooses his targets well, reserving full angry mode for occasions when he detects a genuine injustice, capable of remedy. While he can be scathing about those in power, his attacks are often coated in satire. Less scabrous, more effective. That combination has brought him enemies as well as cautious admiration on his own side. Despite his personal standing, it has frequently seemed to me that Dennis Canavan felt somehow politically thwarted. I am not saying he thought he should have been a government Minister at some point. His whole approach is that of the back-bench debunker. However, I suspect he often felt in his soul he was a more capable politician than those who did make it to the front bench in the Commons.

Throughout his political career, Canavan has been a fervent supporter of devolution. So it was no surprise when he sought nomination as a Labour candidate for the Scottish Parliament. Equally, given his habit of iconoclastic insurrection, the reaction from the party machine was perhaps also unsurprising. He was kept off the list of approved candidates.

No surprise, but a serious blunder by the Labour Party. After twenty-five years as a Labour MP, Dennis Canavan was not about to accept that he was not good enough to represent the party in the Scottish Parliament. He appealed, unsuccessfully, against his rejection, then opted to stand as an independent, automatically disbarring himself from the Labour Party. Again, to no-one's surprise, he was returned for his own constituency of Falkirk West – with the largest numerical majority in Scotland.

Canavan dislikes being called an independent, preferring to style

himself 'the member for Falkirk West'. He is easily the most reluctant member of the three amigos, believing that his party left him
rather than the other way round. Indeed, it seemed at one point as
if an accommodation might be reached with the Labour Party.

Before the UK General Election in 2001, Dennis Canavan
remained both an MP and an MSP, in keeping with the others who
had transferred from Westminster to Holyrood. After Donald Dewar's
death – and with that 2001 contest pending – there were off-stage
discussions aimed at ending Canavan's isolation and resolving a
tricky question for the party.

The only deal possible was that Canavan would join the Labour
Group in the Scottish Parliament, while agreeing to support the
party in retaking Falkirk West in the Commons. In the event,
Canavan ended the speculation, by resigning his Westminster seat
in November 2000 and forcing a by-election which Labour won.
Canavan blamed Tony Blair for failing to investigate claims that his
original Holyrood selection process had been rigged. Labour claimed
Canavan was unwilling to accept group discipline. Canavan retorted
that the discipline practised by the group was excessive and anti-
democratic. And so the split deepened.

In the Scottish Parliament, Canavan has been sporadically effective. He is a standing rebuke to any Minister who appears to him
to be neglecting the plight of those with less. For example, he has
fought a sustained battle to win a better deal for Scottish Transport
Group employees in his constituency who saw a multi-million
pound surplus from their pension fund transferred to the Treasury
after privatisation.

Canavan has never shown any inclination to join another party.
In his earlier days, he was regarded by some as a quasi-Nationalist,
but he is utterly scathing about the SNP. He is firmly on the Left,
but has never joined Sheridan's Scottish Socialist Party. Rather, he
has remained like Ken Livingstone – in the public eye but outside
the Labour Party. I asked him about his plans. He told me, with a
mischievous glint, that he had subjected himself to a rigorous selection interview and had decided, unanimously, that he was the right
candidate for Falkirk West.

Dennis Canavan, then, is distinctive, a one-off. By contrast, the
other two of the three amigos represent a sustained attempt to
expand the relatively limited scope of Scottish politics. Further, they

represent – in different ways and at a minuscule level – nothing less than a fundamental challenge to global capitalism.

Even as I write that sentence, I am aware that it is uncomfortably, if deliberately, grandiose. Brian, behave yourself. This is Tommy and Robin we are talking about. Tommy with the smart suits and the suntan. Robin with the guitar and the garish taste in ties. At one level, that is true. These are two individual members of the first devolved Scottish Parliament. Sheridan in particular is arguably much better known as a personality than most on the Executive or main opposition benches. The public mood may be to welcome them as a dash of maverick colour in the seemingly uniform grey of contemporary politics.

However, they are not mavericks. They are not loners or independents. They represent distinct parties with distinctive ideologies. While appraising them as individuals, I believe it is also right to examine those ideologies. I believe, in short, that it is better for democratic scrutiny to take them seriously as partisan politicians rather than to laud them or patronise them as personalities.

So what about that challenge to global capitalism? Well, Tommy Sheridan's Scottish Socialist Party wants, according to its published programme, 'to replace capitalism with an economic system based on democratic ownership and control of the key sectors of the economy'.[1] This would be 'a system based on social need and environmental protection rather than private profit and ecological destruction'.

Robin Harper's Scottish Green Party wants, according to its published programme, to limit international trade, including air traffic, to move towards local and regional self-sufficiency and to create a system where 'economic growth is no longer an objective of economic policy'.[2] Both parties stress that these objectives form part of their longer term ideology. From their different standpoints, they also each offer a raft of policies which, they argue, would address immediate, practical concerns in Scotland. As Sheridan puts it, they have 'policies for today as well as tomorrow'.

We have grown accustomed to blandness in domestic politics. It is important to understand that the new parties in Scotland are not remotely bland, at least in terms of their ultimate objectives. When Sheridan talks of socialist ownership of industry and Harper vaunts no-growth ecology, they really mean it. Such ideologies may attract

or repel voters, according to taste. It is only right, however, that
electoral customers know what they are buying. To be fair, both
parties display their ideological wares completely openly.

Let us start with the Greens. Robin Harper is universally popular
in Parliament. I believe there are two reasons for that. One, he is a
thoroughly decent guy, open, friendly and approachable. Two, others
occasionally like to enlist him to their cause in order to add a Green
tinge to a particular cross-party initiative. It is cool to be Green.

Harper was born in 1940 in Thurso. After university and a spell
working in Kenya, he taught Modern Studies at Boroughmuir High
School in Edinburgh for twenty-seven years until entering the
Scottish Parliament on the Lothian list in 1999. In appearance, he is
almost a stereotypical Green. Loud ties, a long Dr Who scarf, folk
guitar and a bike. He has easily the broadest permanent smile in
Parliament, as if he is endlessly surprised and delighted to be a prac-
tising politician. In chamber and committee, he intervenes on
environmental matters, naturally, but does not confine himself to
that sector, offering a Green perspective on everything from public
services to the economy.

By his own account, however, he is not entirely typical of his
party. Many are well to the Left of him, perhaps more in keeping
with the European Green movement. There are limits to Harper's
iconoclasm. For example, he could not bring himself to vote against
the Parliamentary tribute to the Queen on her golden jubilee in
2002. He told me it would have been 'bad manners'. More generally,
he categorises himself as a 'moderate radical'. Most will generally
associate the Greens with protecting the environment. Relatively
few, I suspect, will be aware of their full policy programme. They
believe in replacing competitive growth with self-sufficient regionally
based economies; including an agriculture system which they
describe as 'local protectionism', with strict limits on wider distribution and trade, plus land value taxation and regulated planning.
They want public utilities under 'locally accountable democratic
structures'.

They back a Citizens' Income scheme whereby a guaranteed
wage for all would largely replace the need for benefits. They
support sustainable public transport, discouraging air travel except
to island communities and halting all major trunk road building.
They want full recognition for same-sex partnerships. They support

the legalisation of cannabis. They group all their policies under short-, medium- and long-term aims.

Without remotely endorsing that broad programme, the major parties in Parliament frequently appear keen to work with Harper, or at least not to antagonise him unnecessarily. They may find it useful to obtain his fiat for cross-party initiatives in legislation or debate. In essence, they tend to treat him and his party as an environmental pressure group whose support can be valuable.

Harper is aware of this – and offers no real objection, although the Scottish Greens have discussed the issue of their relationship with other parties. There is no fixed policy but the broad view appears to be that the Greens should be willing to advance ecological aims, wherever possible. Certainly, that is the strategy Harper mostly pursues. He prefers to secure a practical amendment to the law rather than to grandstand with purist doctrine which will be roundly ignored.

Obviously, this presents potential difficulties. No party, no matter how small, likes to feel that its wider ambitions are seen as insignificant by the body politic. However, Harper explains that there are sound underlying reasons for his tactics. The Greens believe that our planet is facing an imminent environmental catastrophe. They cannot afford, consequently, to indulge in long-term tactical politics, setting out their stall and hoping for eventual triumph. They suspect there may not *be* a long term. They believe they have to make ecological progress now.

Harper speculates gently that rival parties may not treat him so kindly if and when ecological collapse presents an actual and present challenge to the global economy and, consequently, to established politics. More prosaically, I would say that the major parties would very swiftly become more combative if the Greens showed signs of presenting a significant electoral threat. As it is, each of the main parties likes to display Green credentials.

However, for now, the bigger players in politics tend to regard Robin Harper benignly. He has become a protected Parliamentary figure rather like Lord James Douglas-Hamilton: it is forbidden to be nasty to him. A rather different attitude is displayed towards the third amigo – Tommy Sheridan. More accurately, a different attitude is displayed by the Labour Party. Sheridan is a Marxist who was formerly a prominent member of Militant, the Trotskyite organisation which worked within Labour, seeking to take control of constituencies and influence policy. Key Militant supporters were purged from the party, particularly after Neil Kinnock condemned them in a powerful party conference speech in 1985.

For some Labour activists who remember that inner turmoil, Sheridan's background prompts loathing and mistrust. But Tommy Sheridan went on to found the Scottish Socialist Party, which is now seeking to usurp Labour support in Scotland's housing schemes and elsewhere. Among Labour activists, this provokes fear.

Tommy Sheridan himself is a remarkable individual, easily one of the most well-known and charismatic characters in Scottish politics. He is a powerful platform orator – and Parliamentary speaker – with a line in controlled, measured invective. Sheridan may occasionally appear to rant, but every word is weighed, every image calculated to move the listener or antagonise an opponent. A disciplined, dedicated socialist, he plans every strategy, with the objective of advancing his own aims and causing maximum embarrassment to his former colleagues in Labour.

Sheridan is a 24/7 politician, seeming almost wary of relaxation. He does not smoke, he does not drink, he never socialises in the Scottish Parliament. He takes the wage of the average skilled worker, handing the rest of his Parliamentary salary to his party. There is a puritanical, almost Cromwellian touch about him, although a more accurate comparison might be with the late nineteenth- and early twentieth-century Scottish socialists who advocated abstinence along with the political transformation of society. Neddy Scrymgeour – the Prohibitionist who defeated Churchill in Dundee – would be proud of him. The answering message on Sheridan's mobile phone used to say that he was 'probably out fighting the Tories'. Now it says that he is 'probably out fighting Blair's new Tories'. Each is designed to present an image of incessant struggle for the cause. When he was due to be presented with a Parliamentary award at the prestigious annual ceremony hosted by *The Herald*, he declined to attend, noting that he had a housing benefit meeting that evening. His vivacious wife Gail went in his stead.

Cynics might say there was more than a speck of vanity in the deep Sheridan tan, carefully topped up by regular sessions under the sun bed. Supporters might say such criticism displays a bourgeois attitude, that the honest working classes are entitled to look their best, that Sheridan is a handsome man who takes care of himself.

Born in 1964 in Glasgow, Tommy Sheridan was educated in the city before graduating in Economics and Politics from Stirling University. He cites football as his passion outside politics: he is a keen amateur player and a Motherwell fan. His blend of interests is reflected in Parliament, where he is a member of cross-party groups on: animal welfare, Cuba, nuclear disarmament, Palestine, asylum seekers – and sport. He lists his heroes as John MacLean, Leon Trotsky, Lenin, Che Guevara, Fidel Castro and Tony Benn.

Sheridan first came to political prominence in the late 1980s with the campaign against the poll tax. For Sheridan and the Marxist Left, this was a perfect target. First, the tax was genuinely detested as an attack on the poorer sections of society. Second, it provided a political weapon to attack the Tories. Third, by leading a non-payment campaign, Sheridan was able to criticise the Labour leadership, who were reluctant to sanction defiance of the law. His next target was warrant sales – the Scottish system of confiscating and selling a debtor's household goods. Sheridan was jailed for six months early in 1992 for breaching a court order forbidding him from attending a particular warrant sale. During his spell in Saughton Prison, he was elected to Glasgow city council on a Scottish Militant Labour anti-poll-tax ticket. He has subsequently been back inside for refusing to pay fines imposed over his protests outside the Faslane nuclear base on the Clyde.

Labour has frequently seemed unsure about handling Sheridan and his party. Some MSPs ignore him. Others patronise him as 'Tommy the Trot', or as a slightly risky Red who, with a bit of effort, can be brought into the mainstream. Others – particularly Glasgow members – think Labour should confront him as a Marxist revolutionary, subjecting his policy programme to tougher scrutiny.

This quandary appeared to be reflected in the *Daily Record*, the main Labour-supporting tabloid. Sheridan used to be a columnist in the *Record*, billed as 'the radical voice of politics'. The paper later described him as 'Pillock Number One' in an article ridiculing his arrest outside Faslane as a stunt.[3] (Number Two was the Labour MP George Galloway, who was also arrested.) It subsequently condemned his support for the legalisation of cannabis. The *Record* would say it saw through him. Sheridan traces the switch to a change of editor – and Labour influence.

The Scottish Socialist Party makes no secret of its longer term ambitions. It wants to 'replace global capitalism with global socialism'. It would renationalise all privatised industries and utilities while extending public ownership to the banks, the North Sea oil industry, major manufacturing companies plus key players in the construction and transport sectors. Companies who fled Scotland in search of greater profits would have their assets confiscated. Further, according to the 2001 Scottish Socialist Party manifesto, the party backs the public ownership of all 'under-used' land, including sporting estates. Land holdings would be set at a maximum acreage. The party would squeeze the rich with higher tax, halt all motorway construction, provide free travel for all needy groups, reinstate student grants, legalise cannabis, end means testing of benefits, ditch all 'anti-union' laws, abolish the monarchy, scrap nuclear power, pay pensioners £150 a week and hike the minimum wage to £7. Those latter figures will have been revised upwards since.

The party insists its programme has 'nothing in common' with either 'Eastern European style Stalinism' or 'old Labour bureaucratic corporatism'. It says it is interested in bringing real power to the ordinary people of Scotland. It says its three pillars are Scottish independence, socialism and internationalism. Labour critics say the programme is an uncosted fantasy, guaranteed to wreck the economy and betray the hopes of the poor.

Sheridan, then, is openly seeking to overturn the entire structure of society. However, he commonly narrows his focus upon smaller, individual issues which resonate with poorer Scots, and create a problem for the Labour Party. In essence, this is a repeat of the strategy deployed over the poll tax. The Scottish Parliament presents an ideal forum because of its system of members' Bills.

Under this system, proposed legislation can be advanced by an individual MSP. At Westminster, such private members' Bills occasionally prosper, but, much more frequently, vanish into oblivion. They are often advanced by MPs simply seeking a debate – or publicity. At Holyrood, by contrast, members' Bills are serious. MSPs are strictly limited in the number of such Bills they can introduce, so they tend to avoid frivolity. Once introduced, a member's Bill has, technically, the same status as a key plank of the Executive's legislative programme. It cannot be ignored. It must be discussed, and put to the vote.

On 27 April 2000, the Scottish Parliament had to vote upon the principle of Tommy Sheridan's Bill to abolish warrant sales. Again, like the poll-tax campaign, this had a double edge. Sheridan genuinely detests the Scottish system of diligence, or debt enforcement. He believes it is primitive and brutal. Equally, though, this was a direct challenge to Labour MSPs. Would they have the stomach to vote for abolition, when the Executive was warning that there was no immediate replacement system available for ensuring that debts were paid? It turned out they did. As I have already described, it fell to Jim Wallace to announce the eventual Executive climbdown in the face of a Labour back-bench rebellion. Ministers would back the Bill, with the caveat that the search would continue for alternatives. As I write, those alternatives are still being hotly disputed.

However, the key political point was Sheridan's victory. His Bill had been supported by Alex Neil of the SNP and Labour's John McAllion, who are both on the Left. But this was Tommy Sheridan's Bill. Labour MSPs had bluntly told their whips that they simply could not vote to retain warrant sales, particularly when the main advocate of abolition was Sheridan. The back-bench MSPs heard and acknowledged the practical problems, the lack of an alternative system, but this was pure politics. They could not tell their constituents they had voted for warrant sales.

Tommy Sheridan generated a similar problem for Labour in 2002. Again with support from Neil and McAllion, he had introduced a Bill to provide free school lunches for every pupil, regardless of income. He argued this would end the stigma attached to those receiving free meals and boost uptake, potentially improving the poor nutritional record among Scotland's children. He managed to muster substantial external support for the measure.

Once more, a difficulty for Labour MSPs. They knew there were significant cost implications, and doubts as to whether universal free provision would actually succeed in tempting kids to stay in school for their mid-day meal. But could they really vote against free meals for their constituents' children?

Again, this was a double edge from Tommy Sheridan. Yes, he backed free school meals: it matched his party's ethos of ending means testing for benefits. Equally, though, while campaigning on nutrition for the young, he could spot a tasty problem for Labour. He was offering simple fare: free meals for kids. They had the leavings: the cost, the complexity, the practicality.

On 14 June 2002, the Parliament's education committee voted against endorsing Sheridan's school meals Bill. They acknowledged a genuine effort to remove stigma and improve nutrition. But they voiced practical concerns. They argued there were other disincentives which kept pupils away from school at lunchtime. They questioned whether free meals would bring them back. They suggested further that the cost of universal free provision might forestall other much-needed initiatives in boosting the nutritional content of school catering. They argued that stigmatisation could be addressed by other means, such as swipe cards to obtain food, which would not show whether the card had been paid for or freely received. The committee's verdict was backed by the full Parliament on 20 June 2002.

As I write, Tommy Sheridan intends that his next big campaign will be to replace the council tax with a Scottish Service Tax which would load charges upon the better-paid. To some extent, this recalls his 'glory days' fighting the poll tax. I may of course be proved wrong but I would doubt, at this stage, whether this campaign will present Labour with the same political quandary as warrant sales and school meals. I feel this issue lacks the simple pitch of the others.

It seems likely, however, that Tommy Sheridan will continue to find campaigns which appeal to the disadvantaged – and irk Labour. But will the party prosper as a consequence? It does appear to be growing, claiming some 3,000 members. Self-evidently, its biggest asset by far is Sheridan himself. Doubtless, he attracts support or at least sympathy from voters who may pay little heed to the party's detailed programme. There was little sign, for example, that voters were flocking to other campaigners on the Left such as the Socialist Workers Party (SWP). In Scotland, the SWP has gone in with Sheridan's party.

Sheridan insists that the SSP is much more than a personal fan club. He says it attracts idealists, either fleeing Labour and the SNP or entering party politics for the first time. He says further that it is not easy to be a member of the Scottish Socialists. Members, he says, are routinely vilified by rivals as either dinosaurs or wreckers. He forecasts that the party will gain further elected members, lessening the identification of the SSP with him, personally. It seems likely that the existence of the SSP – and the personality of Sheridan – will exert an influence on politics more generally, perhaps pulling grassroots Scottish Labour a little to the Left of the party in England, in rhetoric at least, if not in policy.

Furthermore, might sections of the Labour, or indeed Nationalist, Left drift to the SSP? Individuals will, certainly, but large-scale or high-profile defections seem unlikely. Labour's prestige and power exercise a mighty pull in the other direction. Similarly, the Nationalists will continue to attract those who place a primacy upon independence, rather than overturning the economic structure.

In addition, key figures on the Labour Left say they find much of the SSP programme unpalatable. One influential Labour left-winger told me the involvement of 'ultras' from the SWP made it impossible to contemplate working with Sheridan's party. This source said Tommy Sheridan had succeeded in drawing at least part of the focus of the Left away from Labour and the SNP, but would require to 'moderate' in order to create a serious, sustainable left-wing party. Other Labour MSPs insist they are engaged in advocating sensible, left policies within their own party – not looking to rivals.

Sheridan appears relaxed. Naturally, he would welcome defections, perhaps more than his calm demeanour on the topic would suggest. However, he insists he is happy for the SSP to grow from the grass-roots. Other parties, of course, say that the scope for such growth is strictly limited. Longer term, it seems likely that the proportional voting system at Holyrood – and the apparent disaffection with mainstream politics – will continue to offer at least a place to minority parties. The amigos may find they have a few other chums.

Notes

1. Scottish Socialist Party manifesto, 2001.
2. Scottish Green Party policy programme, published on its website, scottishgreens. org.uk
3. Article in the *Daily Record*, 13 February 2002.

13 A Question of Money

The former Secretary of State for Wales, Ron Davies, was fond of describing devolution as a process rather than an event. Davies, of course, had two targets in mind with this remark. He wanted to counter Plaid Cymru, the Welsh Nationalists, who were urging more extensive devolution of powers to Wales and he also wanted to remind members of his own party that they must not put their feet up after the establishment of a devolved Assembly, thinking that their work was complete.

This analysis, however, has wider application than in the particular circumstances of Wales, where sections of the Labour Party have been decidedly reluctant devolvers, where the scheme was only endorsed by the narrowest of margins in the Welsh referendum and where those who want to entrench the Assembly cast envious eyes towards the powers held in Edinburgh. Devolution is structurally dynamic, not static. To some extent, this dynamism is true of all politics. Solutions emerge, positions change, often just when it appears that argument has been exhausted on all sides. Personalities play a part as do shifting allegiances within parties. Think of the European Union. Even as the bound copies of one Union treaty – such as Maastricht or Amsterdam – are being translated into a multitude of languages, the process of advancing the next stage of reform is under way. There is simply no fixed point which can sensibly be said to be the established political structure of Europe, and now of course the entire structural future of the EU is under review by the Giscard convention.

Similarly with Westminster. The decline in relative importance of the House of Commons cannot be traced to a single event, however much analysts may try to blame Tony Blair or over-powerful whips' offices or sycophantic backbenchers or televised debates or the development of non-partisan community politics or, indeed, devolution. Almost intangibly, however, the Commons is a lesser chamber.

It is also absurd to assume that a Westminster government legislates for one precise form of devolution, and that is it. To be fair to Donald Dewar, he never pretended that there could not be further reform of the system. Indeed, he pointed out that the package of powers might be altered in the light of experience or evident public demand. In government, however, Dewar and his successors have been understandably anxious to play down this prospect. For one thing, such talk would appear like excuses in the face of perceived Executive failures to make the best use of the existing powers. For another, it would exasperate London for little practical gain. For another, it would encourage or appear to encourage Nationalist ambitions to 'complete' the powers of the Parliament, as they put it. Consequently, each time the SNP leadership has spoken of devolution as a bridge to independence, Labour has tended to react by depicting devolution in relatively static terms, to talk of a 'settlement' as if the precise Parliament introduced by the Scotland Act were the final word.

To the detached observer, two things seem self-evident. First, the 'settlement' will be in a process of semi-permanent change. These may not be big changes such as the acquisition of further, specific powers. More probably, the relationship with Westminster or the intrinsic dynamic of the new Parliament itself will develop. Circumstances, which could not be envisaged at the time of the legislation, will forge the nature of the newly devolved structure.

Second, independence is not implicit in devolution. There is no guaranteed path from one to the other, no fixed route which one can track whereby a devolved Scotland definitely and finally breaks the Union with England. It may happen or it may not. The establishment of a devolved Parliament, however, is not a guarantee that independence will follow 'as night follows day', as the Tories used to claim before their conversion to accepting devolution. In both cases – the development of devolution and the potential arrival of independence – there will be two interacting forces: the structural tensions which may arise within the UK's new constitutional set-up and the popular response to those tensions. It is important to note that neither force is purely in the hands of Westminster or the devolved Parliament.

Devolution is not simply the creature of Westminster, and this is demonstrated by the very different nature of the packages advanced for Scotland, Wales and Northern Ireland. There is an attempt, admittedly, to impose some form of central order upon the three, to allow some cross-comparison. The differences, however, tend to out-weigh the similarities. For example, Wales has a power of secondary legislation to amend and refine the main statute laws, which will still be laid down by Westminster. Scotland has primary legislative powers. The package laid down for Northern Ireland features areas of competence which are substantially different from those in Scotland.

These evident differences reflect the different nature of political reality and cultural identity in Scotland, Wales and Northern Ireland. Devolution is not centrally driven. It is a Westminster response, not an initiative. As a policy, devolution differs from Westminster's agenda with regard to education or health or defence in that Westminster would never have turned its attention to devolution without evident prompting. Again, let me stress that I intend no implicit criticism with such remarks. It can be thoroughly sensible politics to respond to powerful, identified popular pressure, although of course there will be partisan dispute about the nature and strength of the demand and the justice of the response.

Self-evidently, Westminster retains a substantial influence over the future dynamic of devolved politics in the UK. It would be decidedly oversimplistic to suggest that the future nature of the devolved bodies lies entirely in popular hands or under the control of politicians in the devolved organisations themselves. At the very basic level, any substantial alteration of the package of Scottish powers, for example, would require further Westminster legislation. I would argue, however, that Westminster's role is now interactive, rather than pro-active. No longer will it be credible to maintain that the UK government is all powerful, however frequently the Scotland Act stresses the sovereignty of Westminster. Just as there have been shifts in the balance between the UK administration and the supervisory Commons, so there will be shifts in the balance of power between Westminster and the devolved bodies. This will become more evident still when, with the passage of time, the politicians who are elected to the Parliament in Scotland owe their entire allegiance and have spent their entire career in devolved politics, rather than at Westminster.

That change need not be linear, the difference need not be marked or dramatic. It will be one of tone, of perception. Look at the difference in stance between the three Executive leaders. Donald Dewar, the last full-power Secretary of State as well as the first First Minister, a Westminster politician with residual Westminster habits. Henry McLeish, the first post-devolution First Minister who seemed occasionally to feel the need to define himself at least partly in terms of defying Westminster. Jack McConnell, never a member of the Commons, who works pragmatically with Westminster but neither inflates nor denies its importance. In practice, the shift was perceptible from the moment the referendum carried in September 1997. Those Westminster MPs who had declared for Holyrood started immediately to talk as if they were already Members of the Scottish Parliament.

For example, I recall the experience of Henry McLeish as Minister of State at the Scottish Office prior to devolution. He had declared his intention to pursue his career in the Scottish Parliament. Almost instantly, he told me, he found that he felt it rather odd to be at Westminster. In a curious way, he wondered what he was doing there when his political inclinations now tended towards Edinburgh. I believe this is a tendency which is becoming still more marked. Politicians have become immersed in Scottish Parliamentary politics. Their concerns, their style, their manner of address and, above all, the loyalties which shape their personal future will be different from the Westminster pattern, even for those who were previously members of the House of Commons. They have become institutionalised in the Scottish Parliament, owing their allegiance to that body.

Their political careers now depend solely on advancing Scotland's interests or at least on appearing to advance Scotland's interests. This may well bring them into explicit conflict with Westminster, including with members of their own political party at Westminster. This factor, I feel sure, will add to the structural tensions which exist within the new constitutional set-up.

By that analysis, I do not mean to imply that devolution is fatally flawed or dangerously unstable. It may be said, indeed, that all political structures are unstable in so far as they are all subject to change, often substantial change. The ambition of despots down the centuries has been to create 'stability' in the shape of their own entrenched, unchallenged rule. All, to date, have ultimately failed.

Similarly, there will always be tensions as long as one ambitious political person attempts to oust or thwart another ambitious political person. Provided they play reasonably fair, such a situation can be creative and productive. The key question is whether the tensions inherent in the new constitutional set-up can be harnessed to creative effect or whether they will tend towards political stalemate, friction or collapse.

Aside from the unpredictable events and incidents which will inevitably create continuing difficulties between the various administrations within the UK, I believe there are three structural elements which may provoke continuing tension: finance, Europe and the future governance of England. By structural, I mean these are inherent problems where the difficulty arises from the nature of the constitutional settlement. These are not transient disputes: for example, over an item of legislation or harsh words at a party conference. These are fundamental issues which, I believe, may ultimately require further fundamental reform.

To varying degrees, each issue – money, Europe, England – has featured in the life of the first Scottish Parliament. I believe there are constant motivating factors which will ensure that these issues continue to resurface until they are resolved or at least seriously addressed. That does not mean that there will be permanent, daily conflict over such matters, nor that the solution will be required next week or month or year. Rather, there will be a background of mumbling disquiet, occasionally bursting into frenzied argument, as long as these structural problems remain extant within the UK's constitutional set-up. I intend to address each in turn.

First, finance. To recap, the Scottish Parliament receives a share of United Kingdom public expenditure from the UK Treasury. This is broadly in line with the previous block grant system for disbursing cash to the Scottish Office to enable it to carry out its task of administering Scotland on behalf of the UK. The sum is, of course, subject to regular review.

As I write, the Executive is deciding how to spend the extra money allocated to Scotland as a result of the latest Comprehensive Spending Review (CSR) by the Chancellor, which will determine expenditure for the years from 2003/4 to 2005/6. Gordon Brown announced the details to the Commons on 15 July 2002.

As a consequence of this announcement, the budget assigned to Scotland will rise to £22.31 billion by 2005/6. That is £4 billion more than the existing assigned budget for 2002/3, which is £18.2 billion. In line with the principle of devolution, it is up to the Executive and MSPs to determine how this money should be spent.

The Executive, of course, had been preparing for the CSR statement for months, working to published forecasts of expenditure. The Finance Minister Andy Kerr had taken the opportunity of the CSR process to return to basics, obliging each spending department within the Executive to prove that it was achieving maximum productive return for expenditure.

Quite apart from that challenge, this exercise in determining long-term Scottish priorities was tricky for two reasons. One, the global spending total was, of course, in the hands of the Treasury, not the Executive. The Executive could cajole to a limited extent. However, it was largely a case of awaiting the detailed outcome of Whitehall discussions, while preparing plans for allocating the anticipated sum to individual services.

More generally, the change in the Executive's budget is linked to that of comparable Whirehall departments. Those are the departments that fund, for England, domestic items like Education and Health which are devolved to Scotland. If they gain, Scotland gets a share of that gain. There is no such link with non-devolved departments like Defence. That means, crudely, the Executive is permanently hoping that the Treasury will look favourably on its English 'buddies', and play down the areas where there is no knock-on gain for Scotland. So, as one Scottish insider confided to me with a grin, the Executive wished all power in the CSR to the Department of Health and penury to the Ministry of Defence. He was, of course, jesting.

The second fundamental problem with the latest CSR is that it bridges the period of the next Scottish Parliamentary elections. Ministers are being asked to contemplate long-term spending plans in the knowledge that they or their party may lose power in the interim. I am told that even experienced Ministers cannot resist the occasional nervous giggle when civil servants raise the prospect of planning beyond 2003. Such is politics.

In principle, the Scottish Parliament has complete freedom to determine its own spending priorities, although in practice that freedom is constrained by the obligation to provide statutory services such as education. The Parliament has a limited power to vary the standard rate of income tax: accruing additional revenue if it raises tax or returning cash to the Treasury if it lowers the rate.

As outlined above, the budget assigned to the Scottish Parliament and administration by the UK Treasury is regularly varied in accordance with a mechanism known as the Barnett formula. This takes the established, historic spending level in Scotland and alters it according to the change which has been effected in comparable spending departments for England alone or for England and Wales.

The formula, consequently, governs only the changes in Scottish spending relative to England. Contrary to the impression fostered by some, it does not govern the base level of Scottish spending itself. That has been built up by historical precedent and past political haggling. The Barnett formula is named after Joel Barnett, Labour's Chief Secretary at the Treasury in the late 1970s, who devised a funding mechanism to cope with the expected onset of devolution to Scotland and Wales at that time. Devolution, of course, was frustrated by the outcome of the 1979 referendums, but the formula survived.

Joel Barnett conducted an assessment of the relative needs of areas of Britain. He wanted to find out whether the available money was fairly spread across the kingdom as a whole. This analysis disclosed that there was a spending bias in favour of Scotland and Wales, and, consequently, to the detriment of England. He produced a formula to remedy that perceived problem which now governs the annual alteration in territorial budgets for Scotland, Wales and also for Northern Ireland. This simple arithmetical formula has more recently stirred a quite remarkable brew of bile and bogus patriotism.

Listen to some English MPs, listen to the Mayor of London, and you would think Barnett amounted to largesse on the scale of the

South Sea Bubble and the Millennium Dome combined. Listen to some contemporary Scottish politicians who affect to regard the Barnett formula as if it were Holy Writ. Any criticism of its operation, any suggestion that the Treasury might be looking on it with disfavour is regarded as nothing less than treachery to Scotland. When it was indicated, in the latter years of the previous Conservative government, that the Barnett formula was being called into question, politicians from across the party divide mounted a crusade to preserve this magical elixir for the nation.

The Barnett formula, of course, is nothing of the sort. It is critical to realise that, when it was first introduced by Joel Barnett, it was firmly intended to narrow the gap in spending between Scotland and England. Admittedly, it was envisaged that this gap would be narrowed over an extended period of time but the intention was clear: Barnett meant to rein back Scotland's cash lead over England.

Barnett was designed to introduce stability, certainly, but stability which was predicated upon Scotland suffering a progressive disadvantage relative to England as each annual spending review came into effect. The intention was to settle the topic of Scottish spending on a relatively fixed basis and allow annual negotiations between competing Ministers to focus on English spending departments, to give the Treasury less to worry about, in other words. Again, it is important to stress that Barnett does not dictate the overall level of Scottish spending. This has developed historically. Barnett only governs the annual or regular change in the total allocated to Scotland. For example, if an English spending department like Health gets a budgetary increase, a fixed proportion of that sum – roughly a tenth – will be added to the Scottish Block. Under the rule of budgetary freedom, Scotland may spend that available money according to choice. It does not have to be spent on health.

As noted above, the comparison is only made with like-for-like departments: in other words, with domestic spending departments like Education where there is a comparable remit governing Scotland. Scottish spending is not compared with departments like Defence or the Foreign Office because there is no military or diplomatic remit under Scottish devolution. Barnett provides, consequently, that Scotland gets a fixed share of the regular change in all the comparable Whitehall budgets. To repeat, if they can extract a big cake from the Treasury, Scotland gets an agreed slice.

There are one or two budgetary areas that are settled specifically for Scotland. For the most part, however, Scotland has not negotiated directly with the Treasury since Barnett was introduced in 1978. The change in Scotland's budget has depended, second hand, on the change in comparable English departments like Education or Health – on the political clout of their Ministers in combating the Treasury, in other words.

The division of cash between Scotland, England and Wales was meant to be based upon population. When the Barnett formula was introduced, the percentages were set at Scotland 10 per cent, Wales 5 per cent and England 85 per cent. In other words, from every additional pound of public spending, 10p went to Scotland, 5p went to Wales and 85p went to England.

This arithmetical calculation was structurally more favourable to England than the historic division of cash between the territories. In other words, with each successive annual spending round, it was envisaged that England would do marginally better while Scotland and Wales retrenched fractionally. Over time, naturally, the gap between the territories would close. Again, for the avoidance of even the remotest shadow of doubt, this was not an accidental consequence of Barnett but its entire purpose.

However, for many years the formula did not achieve that purpose. First, the population of Scotland continued to decline relative to England while the formula remained unchanged. Spending per head in Scotland, consequently, stayed high because, simply, there were fewer heads upon which to lavish that spending.

Second, a key element of state spending is public-sector pay. These pay settlements continued to be calculated and funded on a UK basis. This meant Scotland receiving every bit as much as England, per head, for pay when a strict application of the Barnett formula would have meant that precise equivalence should not have applied. As long as this happened, pay was effectively removed from the Barnett effect. Barnett was restricted to working on the non-wage element of public-sector spending. In addition, other technical and political devices were found to bypass Barnett.

Steadily, however, these holes were plugged. In 1992, the Conservative government reconfigured the formula, tightening the calculation to reflect more accurately the relative population numbers. By 1996/7 – the last year of the Tory government – Scotland was receiving 10.66 per cent of the cash available to purely English spending departments and 10.06 per cent of the money that went to services like law and order which covered both England and Wales.

Also, over a period of years, the Conservative government obliged spending departments to fund certain key public-sector pay rises – including local government – from 'efficiency savings'. This meant that Scotland's protection from the Barnett impact on pay had been severely eroded. Whitehall was no longer offering universal provision for pay. Consequently, Scotland had to find the cash for pay rises from a budget which was now affected by a tighter Barnett deal. Finally, the Treasury steadily plugged the technical gaps in the formula. Barnett, in short, began to bite. The impact of these cuts in spending, which was discernible in the final few years of the Conservative government, has been substantially increased during the period of the subsequent Labour administration at Westminster.

The key decision, announced by the Treasury on 9 December 1997, was that the Barnett formula would in future be updated annually according to changing population ratios and might be altered at other times to take account of technical changes. This transformed the nature of Barnett, preventing its intended impact from being distorted or weakened. From 1999/2000, when this change took effect, Barnett applies strictly.

Barnett was tightened at the time of the Comprehensive Spending Review in July 1998 and again subsequently. The latest figures – from November 2001 – left Scotland getting 10.23 per cent of the annual alteration in English spending and 9.66 per cent of the alteration in budgets affecting both England and Wales. It will be noted that these are perceptibly lower than in previous years. In future, Barnett will be further refined, based on a mid-year estimate of relative population numbers.

It is important to understand that this does not mean that Scotland's budget is being cut, as some of the less precise or politically motivated analysts would argue. Scotland will continue to receive a budget increase under normal circumstances: at least as long as English spending departments are receiving an increase. The difference is that – with Barnett biting – the percentage increase will be less than in England. This is inevitable; indeed, planned. Scotland, historically, has received more in public spending than a strict population comparison with England would promote. This is arguably justified by higher spending needs – for example based upon sparsity of population or relative disadvantage – although the differential has been a cause of sharp political dispute.

From now on, the annual changes in the Scottish and English budgets are to be determined strictly by population. That means Scotland's increase will now lag behind its historically high level of spending, while England, slowly but surely, catches up.

· The spending gap is generally calculated by UK government analysts as around 20 per cent per head. In other words, Scottish spending has been a fifth more favourable than that applying to England. I am, of course, aware that these figures are estimates and are open to dispute. I have followed and analysed Nationalist claims, for example, that the calculation takes little account of hidden subsidies to the south-east of England through the disproportionate impact of, for example, defence spending and public-sector jobs. My purpose at this point is not to enter that fascinating, partisan debate. I do not intend in any way to belittle the argument between the Nationalists and the other parties over Scottish spending. It is in many ways critical to the future prospects of the various parties and, of course, to the future of Scotland. Equally, it can become somewhat sterile with untested assumptions thrust into conflict with imponderable statistics. Rather I intend to dwell for the moment upon another element: the spending challenge which will potentially face a Scottish administration of whatever political colour. If we work with the grain of the UK government's calculations, it is clear that Scotland is now facing a relative squeeze, a Barnett squeeze.

Again, that does not imply instant penury. Indeed, most detached analysts confirm that the relatively high cash levels implied by the current three-year Comprehensive Spending Review and future plans should mean significant increases in spending for Scotland. As opposition politicians frequently point out, these increases follow two exceptionally tight years in which the Chancellor Gordon Brown initially adhered to Conservative spending plans and, indeed, contrived to produce an outcome tighter than the Tories had intended.

More generally, though, the point is a structural one rather than being based on an immediate – and possibly transient – assessment of Scottish spending. Scotland has received more money in the

CSR, and will do so in the next round, but England has received more still as a consequence of the new, tighter, fitter Barnett.

In years of stringency, this may have a sharp impact on Scotland. If, for example, England receives a spending increase at some future date which is calculated barely to cover the prevailing rate of inflation then it is axiomatic that Scotland's increase will be below the inflation figure. Scotland could do little or nothing about that under the established rules. This potential impact has been identified by economists. In April 1999, the respected Fraser of Allander Institute (FAI) published an analysis of the UK government's CSR spending plans for the period up to 2001/2 as they affected Scotland relative to the rest of the UK.[1] This report found that Scotland had indeed, as intended by Barnett, lagged behind England in the spending calculations. Adjusting for price changes, the FAI report estimated that the Scottish budget would increase by some 6 per cent or 1.9 per cent per year, while the increase for the rest of the UK was 10.7 per cent or 3.4 per cent per year.

Again, to stress, this is not a cut in Scottish spending. Scotland is getting more money. The FAI report however noted: 'These comparisons imply that while Scotland is to receive an increase in public expenditure, the country fares much worse than the rest of the UK.' This is simply a demonstration of the new model Barnett in action. Scotland's increase is behind England's. For the future, it is envisaged that Scotland's increase will always lag behind England's. This is structural arithmetic, not political manipulation, although of course the arithmetic has a political origin. In years of relative generosity to England, there may not be an apparent problem for Scotland. In years of relative stringency for England, Scotland could face spending difficulties.

It is fair to say that Barnett is not – yet – an issue at the forefront of contemporary politics, as far as the voters are concerned. Rather, there is a permanent debate over the global total of UK public spending and its consequences for services and taxation. In a popular context, that has tended, so far, to overshadow the question of the internal division of funds between constituent parts of the UK.

The issue, however, is under academic examination by writers who are respected in the field, and, politically, there is evidence of growing scrutiny. Scrutiny which, I believe, may lead to pressure for substantial change.

First, the academic analysis. The potential for spending problems in Scotland was trenchantly analysed by Professor Neil Kay of Strathclyde University, writing in December 1998.[2] He argued that Scotland had received a relatively favourable deal on spending, because Barnett had been neglected over the preceding years. Now that Barnett was being dutifully implemented, he foresaw problems for the devolved Parliament in Edinburgh as a direct consequence. Kay wrote: 'The corrosive effects of the Barnett squeeze on Scottish public spending could institutionalise a source of tension and conflict between Holyrood and Westminster.' It should be stressed once more that Kay envisages such a potential development over a long period as a result of the structural squeeze implicit in Barnett.

Equally, it should be stressed that there are other economists who believe that the potential impact of the Barnett squeeze is exaggerated. Professor Arthur Midwinter of Strathclyde University is an established and highly respected economic analyst, with a particular expertise on the funding of the Scottish public sector. He has been consulted repeatedly over the years by government and local authorities.

Professor Midwinter told me that he thought any Barnett squeeze would be 'minuscule'.[3] Further, he insisted that the Treasury's aim had never been to close the spending gap entirely between Scotland and England. Rather, they had nurtured a long-standing aim to narrow the gap and had tried to carry out that purpose over many years, under successive Westminster administrations. There was, in short, a political element which would mitigate any technical Barnett squeeze. Professor Midwinter told me he had received private assurances from senior Ministers that Barnett would be renegotiated should that technical prospect of convergence between Scotland and England come anywhere near completion.

In private conversations with Treasury sources, it has been similarly stressed to me that Barnett would not necessarily be applied rigidly at all points in the future. There might, for example, be distinctive and individual allocations of cash which benefited Scotland in percentage terms. An example suggested to me was the product of the windfall tax on the profits of the privatised utilities, introduced by the new Labour government shortly after winning the 1997 election. This, arguably, was used substantially to benefit a jobs programme in Scotland, although relatively little of the cash had been raised from Scottish firms.

There is, however, at the very least an internal Scottish question mark over Barnett and the structural nature of the funding relationship between Scotland and England. This question is posed most frequently by Nationalist politicians. For understandable electoral reasons, they are keen to argue that England is gaining proportionately from the current application of Barnett. For example, they argue that, during the period of the CSR from 1999 to 2002, spending on comparable services increased two and a half times faster in England than in Scotland.

The SNP noted in a party briefing in 2002 that 'the application of the formula is placing continued strain on Scotland's public services'. In response, Executive Ministers tend to dismiss such arguments by pointing to the steadily increasing global total. Privately, though, one or two have acknowledged to me that the SNP has a statistical point which is hard to counter, particularly when it is delivered with such persistence.

Civil-service insiders readily concede the technical point about a planned relative squeeze, but argue that this misses the point, which is that any real debate over spending should focus upon the block totals available to the territorial departments, rather than the annual alteration. Those who attack Barnett as a Caledonian benefit scheme frequently get their facts wrong. From misinformation or malice, they ignore the undisputable fact that Barnett is designed to reduce the gap in spending between Scotland and England, that it is designed to curb Scotland's historic advantage. They are using Barnett, in other words, as a totem, as shorthand for a wider, political attack upon Scottish spending levels relative to England. One senior source at Westminster suggested to me that such shorthand was occasionally deployed by Cabinet Ministers seeking to 'carp about Scotland and needle Gordon Brown'. The source suggested that Ministers such as Jack Straw, David Blunkett and – before his departure – Stephen Byers felt that Brown was vulnerable on Scottish spending levels and took every chance to raise the issue: sometimes in a semi-whimsical way but always with a serious purpose. Similarly – and understandably – regions of England such as the north-east frequently complain about Scottish spending.

I believe these complaints need to be addressed, not dismissed. Those who defend Barnett frequently dodge the question of the issue of the historically high spending block upon which the formula is based. In other words, they focus narrowly on the annual pay negotiations, without considering or attempting to defend the block budget, the basic salary upon which those negotiations are predicated. I believe, then, that there is a genuine issue to tackle: either within the context of devolution or within the wider framework of independence. However, it is rather bogus to base this debate solely upon Barnett. It is an arithmetical formula for settling Scotland's annual pay round. As it stands, it is slowly but steadily eroding the spending gap between Scotland and England.

Tweak the formula, and you make only a marginal difference to the pace of that erosion. That is because the annual changes in UK expenditure – however fiercely argued – are inevitably relatively small by comparison with the huge, aggregate block upon which they are calculated. Scrap the formula as it stands and you either have to devise another formula in its stead or revert to annual haggling between Scotland and London. The alternative, of course, is financial independence.

Arguably, then, the real issue within devolution is not whether Barnett is fair or unfair. The underlying debate, which is beginning to emerge, is whether Scotland's overall service needs are fairly or unfairly met by the budget. In short, a much more comprehensive and fundamental debate than has taken place so far. I believe that debate will grow in importance, encouraged more by external factors rather than the internal factor of agonising over the impact of Barnett upon Scotland. Those external factors include the attitude of England, the stance of the other territorial administrations and the long-term view of the Treasury.

Within this debate, most attention so far has been paid to the attitude of England. It is a commonplace at Westminster for MPs from English constituencies to challenge the level of expenditure upon Scotland. Indeed, the Barnett formula is now almost a permanent fixture in the monthly sessions of Commons questions to the Scotland Office.

For example, on 15 January 2002, Nicholas Winterton, the Tory MP for Macclesfield, argued that Barnett currently 'produces levels of public expenditure per capita in Scotland far greater than in many areas of England where there are equal problems of poverty and deprivation'. In response, the then Scotland Office Minister George Foulkes deployed a classic tactic of triangulation, stressing the contrary views of Barnett held by English Tories and Scottish Nationalists. He said: 'The truth is that the Barnett formula is stable, flexible and fair. If the English Tories think that it is too generous and the SNP thinks that it is too mean, I think that it is just about right.' A neat, effective answer. But, as George Foulkes well knows, far from the end of the matter. Just because Tory MPs frequently ask the wrong question – spotlighting Barnett rather than the overall block – does not mean that they will get it wrong forever. Sooner or later, Scottish spending may face a more fundamental challenge.

However, you may say that Labour Ministers can afford to ignore Tory complaints. They can indeed, but what if those complaints come from their own side. Joyce Quin is the Labour MP for Gateshead East and Washington West. She is a former Minister and a near constituency neighbour of the Prime Minister. On 19 July 2001, in the Commons, she challenged the Treasury to defend Barnett, noting that it continued to be 'the focus of public concern and public attention, especially in the north-east of England'. She urged a review of needs, covering the whole of the United Kingdom. Her stated aim would be to cut the money available to Scotland in order to assist English regions like her own.

On this occasion, the Minister did not resort to triangulation. Rather, Andrew Smith (then Chief Secretary to the Treasury) described Barnett accurately. He said it was a 'convergence formula', noting wryly that this was 'something on which we receive representations from other parts of the United Kingdom'. He conceded – as obliged by arithmetic and logic – that Barnett is designed to squeeze the money available to Scotland. Mr Smith also advised his party colleague that those with concerns about the Barnett formula were rather missing the point. It was not the formula, he noted, which was responsible for 'the inequalities in funding' which prompted cross-border concern. Rather, those were 'historic matters', which Barnett attempted to address.

Joyce Quin's question was not an isolated exchange. As mentioned earlier, MPs from the north-east of England frequently criticise the level of expenditure in Scotland. From their perspective, this is good, common sense. They are protecting their own political backs, reflecting a mood which is growing in that region and in other areas of England experiencing relative deprivation.

It is a core element of the campaign for a north-east Assembly that there should be a cash transfer from Scotland to the English regions. Indeed, it is arguably the single most important element, the banner under which disparate elements can rally. The campaign for regional assemblies, even in the north-east of England, has few of the parameters which featured in the much more established campaign for a Scottish Parliament. There is no sense of nation-hood, no sense of ancient grievance, no serious and sustained party political issue, no consensus over what such Assemblies might do, no England-wide evidence of lasting popular demand, no grid map for how to achieve such reform, no uniform agreement on which areas want or merit assembly status.

There is, however, one outstanding element in those areas, like the north-east, where there has been discernible agitation. One common factor which unites those pressing the demand. The north-east wants an Assembly to bring it more financial bargaining power, more clout to attract jobs. It wants more cash, and it knows where to get it: Scotland.

This argument is addressed bluntly in the statement on the Barnett formula in the planning document published by the Campaign for the English Regions on 15 January 2002. Having canvassed other funding options, it stated: 'The case is then made for the financing of the assemblies to be by block grant, but with a commitment that the Barnett formula is subject to a radical review. The principle that underpins the allocation of funding should be need assessment, not nationality.'

Note the reference to nationality. The document is stating baldly – as countless north-east politicians have done – that Scotland is fiscally feather-bedded, comforted by largesse from the UK tax-payer. And that this must stop. I should stress in passing that I am not remotely criticising those politicians from the north-east of England for pursuing this case. They would be failing in their duty to their constituents if they did not argue for increasing the resources avail-able to their region, and challenge the apparent diversion of cash elsewhere. It is up to Scottish politicians to deliver their response, and to base it upon evidence.

In an article on the Barnett formula in *The State of the Nations*

2001, David Bell and Alex Christie picked up on this potential combat between the various parts of the UK over funding. While they perceived 'an uneasy truce' over the question for now, they added: 'Unless this issue can be satisfactorily resolved, the tensions caused by the perceived unfairness of the system of allocating resources between the constituent parts of the UK will undermine the legitimacy of devolution.'[4] They said the formula itself was now almost without friends.

Less attention has to date been paid to another factor. This is the attitude towards Barnett not just in England or Scotland but in the other territories of the devolved UK. Wales and Northern Ireland are getting bothered about Barnett. They are growing restless.

In Wales, the issue of funding was brought to a head by a remarkable row over European aid which ultimately cost Alun Michael his job at the head of the Welsh devolved administration. The European Union had determined – in its round of Structural Fund grants covering the years from 2000 to 2006 – that Wales merited special aid, because of the decline in traditional industries.

The EU proposed, consequently, that Wales should receive much more, as a proportion, than England. However, EU spending is counted by the UK within the overall budget allocated to devolved territories. Hence, Barnett kicked in and calculated that, taking the EU money into account, Wales would be receiving much more than its due as things stood. The prospect arose that – in order to receive the EU structural money – Wales would have to compensate with cuts elsewhere in the budget. This was, as Bell and Christie note, 'so plainly crazy' that the rules were eased and further resources were made available by the Treasury.

Wales, then, has cause to distrust Barnett and the present system of allocating resources. Northern Ireland has gone further, however, instigating a formal review of the issue. The suspicion in Northern Ireland is that the formula for dividing up cash across the UK is beginning to hurt them. For a range of reasons, including relative disadvantage and, less tangibly, political sensitivity, public funding at a substantial level has generally been accepted for Northern Ireland. Those English MPs who complain about Scotland's money tend not to lodge similar complaints about cash going to Belfast.

However, it is important to understand that things are seen rather differently in Northern Ireland. They do not believe they are funded generously. Indeed, Ministers in Belfast believe that convergence may already have been reached. In other words, they believe that Barnett has squeezed Northern Ireland's budgetary advantage completely out of the system. The Northern Ireland Executive has announced to the Assembly that it has commissioned evaluations of 'needs and effectiveness' in six key areas: health and personal social services; education; housing; vocational training; selective financial assistance to industry; and culture, arts and leisure.

In a statement, the Executive in Belfast told me that the purpose was to gather the data on 'the strategic spending issues affecting some major public services'. The work would include 'comparisons of spending levels and what is being delivered with other regions'. The studies are being led by the office of the First and deputy First Ministers, along with the department of finance and core spending departments. Plainly, this is not a minor book-keeping exercise. Politically, it is led from the top. Equally, it is not confined internally to Northern Ireland; the Executive intends to make comparisons with other parts of the UK.

In short, Northern Ireland suspects that it is losing out, or that it may be about to lose out under the continuing application of formula-based spending rules. It is looking for data to confirm that suspicion. Data, presumably, with which to confront the Treasury. This is, in effect, the prelude to a potential demand for a rethink of the formula which governs the allocation of money to the UK's devolved territories. It is the equivalent – from an entirely different standpoint – of English regional demands for a UK-wide needs review. Northern Ireland is arguing that the present formula system provides too little to the devolved territories. The English regions – and many English MPs – are arguing that it provides too much.

From either perspective – or both – this could prompt a comprehensive assessment of spending needs: starting from scratch, in other words, with a full analysis of what the various territories of the UK actually need to meet the requirements of their citizenry as opposed to what they have historically received. This has an apparent logic of its own. It would, arguably, clarify matters. If Scottish politicians believe they can defend the present level of expenditure north of the border, presumably they would be prepared to argue this case in a wider forum.

However, as the former Conservative Scottish Secretary Michael

Forsyth never tired of pointing out, such an approach could bring difficulties for Scotland. A needs assessment might simply hasten the spending convergence which Barnett is due to generate over time. The outcome of such an assessment would depend on the statistics and assumptions used. It might also depend on who had the final say.

There are obvious practical problems. How, for example, do you calculate need as between Scotland and England when there are different policies and practices in the public sector? How do you compare two different governments, with different policies? Who judges which spending policy is an actual 'need' – or a political whim?

Arguably, this problem might even arise ahead of a general needs review. Scotland's annual spending increase is based upon the changes in budget at comparable London domestic spending departments. Historically, Scotland has relied almost entirely upon public-service provision, with minimal use of the private sector.

But what if *England* progressively moves to make more use of the private sector or private insurance to provide, say, education and health? That might mean a lower demand upon the public sector in England. That would, in turn, mean a lower annual increase in purely 'public' spending on English schools and hospitals. That would mean, under Barnett, that the money going to Scotland was similarly constrained. However, Scotland would still be operating under a predominantly public system. The same, continuing demand for services, but less money to meet that demand.

That conundrum would also arise in any comprehensive needs review. What is 'need' – and how is it assessed when policies differ? The Scottish Executive has determined, politically, that there should be free personal care for Scotland's elderly. The UK government has determined, politically, that England should not receive free personal care. At present, the Executive is choosing to fund that promise from within its Barnett-varied block, making consequent savings elsewhere. But how do you take account of this difference in policy and practice if you are starting from scratch, if you are attempting to calculate basic 'need'?

Does Scotland 'need' free personal care? Or free upfront university tuition? Or any of the other policy pledges which differentiate Scotland from England, now and in the future. Who decides Scotland's 'needs'? The Executive? The Treasury civil service? The politicians in the UK government, an administration that already has a different political colour from Scotland's coalition Executive and might be markedly different in the future? How do you assess need across boundaries where domestic political choices are driven by two different – and potentially competing – administrations?

A Treasury-driven survey might not be especially favourable to Scotland, particularly with Scotland governed and administered by a distinctive Scottish Executive and Parliament which might have relatively little influence in Whitehall.

When the devolution White Paper was published, most attention in the financial area focused upon the promise that Barnett would be retained. As I have discussed, there was some comment upon the fact that the White Paper envisaged the formula being 'updated from time to time to take account of population and other technical changes'. There was relatively little attention paid to the sentence which followed: 'Any more substantial revision would need to be preceded by an in depth study of relative spending requirements and would be the subject of full consultation between the Scottish Executive and the UK Government.' This sentence postponed a full-scale needs assessment, but it did not preclude one entirely. Indeed, it might be argued that it raised the prospect.

So there are external and internal pressures for a more fundamental examination of funding. I am aware, however, that it can be a mistake to equate pressure with outcome, to equate volume with consensus. Loud repetition of the case for a review does not mean such a review will be conceded in the near future.

There are mitigating factors. For one thing, such a fundamental review, if carried out properly, would require substantial resources of brainpower, cash and time. This would not be welcome to a UK government or a Scottish Executive desperate to deliver improved public services within the current structure.

Tony Blair's north-east of England constituency might be looking enviously towards Scotland's budget. However, as Prime Minister, he has other matters on his mind. He would not instantly welcome an approach which might look like a tactical diversion, and would risk antagonising the Scots for little instant political reward.

Second, one should never underestimate the inertia factor in British politics. The UK has been through an enormous upheaval in devolution. The British body politic might prefer for the time being to exercise its new limbs rather than contemplate the fluff in its navel. Taking those factors into account, it is unlikely, therefore, that the cash allocation system within the UK will be fundamentally reviewed within the immediate future. I do not believe, however, that such scrutiny can be postponed indefinitely.

Should such a review arise, Scotland has answers mustered. Broadly, Scotland's case is that spending needs are measurably higher north of the border: with a relatively poor health record placing greater strain on hospital resources; with the public sector playing a larger part in Scottish life because of the low dependence on private provision in, for example, education; with a scattered population across a large land-mass placing greater demands on spending in areas like transport; with sectors like the water industry remaining within public funding in Scotland while they are privately run elsewhere. In addition, Scotland argues that comparisons are inevitably imprecise because there is relatively little all-England, all-service data with which to make comparisons. Scottish spending is grouped in a block while spending in England is dispersed across a range of departments and regions.

These are powerful and substantial arguments, which make the case for Scotland receiving more funding per head than England. They do not, however, make the case for that funding being at a particular level. Again, the disparity between the two territories might in future require to be established by an overall assessment of needs.

For now, though, Scotland is likely to have to contend with Barnett and the Barnett squeeze: with its potential impact, minor or substantial according to taste and economic analyst. The Barnett squeeze is not simply an arcane debating point. It could have a direct effect on people. If, over a long period, the Barnett squeeze were to have a substantial impact, or if it were to be felt by the Scottish population or by the political parties that Scotland was starting to slip in the spending stakes, then there could be pressure to use the Tartan Tax, the Parliament's power to vary the standard rate of income tax. (I make no apology, incidentally, for using the phrase 'Tartan Tax'. I am aware that it was originally a pejorative term devised by the Tories. The word 'Tories' itself was also originally a pejorative term. Usage alters. Who now remembers the poll tax as the 'community charge'?)

There might be pressure, then, to use the Tartan Tax to fill an actual or perceived deficit in spending increases between Scotland and England. The Tartan Tax was designed to give the Parliament financial flexibility. It might reasonably be argued, particularly from a London standpoint, that, if Scotland wants to sustain historically high levels of expenditure, then Scotland has an available remedy in its own hands.

This is one reason why some Nationalists were unhappy with their party's pledge, during the 1999 Scottish Parliamentary election campaign, to make use of the Tartan Tax if the SNP won. The SNP leadership offered to reverse for Scotland alone the Chancellor's planned cut of a penny off the standard rate of UK income tax.

The Nationalist case – advanced in a campaign styled 'A Penny for Scotland' – was that the people of Scotland had the chance to reject what the party called a 'bribe' by Labour and to divert the product of the penny tax to productive public expenditure. SNP strategists now concede that they did not prepare the ground sufficiently for this policy while noting that they were simply seizing an apparent opportunity presented by the Chancellor's decision. Equally, SNP leaders continue to insist that this policy played well on the doorsteps in Scotland. They say people were open to the argument that they would not be paying more than at present in tax, because it was not a tax increase but rather the reversal of a planned tax cut. The SNP leadership adds that voters in Scotland were prepared to accept that they would end up paying more than comparable taxpayers in England in order to fund targeted spending on Scottish services.

One or two internal critics, however, feared that the SNP fell into a Unionist trap. By offering to use the very limited tax power of a devolved Parliament, it was argued, they gave London an excuse in future to trim the central budget made available to Scotland. Further, according to those critics, the SNP and the cause of independence more generally risked becoming associated in the public mind with tax-raising.

Whatever the internal strategy of the SNP, Labour's response was instructive, then and since. Labour leaders were initially worried that the SNP would gain ground with their promise to spend more on health, education and housing. As the 1999 campaign progressed, however, Labour strategists claim they were able to contain this by, in effect, pointing out the inherent 'unfairness' of Scotland paying more than England in income tax. Labour insists that this argument applied purely in the circumstances of Gordon Brown's carefully balanced budgetary mechanisms. However, I believe Labour has created fundamental doubts about the nature and use of the Parliament's tax powers.

Listen to Labour Ministers, especially the Chancellor, on this question. If they mention Scotland's tax powers at all, which is rare, their attitude is almost universally dismissive. Yes, one or two Labour figures on the Left – including Mike Watson, while a backbencher – have noted that the Executive should stand ready to use the fiscal powers available in the interest of enhancing public services and improving the lot of the poor.

Far more commonly though, Labour leaders will talk of tax equity and the need to foster enterprise. For example, on 6 February 2002, Scotland's Cabinet agreed to refocus the Executive's approach to regional selective assistance as part of a shift in economic strategy. Ministers agreed to target aid in future upon indigenous industries following the closure of major projects which had been brought to Scotland from overseas by attracting inward investment.

The First Minister Jack McConnell noted: 'That is the way forward: for Scotland to compete in the global economy and for Scots to enjoy more secure, long-term employment.' Again, in a speech to business leaders in St Andrews on 22 March 2002, the First Minister said he wanted 'a Scotland bursting at the seams with opportunity'. The immediate challenge, he said, was to boost competitiveness and get Scotland growing again. Certainly, Scottish growth is sluggish, and, averaged out over a protracted period, has lagged behind the rest of the UK.

Such pro-enterprise statements voiced by Ministers do not, of course, rule out in themselves higher public spending or use of the Tartan Tax. Indeed, in his St Andrews speech, McConnell made much of the need for productive investment in education as one route to economic growth. However, at its simplest, higher personal income tax for employees and small enterprises might be thought to be somewhat contrary to the Executive's stated aims. Further, take those aims together with a UK Treasury strategy, which is to diversify the tax take beyond the standard rate, and the use of the very limited powers offered by the Tartan Tax seems increasingly unlikely.

On other occasions, Labour Ministers – notably Gordon Brown – have noted that the Tartan Tax would impact disproportionately on the lower-earners. That is because it is applied only to the basic rate of income tax and not to upper brackets. It is important to understand that this is a fundamental objection to the tax power, not simply a transient complaint about its application at a particular time and for a particular purpose. If the problem is that the Tartan Tax hits the poor, then that is a structural flaw in the tax itself, which is not removed by deferring the decision on implementation to a later date. It is a reason *never* to use the tax.

What has not previously been disclosed is that this structural flaw was recognised by the team drafting the original White Paper on devolution. It is important to remember that the tax power was itself something of a hangover from 1970s devolution, when it was felt that the proposed Assembly would be toothless without fiscal bite. Throughout the Convention – as I have discussed in earlier chapters – the tax issue became a totem. This would be a big, grown-up Parliament. It would have tax powers. It was a badge to wear, a banner to wave. Those campaigning for devolution honestly felt that such a statement was important to underpin the extent of the proposed reform.

Subsequently, though, the tax gesture confronted hard politics. First, as I have outlined, the power was refined within the later stages of the convention, dropping the notion of full Scottish-controlled revenue raising. Second, the Tory campaign against the tax obliged Labour to play down the prospect of the tax being used. A power was not a tax, we were repeatedly told. Third, the implementation of devolution – and hard bargaining within the UK Labour Cabinet – posed tough questions about the potential use of the new tax power.

Those around Donald Dewar who looked seriously at the tax power were aware of its limitations. They were aware of the structural flaw discussed above, that the tax as it stood was regressive, that it would impact most substantially, as a proportion of income, upon the relatively poor. This meant any use of the tax by the Scottish Parliament – presumably to improve services and better the lot of Labour's traditional supporters – would disproportionately hit those on lower incomes, those just inside the standard-rate tax band. Spending to help those on low incomes would end up penalising those on low incomes.

Team Dewar could see that. They readily grasped the concept. So, at one stage during Cabinet committee negotiations, they attempted to remedy that flaw. I am reliably told that a proposal was drawn up whereby the Scottish Parliament's tax power would apply beyond the standard rate of income tax. It would apply to the upper band of income tax, too.

Further, it was envisaged that rules would be framed to enable the tax power, the Tartan Tax, to cope with any subsequent remodelling of UK tax bands. The Scottish Parliament's power to vary income tax would, potentially, apply to the full range of UK tax bands, however they might develop, allowing Scotland's fiscal regime to keep pace with UK changes. Under this proposal, the Tartan Tax would not have been the relatively powerless beast we know now. It would have ranged more widely and raised more money. It would arguably have given the Executive and MSPs more discretion.

However, this proposal was swiftly disavowed by Ministers from other departments who were scrutinising the devolution deal. They were keen to contain the scope of devolution, not to extend it. Dewar's team did not push the point. It was difficult enough, in truth, to preserve the Convention scheme from the depredations of Whitehall Ministers and departments. It was concluded that arguing forcibly for a tax plan which went beyond the Convention would not succeed and might backfire.

This internal recognition that the tax power was limited helps to explain Labour's reluctance to sanction its use now. In truth, from a Labour ministerial perspective, the Tartan Tax raises too little money for too much grief. Estimates vary but it is thought that a penny on the standard rate of income tax in Scotland might bring in some £230 million. A tidy sum, but minuscule in comparison with Scotland's £22 billion budget. Why, a penny on income tax by that calculation would not even pay for the cost of a new Parliament building, at present (and rising) prices.

So much for the limited gain. Consider, next, the pain. According to the White Paper, the cost of raising the revenue in Scotland would be some £8 million for government and £6 to £15 million for business. No doubt those figures should by now be updated. Next, the political pain. People do not like paying tax, whatever they may tell eager opinion pollsters. Still less do they like paying a tax which might be perceived as unfair, imposing as it would a higher tax burden on Scotland than England, leaving the citizens of Dumfries paying more than their near neighbours in Carlisle.

Scotland might be persuaded to bear such a burden – *if* it could be demonstrated that the money was required, *if* it could be further demonstrated that the money was definitely being spent in the target area and *if* it could be shown that the expenditure generated productive investment which could not be derived from other means. As many politicians have recognised, those are fairly big *ifs*. Such quibbles do not rule out one party or another advocating use of the tax. We might, for example, see a revival of the notion very briefly floated by Donald Dewar that the tax power should only be used for specific, worthy capital projects.

Again, in the future as in the past, the SNP or the Liberal Democrats might see political gain in vaunting increased spending above total tax restraint. However, they will presumably take note of the particular pitfalls associated with Scotland's distinctive tax power.

Labour and the Conservatives before them have faced a political dilemma over this question of Scottish spending. On the one hand, they want to boast about the cash which Scotland receives: both for their own partisan credibility in Scotland and in an effort to undermine the SNP case for independence. On the other hand, stressing Scotland's spending advantage has had the effect of prompting tough questions in the Commons and elsewhere, particularly from English MPs, as we have already discussed. The quandary is: attempt to taunt the SNP and find that you infuriate your own English back benches.

Despite this backlash, however, successive Secretaries of State for Scotland thought it right to publish detailed assessments of Scotland's claimed spending advantage. Ostensibly a statistical exercise, this became a political hammer with which to hit the SNP. Begun under the Tories, this initiative was pursued by Labour when they took office. In November 1998, for example, Donald Dewar as Scottish Secretary published an analysis of Scottish spending relative to the rest of the UK.[5]

This indicated that total government spending for Scotland in the year under scrutiny (1996/7) was £31.8 billion or 10.1 per cent of the UK total. That was broken down as £24.7 billion of identifiable cash spent specifically to benefit the residents of Scotland plus £3.1

billion of non-identifiable money, Scotland's estimated share of more general UK spending, and £4 billion of other expenditure including debt interest.

For the same year, government revenue in Scotland from tax and other sources – but excluding North Sea oil revenue – was put at £24.7 billion or 8.7 per cent of the UK total. The gap, supposedly filled by borrowing, was therefore put at £7.1 billion or 11.25 per cent of Scottish gross domestic product (GDP). For the same period, it was calculated that the UK's debt ratio was much lower, at 4.25 per cent. Even including revenue from the North Sea in Scotland's budget, the report noted that there would be a deficit of £3.2 billion or 4 per cent of Scottish GDP. Under these circumstances, the UK debt ratio was said to be 3.25 per cent.

The exercise is repeated annually. The latest version emerged on 17 December 2001. By then, the non-oil deficit was put at £4 billion. Net borrowing including an estimate of oil revenues accruing to Scotland was put at £1.6 billion or 1.8 per cent of Scottish gross domestic product (GDP).

This annual exercise regularly concludes, in short, that Scotland spends more than she earns. The political interpretation placed upon this by politicians who adhere to the Union is that Scotland would struggle under independence, that services would have to be cut or taxes would have to go up or both.

Naturally, this conclusion – and indeed the entire exercise – have been subject to challenge from the Nationalists and from some economists. Broadly, the SNP claim that the government exercise undervalues the extent of Scottish revenue and overplays the amount of spending. They note the regular admission by the report itself that the calculations are 'subject to imprecision' due to the need to use estimates. For example, responding to the 2001 version, the SNP's Alex Salmond argued that the variation in Scottish income tax estimates – down, apparently, by one billion pounds on the previous year – was, literally, incredible and vitiated the entire exercise. He further disputed the argument that there was a deficit once oil revenues were included.

Executive insiders concede that the exercise is inevitably 'crude' because the required Scottish data on, for example, income tax is simply not available from the Inland Revenue in the detail required. The hunch is that Salmond may have a point on this, that the income tax estimates for Scotland may indeed be too low. The same sources, however, insist that – even including oil, even factoring in the 'underestimate' of income tax – Scotland has a deficit. Not a huge deficit in terms of the Maastricht criteria. But a deficit.

Accepting that point for the purposes of argument, the debate would then revert to politics. Would growth under independence boost the Scottish economy and hence spending capacity, as the SNP forecasts? Or would the disruption of ending the Union lead to greater economic problems, as the other parties argue?

At an earlier point, in January 1997, the SNP seized upon a Commons written answer from William Waldegrave, then the Tory Chief Secretary to the Treasury. Waldegrave had been asked by the SNP to show the relative financial position of Scotland and England from 1978 to 1995, assuming that 90 per cent of oil revenues had been attributed to Scotland. The Nationalists argued at the time that 90 per cent was a reasonable estimate based on international comparisons, although they used lower estimates for more detailed calculations during the Scottish election.

Waldegrave's answer suggested that, under these hypothetical circumstances, there would have been a net transfer of £27 billion from Scotland to England. That means, say the SNP, that Scotland subsidised England during that period. Sceptics say the outcome reflects the boom in the North Sea of the early 1980s and would not be a permanent feature of the spending relationship between Scotland and England.

Certain economists, notably Professor Andrew Hughes-Hallett of Strathclyde University, have argued that the whole method of analysing Scotland's independent financial position is misplaced. Professor Hughes-Hallett says there is a structural problem in that spending incurred entirely in England may be assumed, under the formula procedure, to have an automatically corresponding impact in Scotland, although that may not truly be the case. He argues further that the approach adopted by those politicians who place a dismal interpretation on the statistics is misdirected. They assume, he says, a static budget whereas Scotland might reorder priorities: for example, opting to reallocate its share of defence and diplomatic spending to other areas.

Professor Hughes-Hallett later led twelve economists in arguing that the issue of full fiscal autonomy for Scotland should be given serious consideration. Under such a system, Scotland would be responsible for controlling all revenue-raising north of the border. While recognising these significant challenges to the claim of a fiscal deficit, it is also fair to say that many other analysts – and, of course, almost all non-Nationalist politicians – have tended to endorse the claim that Scotland's budget does indeed operate at a deficit. The point, they argue, is not that there is a deficit. The United Kingdom and most other established economies have regularly operated a deficit in the past, borrowing in order to finance expenditure or investment. The point is that Scotland's estimated deficit would appear to be disproportionately high: it is a structural deficit, in other words, rather than a temporary phenomenon dictated by prevailing economic circumstances.

This claim of a structural deficit is sharply contested by the Nationalists. The essence of their argument is that Scotland is a rich country, potentially the seventh richest in the world. This claim is advanced further in an economic briefing, already discussed, which has been taken round businesses and others by Jim Mather, the party's Treasurer.

Far from a structural deficit, the Nationalists argue that an independent Scotland could thrive and would be able to cut taxes or improve public services, according to political taste. SNP strategists have long, privately, accepted that they cannot win the war of numbers outright. Their best hope, realistically, is to neutralise an extremely potent fear in the popular imagination, fostered by the SNP's rivals. The charge lodged by Labour and others is that independence would inevitably damage Scotland's economy. Like a defence advocate, the Nationalists hope they can plant a doubt in the public mind over this charge by offering an alternative explanation of events. They plead 'not guilty' in the hope of the charges being found 'not proven'.

No matter how much either side attempts to argue that their economic claims are precise and defensible, the decision for the voters remains broadly an act of faith. Either they believe that Scotland is, broadly, better off in tandem with the rest of the UK or they believe that the economic advantage would lie in setting up an independent state or they believe that the advantages of independence outweigh any financial problems and they are prepared to take the risk.

That assessment is not purely an academic exercise. Naturally, it has an immediate impact in terms of the voters' view of devolution. To be precise, they may be more inclined to look favourably on the decisions of a devolved Parliament if they have firmly implanted in them the conviction that independence would be damaging. By contrast, if the Nationalists can gain the edge in the argument over the cost of independence, then the devolved settlement might come under question.

To conclude this chapter, let me revert to looking at the potential challenge which may confront Scottish spending under devolution: the Barnett squeeze. When I discussed the matter with Donald Dewar, he described Barnett – in customarily cautious language – as 'a mixed blessing'.[6] On other occasions, he was heard to suggest that there might come a time when the Scottish body politic begins to urge a rethink of the very formula it was once so keen to defend. Add that thought to the external pressure previously examined and it is hard to avoid the conclusion that a fundamental review of spending might have to be undertaken at some point.

Of course, should such a review be instigated, Scottish politicians would not necessarily be in purely defensive mode. They might usefully urge remedies to other perceived flaws in the Scottish funding system. Some might point to the lack of significant capital borrowing powers which has led, for example, to the ludicrous situation whereby the bill for a Parliament building designed to grace the Edinburgh skyline for centuries has to be paid from current expenditure over a few years.

This absence of borrowing powers is, arguably, a substantial impediment to the work of the Executive. Certainly, several Scottish Labour politicians – including one or two Ministers – raised a quizzical eyebrow when it was announced that the planned regional assemblies for England were to have limited capital borrowing powers. Admittedly, the budgets to be controlled by these assemblies are tiny by comparison with the extensive scope covered by the Scottish block. In addition, the White Paper[7] on the English regions made clear that capital projects would normally be funded by central government grant. However, the White Paper explicitly envisaged that the regions might want to borrow to fund particular projects, provided they could finance this from revenue.

Again, looking at the Scottish set-up, others might argue that the present system does not contain sufficient fiscal incentives for the Executive to grow the economy. If a Scottish company thrives, then the corporation tax, income tax and VAT which that growth generates all return to the UK Treasury – and not to the Executive.

This factor was present, behind the scenes, in the debate over whether Scotland should go it alone with a bid for the Euro 2008 football championships. Ministers looked extremely sceptically at the estimates of benefits for Scotland, noting glumly that the Executive would fund the investment while any returns went to the Treasury (increased tax take) or to the private sector (hotels and service providers).

Certainly, there are huge political incentives for Executive Ministers to promote growth. No politician wants to be answerable for a stagnant economy or industrial sector. Arguably, those are sufficient to outweigh the lack of fiscal incentive. This need not prevent Scottish politicians raising such issues in any wider debate about public spending and tax.

To conclude, a wide-ranging review is not in the present thinking of the UK government, but it could emerge at some future point, perhaps under a different Chancellor or in different economic circumstances. Such a review could, as I have noted, present a further spending challenge to Scotland. However, there could be pressures in the other direction. As one senior Labour source cautioned me, one should never underestimate the desire of the British state to placate Scotland.

Notes

1. Fraser of Allander Institute, Glasgow: *Quarterly Economic Commentary*, April 1999. Paper by Professor Brian Ashcroft.
2. Fraser of Allander Institute, Glasgow: *Quarterly Economic Commentary*, December 1998. Paper by Professor Neil Kay.
3. Interview with Professor Arthur Midwinter, 24 March 1999.
4. David Bell and Alex Christie (2001), 'The Barnett Formula: Nobody's Child' in Alan Trench (ed.), *The State of the Nations 2001*, London: Imprint Academic, the Constitution Unit, University College London.
5. *Government Expenditure and Revenue in Scotland 1996/97*, published by the Scottish Office Statistics Division, November 1998.
6. Interview with Donald Dewar, 16 January 1998.
7. White Paper, *Your Region, Your Choice – Revitalising the English Regions*, published by the Cabinet Office and the Department for Transport, Local Government and the Regions, 9 May 2002.

14 The European Question

Scotland is a marvellous place for mythology. Indeed, Scots have such a love of legend that they often seem capable of sustaining two mutually contradictory myths at one and the same time. At the most basic level, my fellow citizens can, simultaneously, remain alert to the realities of modern Scotland while painting a picture straight out of Ossian or Brigadoon for visitors. I have frequently done it myself. It is part of our charm.

In one breath, the Scot will praise the Scottish education system and laud the value of well-directed schooling. There may be hints that Scotland's system is superior to that of England or indeed the rest of the globe. The very next moment, scarcely pausing for a second breath, the Scot will talk cloyingly of our native intelligence, of those who display rare talent without the requirement to trouble the education system.

There will be much mention of Rabbie Burns. The scene will be unfolded whereby Burns tramps home from the field, casts aside his plough, scrapes the sharn off his calloused hands, and dashes off a perfect neo-Augustan mock-epic, devising his own verse form in the by-going.

Both self-images are, needless to say, economical with the truth. Burns absorbed as much Classical education as was possible within the limited resources of his family circumstances. By dint of his own efforts, his reading was relatively extensive. An untutored ploughman poet, he certainly was not. Equally, while Scotland's early establishment of a system of parish-based schooling is praiseworthy and its universities, ancient and modern, well worth defending, it may be self-deluding to categorise Scottish education as being of unquestioned international renown.

In the political field, there are several Scottish myths: some with a foundation in fact but often with an added varnish. For example, we are frequently told that Scotland is inherently more egalitarian than England. Such assessments are often based on no more than a left-of-centre voting pattern which may depend rather upon sociological make-up or historical loyalties or the decline of the Tories over the identity question. There are sporadic indications of a somewhat more collectivist approach in Scotland but the prevailing myth substantially overstates this factor.

Perhaps the most persistent contemporary myth is that Scotland is intrinsically pro-European while England is anti, that Scotland adores the European Union while England abhors it. Again, myth does not mean straightforward falsehood. This collective self-image has something of a basis in fact. Opinion polls have occasionally suggested, for example, that Scotland might be more amenable to the single European currency. In Scotland, you will encounter less strident anti-European sentiments than might be overt in the south-east of England.

However, if you accentuate the positive and ask for evidence of Scotland's basic love of all things European, you may simply get vague references to the Auld Alliance with France and to long-distant trade with Belgium. In the last resort, you may even hear wild talk of the Hanseatic league. The untested presumption is that Scotland is, at bottom, internationalist and outward-looking while England is self-obsessed and isolationist.

Either way, fact or fiction, this self-image has a practical significance for modern Scottish politics. Myths matter. The wise political tactician will defer – at least overtly – to the conventional wisdom, as J. K. Galbraith called it. At the same time, our tactician may be attempting to bend public opinion in a different direction. You can generally spot such speeches. They will contain phrases like: 'While acknowledging that . . .'

The European myth matters in Scottish politics because parties have had to factor it into their attitudes to self-government. One key test of the devolved Parliament – and rival schemes – has been its capacity to interact with European affairs, to give Scotland 'A Voice in Europe', a phrase generally uttered as if in capital letters.

This has been particularly true since the SNP became pro-European. Since 1988, this previously Euro-sceptical party has definitively viewed sovereign Scottish membership of the European Union as a counterpoint to claims that Scotland would be breaking valuable collaborative links by sundering the Union with England. Scotland, it is argued, would leave the UK but join Europe as an independent nation. This is not, we are told, separation but reunion.

For the SNP, this stance has provoked a few awkward questions, initially from internal dissidents who regarded the switch as watering down the party's commitment to full Scottish sovereignty. What, they wondered, was the point of breaking with London only to hand power to Brussels? Subsequently, rival parties have challenged the SNP on European detail, for example the party's commitment to Scottish membership of the single European currency. Such challenges became particularly acute after the SNP declared during the 1999 Scottish Parliamentary election campaign that an independent Scotland would adhere to sterling during the transition to joining the euro.

Despite such challenges, of varying intensity, the Nationalists have persisted with adherence to the notion of full European membership. As their policy resolution for the party's National Council in March 2002 declared, with admirable brevity: 'Scotland is in the European Union and the SNP wishes Scotland to stay there.' The document envisages a confederal Europe – as opposed to a European superstate – where each state would retain residual sovereignty 'in respect of constitutional, fiscal and other matters'.

Equally, the Nationalists offer an alternative take on the debate over the euro currency. They note that the launch of the euro in January 2002 has been 'a success'. They offer support for British membership of the euro 'as soon as economic circumstances become appropriate, subject to the people's approval being obtained in a referendum': caveats comparable to those lodged by Gordon Brown and Tony Blair. But they go further, arguing that a single currency 'across the whole of Europe' might hasten Scottish independence – if

it has not already happened – because monetary union would
'remove a significant psychological barrier' to Scotland seeking
political autonomy.

Cynics might see this as the political equivalent of a comfort
blanket, making independence more attractive by reducing the
scope of its power, the extent of its capacity to get things wrong.
Nationalists say it is valid to stress the availability of continuing
economic and political structures, while the opponents of independence are painting a picture of utter decay and breakdown.

On the euro, the other main parties in the Scottish Parliament
seem understandably content to leave policy on this extremely tricky
question to the forum where the decision will be taken, at the UK
political level and by the UK people as a whole in a referendum. The
Scottish LibDems are broadly supportive of the euro, the Scottish
Tories broadly hostile, Scottish Labour deeply attached to applying
Gordon Brown's five tests before euro membership is even sought.

Perhaps taking this issue as their lead, observers from outside
Scotland often make the mistake of assuming that Europe will have
very little impact on devolved, domestic Scottish politics. On the
contrary, it is centrally important, and is one of the three key
structural questions left at least partly unresolved by the devolution
settlement. Partly, this is because the issue of 'Scotland in Europe' is
now at the core of the Nationalist psyche. However, the European
Union presents real, practical challenges for the Scottish Parliament.

Throughout the past few decades, the European question has had
a profound impact on the Scottish political scene, and particularly
the development of Home Rule. The SNP standpoint, in particular,
has meant that advocates of devolution have been careful to stress
the potential for the new Parliament to play a role in European
affairs. Devolutionists could not allow their construction to be
undermined by the suggestion that it would have minimal influence
in the new European powerbase. The description of the role which
a devolved Scotland could play in Europe has, however, varied
sharply over the years.

In the first Convention document,[1] completed in 1990, there was
warm approval for the concept of Scottish involvement in European
affairs. It was argued that 'an effective Scottish voice in the EEC is a
pressing priority'. The very phrase 'EEC' instantly dates the document
but there are other elements that have also been overtaken.

The 1990 document, Convention One, stresses its devolutionary roots, repudiating independence with the remarkably confident assertion that Europe as a whole is abandoning such out-dated notions as sovereignty. The document argues that Scotland should desist from 'struggling to re-establish a nation state at the very time Europe is moving away from this narrow concept'. For now, we need not concern ourselves with this assertion which is, at the very least, arguable and open to qualification. It is the detail, later in the document, which provides more substance for analysis.

The document states that 'Scotland's Parliament should establish a representative office in Brussels to facilitate relations between itself and European Community institutions'. There has been little political dissent from this notion. Indeed, the previous Conservative government – while preserving its opposition to devolution – backed the development of an office in Brussels to foster Scotland's trading and lobbying links, although an entertaining leak of a Scottish Office memo suggested that the concept was not universally popular among Ministers, with one voicing concern about subsidised junketing.

The more intriguing element lies in the further assertion in the 1990 Convention document that 'there should be a statutory entitlement for Scotland's Parliament and/or Executive to be represented in UK Ministerial delegations to the Council of Ministers'. By this, it is presumably meant that the legislation establishing a Scottish Parliament would guarantee that Scottish Ministers could cluster round the fabled 'top table' of European negotiations, and that the UK government could not keep them away.

By the time of the 1995 Convention document, the tone has changed somewhat.[2] 'Great importance' is still attached to links with Europe. There is still support for a representative office in Brussels although it is noted that the Scottish Parliament will 'undertake this through consultation and co-operation with other Scottish and UK organisations which operate European offices so as to maximise impact and provide co-ordination among agencies'. While all this may be inherently sensible and even helpful, it is important to note that the independence of action of the Scottish Parliament's European operation has been qualified. So too has that place at the 'top table'. Instead of the statutory representation offered in 1990, the 1995 document states that 'Scotland's Parliament will be represented in UK Ministerial delegations to the Council of Ministers *where appropriate* [my italics] and Scottish Ministers will lead these UK delegations when the areas under discussion are of specific relevance to Scotland.' New links are also proposed, with the European Committee of the Regions and with the Economic and Social Committee (Ecosoc).

Again, this is a shift of emphasis, not the abandonment of a plan. There is, however, a clear distinction between a statutory right to attend talks and involvement 'where appropriate'. The main element, of course, is who decides when that involvement would be appropriate: Edinburgh or Whitehall, the Scottish executive or the Foreign Office. The 1995 document does not make that point clear. However, the relatively firm forecast that Scottish Ministers will have the opportunity to lead UK delegations still leaves open the prospect of a significant European presence for the Scottish Parliament.

Any lingering doubts were cleared up after Labour took power at Westminster and produced its White Paper in 1997.[3] The chapter on relations with the European Union opens in unequivocal fashion: 'Relations with Europe are the responsibility of the United Kingdom Parliament and Government.' In mitigation, it adds however: 'The Scottish Parliament will have an important role in those aspects of European Union business which affect devolved areas.'

Autonomy of action by the Scottish Parliament is clearly constrained. The picture painted is of the UK government taking the lead, but drawing upon the expertise and advice of the Scottish Parliament and the other elements of the new 'regional government' structure emerging in the UK.

It is stressed that Scottish Ministers will be 'fully involved' in UK discussions about policy towards the EU, but equally it is stressed that there must be 'mutual respect for the confidentiality of those discussions and adherence to the resultant UK line'. No question, in other words, of the Scottish team pursuing a different approach. Self-evidently, this section is an attempt to reconstruct or replicate the concept of Cabinet collective responsibility, which, as we have already discussed, is implicitly undermined by the existence of multiple legislatures and multiple executives. Further, the White Paper proposes that Ministers and officials from the Scottish Executive should be able to play a role at relevant EU Council meetings. They are, it seems, potentially back at the top table. However, it is clear that their participation will be by invitation rather than as of right.

It is stressed that 'the UK lead Minister will retain overall responsibility for the negotiations and determine how best each member
of the team can contribute to securing the agreed policy position
so that, in appropriate cases, Scottish Executive Ministers could
speak for the UK in Councils'. Their role, it is stressed, would be to
'support and advance the single UK negotiating line which they
have played a part in developing'. Unlike the Convention documents drafted in opposition, there is no room for doubt here: the
UK government will set the rules for participation by the Scottish
Executive in EU matters. Statutory representation is out.

While this is the kernel of the chapter, there is a range of other
detailed provisions including a requirement for the Scottish Parliament to implement EU obligations which cover devolved matters
and proposals for the involvement of Scotland in the informal
machinery of EU consultation.

Finally, the notion of a Scottish representative office in Brussels is
restated, although it is argued that it should 'complement rather than
cut across' UKREP, the formal diplomatic body which represents
the views of the UK to European institutions. For the avoidance of
any possible remaining doubt, the chapter concludes by stating that
the 'guiding principle' should be the 'closest possible' co-operation
between the UK government and the Scottish Executive on EU
affairs.

The legislation implementing devolution, the Scotland Act 1998,
gives effect to that approach. It states that relations with the European
Union are reserved to Westminster. Given that statement, there is
very little detailed reference to Scotland's role. This, again, is entirely
consistent: the Scottish Parliament's involvement in Europe is not
statutory in the sense originally envisaged by the Convention so
there is no lengthy provision for it in the legislation. Schedule 5 of
the Act provides a role for the new Parliament in 'assisting Ministers
of the Crown' in relation to European matters.

This confirmation of a subsidiary position for the Scottish Parliament in Europe is, of course, entirely consistent with the overall
approach of the White Paper and the government's devolutionary
measures more generally. As must be repeatedly stressed, the Labour
government's reforms are devolution within the United Kingdom,
not a separation of Scotland and England.

From that perspective, the approach adopted within the White

Paper and the subsequent legislation is not only consistent but inevitable. At the very least, however, it is instructive to note that the final approach in the legislation differs measurably from that promised or outlined in opposition. The early, eager ambition of the Convention has confronted the reality that a European member state must offer a united voice in negotiations, that there can be no room for disparity.

Again, I should stress that I am not remotely criticising the approach adopted in the legislation. Within the parameters of a devolutionary settlement, it is entirely reasonable to stress that the UK must take the lead role. Indeed, given the open scepticism of several Ministers and in sections of Whitehall, it is perhaps remarkable that anything has survived at all from the earlier plans to give the new Parliament a voice in Europe.

The inconsistency, if there is one, perhaps lies rather in the earlier Convention documents. As with the notion of 'entrenching' the devolved Parliament against future abolition, the Convention sought to promise what it could not deliver. It was never feasible that a devolved Parliament within a larger state – where state power persists – could have an autonomous or semi-autonomous role in Europe.

For one thing, common sense dictates that there must ultimately be a single member-state position in European talks. European negotiations are difficult enough without the prospect of a multiple-choice menu of policies emerging from a single member. For another, the apparent ambition for a semi-autonomous role in foreign affairs simply diverged from the core element of the scheme being mapped out for Scotland by the Convention. Given the challenge posed by the Nationalists, it is entirely understandable that the Conventioneers sought to highlight the possibility of a European voice.

However, talk of a statutory role inevitably reflects full independence or the shared power of federalism, not devolution. If there is a single member state and a single state government, there must be a single voice, whatever formal consultations may precede the utterance of that voice.

Those, then, were the stated and varying ambitions which emerged during the road to devolution. How has the European dimension been handled in practice? I believe there are three key elements: the Parliament's relations with Europe, the position of the

Executive and finally Scotland's role, if any, in the hugely significant debate over the future of Europe.

First, the Parliament. MSPs have a dual role with regard to Europe. Most importantly, they have a duty along with the Executive to absorb and implement European legislative directives which impact directly upon devolved areas in the competence of the Parliament. Put simply, they have to translate European law for Scotland.

Second, they have a more nebulous role which arises from their responsibility to examine and consult upon issues of concern to the people of Scotland. In this respect, they can also raise and debate non-legislative matters emerging from the EU which might affect Scotland: from citizenship to enlargement of the Union.

Frankly, the Parliament – through its European Committee – struggled in the early days to cope with these requirements. There appeared to be personal and organisational tensions within the committee. Further, there had not been sufficient preparation for the scope of the task, for the vast volume of legislation emanating from Europe: much of it seemingly trivial but other elements crucially important. The committee, bluntly, appeared swamped by the task in the early days. There was frequent private talk that the avenues of information to MSPs appeared closed, that UK politicians were reluctant to co-operate, that even the Executive seemed to distrust the desire of the Parliament for a role in European affairs.

I believe there was substance to these complaints. Knowledge and contacts are power in politics, and this was a decidedly raw new kid on the block, trying to get in the gang and find out what was going on.

However, I believe that the MSPs themselves were also culpable, largely through inexperience. It can take years to comprehend the arcane structures of Europe: where power truly lies and, equally significantly, where it does not, despite outward appearances. The MSPs in Scotland's new Parliament did not have years. They had days before the European directives and issues for debate began to pile up.

Things are improving, though. I recall travelling to Brussels with a group of Scottish Parliamentarians, headed by George Reid, the deputy Presiding Officer and a sage guide in matters European. This was not the European Committee of the Parliament. These were the MSPs heading the subject committees, responsible for Parliamentary scrutiny of health, education, justice and the rest.

As they held wide-ranging talks with their counterparts from the European Parliament, I could see metaphorical light dawning over the permanent building site that is the Belgian capital. This, you could see them concluding, is where we should have been from the outset. One convener, appraised of an emerging directive under consideration in Brussels, said grimly: 'But that is exactly the subject of our present investigation. Why didn't we know about this?' Why, indeed?

It is important to understand why this matters. Yes, politicians are intrinsically nosy. They want to know what is going on. But there is a deeply serious purpose here too. Remember always that the Scottish Parliament has to implement European legislation on devolved matters. Holyrood, not Westminster.

Since the MSPs are going to have to deal with the outcome, is it not reasonable that they should seek some input to the European discussion process, along with Parliamentarians from every other part of the EU? The conveners on that Brussels trip certainly thought so, and new frameworks, both formal and informal, have been put in place in an effort to ensure that MSPs are better briefed. Most importantly, the objective is to ensure that they are informed about emerging issues while it is possible to influence their final shape. To be fair, Scotland's eight Euro MPs, who seem an energetic bunch, with a desire to enhance their role and, of course, their profile, have shown themselves decidedly willing to assist in this process of connecting Scotland to the EU.

So much for the Parliamentary dimension. Where stands the Executive? As with the MSPs, Executive insiders concede that they have been 'on a steep learning curve from the outset' as regards Europe, particularly the emerging debate about the future of the EU.

European politics is fascinating and frustrating, simultaneously. Yes, you repeatedly remind yourself, it is deeply important, it is the future of the Continent, but does it have to be so ponderous, so obscure, so institutionalised? Vast directives, translated into umpteen languages, and not a word of apparent sense in any of it. In groping your way through this fog, it is useful to recall the political definition devised by Walter Bagehot. He divided the constitution into its dignified and efficient parts. The dignified bit was the pomp and flummery to impress the populace. The efficient bit was the real substance, the hard bargaining.

Similarly, with Europe. The subtle Eurocrat – or member state Minister – will pay frequent obeisance at the temple of the European project: unity, co-operation, consensus, partnership, whatever the current (translated) buzz word happens to be. This is dignified Europe. At the same time, our subtle Eurocrat or Minister will make sure to obtain precise guarantees on issues of national interest, whether it be the duty on whisky or the depth of the olive-oil lake. That, in Bagehot's language at least, is efficient Europe.

The Executive, of course, had an advantage over most MSPs. It had a lexicon prepared, it had a crash course to hand on Euro-speak. It could build upon the base of its predecessor organisation, the Scottish Office with its nascent EU links. These links were significantly strengthened with the opening of Scotland House in Brussels in October 1999. This unit is, to some extent, Scotland in miniature, with a lobbying presence for industry and local government as well as the Executive.

As far as the Executive is concerned, the stated remit for its team in Brussels – initially a seconded senior civil servant, three desk officers and two locally recruited staff – is to provide operational support and information to Edinburgh. At the same time, critically, the Brussels unit is required to 'assist in influencing EU policy' and to 'raise Scotland's profile in the EU'. It will be seen instantly that these are overtly diplomatic tasks which might, arguably, clash at some point with the aims and objectives of the United Kingdom permanent representation in Brussels (UKREP), which is just across the road from Scotland House. Theoretically, the Executive might be seeking to influence EU policy in a direction inimical to UKREP, or to raise Scotland's profile at the expense of a competing English region.

In practice, however, this potential for external diplomatic tension, which is privately recognised by insiders, has been assuaged by internal diplomacy. Scotland House works closely and well with UKREP. Back in Edinburgh, the team of civil servants working on the European brief maintain daily contact with Brussels and Whitehall, most notably the Foreign Office and the powerful European Secretariat of the Cabinet Office.

There are key advantages. First, the main players involved are all either career diplomats or members of the home civil service. It is important to remember that the Scotland Act provided that the

Executive's staff would remain firmly linked to the UK civil-service structure. Crucially, the Europe team within the Executive have access to Cabinet Office papers which alert them to emerging issues. This is an important early warning system. Second, there is top-level political direction within the Executive to ensure the system works. As Finance Minister, Jack McConnell was responsible for Europe and external affairs. He made sure he took that remit with him when he was moved to Education. The brief has remained in senior hands under McConnell's leadership of the Executive, although, intriguingly, not exactly as first scheduled. When McConnell took over as First Minister, senior insiders had expected him to retain control of the European brief. He cherished its importance and status.

I had been told that the external affairs brief might form part of a new, beefed-up joint remit for the First Minister and his Liberal Democrat deputy. But, at the last minute, as McConnell was going through the grid of ministerial responsibilities in detail, he turned to Europe and advised a senior civil servant: 'Just give it to Jim.' So Jim Wallace, the deputy First Minister and Scottish leader of a party unequivocally committed to the European 'project', ended up in charge of Scottish links with the EU. However, the First Minister has certainly not distanced himself entirely from such matters. McConnell is keenly aware of the strategic, economic and political importance of Scotland in Europe.

The third factor cementing the relationship between devolved Scotland, the UK and Europe is Her Majesty's office for Foreign and Commonwealth affairs. In Whitehall, several UK and English departments found devolution puzzling, even troublesome. They had been used to taking their own decisions, clearing them where necessary with Downing Street or the Treasury. Now, particularly in preparing for European negotiations, they were constitutionally obliged to consult upstarts in what they instinctively thought of as the regions. Fair enough, they had been used to taking the Scottish Office on board. But this was different. Why, some of these Executive types seemed to think they were a government!

I am keenly aware that that is an utterly simplistic caricature. There were early problems with departments like the old Ministry of Agriculture which occasionally neglected to transmit information in sufficient detail to the Executive and its relevant (Liberal Democrat)

Minister. Further, it seems that the Department of Environment, Transport and the Regions was difficult at first. This massive department, which includes responsibility for English regional affairs within its remit, apparently jibbed at the autonomy of decision-making which devolution confirmed for Scotland.

However, as with any other development, the civil-service machine has generally managed to adapt and the system works, in its own fashion. Things have settled down. By contrast, from the outset the Foreign Office completely grasped the concept and implications of devolution. One senior Scottish Executive insider told me that the Foreign Office was a 'very good friend' of Scotland and the devolution project.

Within the Foreign Office, the issue of devolution is 'main-streamed'. That means it is a key objective for all departments, across the board, to consult and work with the devolved territories. Incoming department heads, incoming ambassadors across the world are specifically briefed on the importance of this task. When the new devolved bodies were set up, the then Permanent Secretary, Sir John Kerr, described devolution privately as the most significant structural challenge facing his department.

Why, you might ask? Well, first, it was the responsibility of the Foreign Office to ensure that the UK's new constitutional set-up did not disturb international links. Diplomatically, the Foreign Office had to make devolution work. The cynic might jibe that the Foreign and Commonwealth Office is used to handling troublesome colonies. Such a remark would undoubtedly produce a watery mandarin smile. However, there is a degree of truth in such satire. The Foreign Office quite definitely wants to make devolution work, but not purely as an academic or administrative exercise. Its corporate concern, the concern of Her Majesty's government more widely, is to protect the state, to show that the present, reformed set-up can provide more than Scottish independence would offer. To defend the Union, if you like.

It is important to understand that this is more than a transient ministerial policy, translated into action by diplomats. This is a core objective shared by Ministers and the administrative machinery of the state. There is common ground, or a 'grand design': a descrip-tion offered to me by one senior civil servant who was undoubtedly well aware that it is the title of an episode of *Yes, Prime Minister*.

I would not want to make *too* much of this. It should not come as a great surprise that the instinct of Her Majesty's government is to protect and preserve the boundaries of Her Majesty's realm. Further, the attitude towards Northern Ireland indicates that the state can be pragmatic in the face of developments. Remember John Major's Downing Street declaration in December 1993 when it was said that Britain retained 'no selfish, strategic or economic interest in Northern Ireland'.

With regard to Scotland – and the SNP policy of an independent Scotland in Europe – I believe the various politicians, from across the parties, who have commented on this were sincere when they said that Scotland could be independent if its people so decided. It is, however, perhaps helpful simply to bear in mind that the defence of the Union is regarded as a core motivation for the standing machinery of government, both north and south of the border. So there is a significant underlying reason for diplomats to ensure that Scotland's voice is at least heard, if not completely heeded, in the preparation for European Council negotiations. Scotland will not get everything – who does? But the Foreign and Commonwealth Office wants to ensure that Scotland has a say.

There is, I am told, a further motivation in taking devolution extremely seriously. The new model UK can be marketed to the rest of the world as a modernised, advanced democracy. Devolution, apparently, sells well. One Executive insider reminded me that Britain had established a new form of government in Scotland 'without a shot being fired'. This, apparently, intrigues visitors from overseas, particularly those from less stable parts of the world.

In the past, when foreign dignitaries visited the UK, they would be shown Westminster and Whitehall as a matter of course. If they inquired about alternative forms of government, they were taken to the City of London to meet the Lord Mayor. Now the devolved territories – and especially Edinburgh with its splendid Castle – are high on the list. Equally, devolved Ministers travelling abroad are fully briefed by the Foreign Office. The view is that anything they can recoup for their area is a plus for the UK. They are given full support.

Initially, there was a diplomatic snag over how to style such individuals. For example, Sir Reg Empey from the Northern Ireland Executive was due to visit China. The Chinese inquired closely as to his status. These things matter, especially to the Chinese. It would affect whom he met, the extent of the reception. The Foreign Office thought for a bit and tried out a few formulae such as: 'He is a member of a power-sharing coalition executive within a territory of the UK which has devolved administrative and partial legislative powers over most domestic matters.' They gave up and informed the Chinese: 'He is a government Minister.'

With regard to Scotland and Scottish Executive visits abroad, Foreign Office insiders talk about 'a two flags' solution. Yes, devolved Scottish Ministers are flying the Saltire when they travel abroad, but, with Foreign Office back-up, they are waving the Union Flag too. New Britain, new diplomacy.

At first, the Foreign Office handled such liaison through the Devolved Administrations Department. DAD, if you will forgive an appalling pun, took a keenly paternal interest in his new charges. Things have moved on and such matters are now tackled by a reconstituted Parliamentary Relations and Devolution Department (PRDD). Either way, the Foreign Office takes devolution deeply seriously.

However, is there not a potential problem down the line, particularly with regard to European negotiations? It is not difficult to envisage circumstances in which there could be an awkward dilemma. Let us suppose that at some point in the future the European Union is considering a substantial revision of the rules governing fisheries. Perhaps the quota or the available fishing areas are to be altered. Let us suppose that the UK's interests in this matter are not uniform, that, for example, the Scottish fleet broadly wants one approach to be adopted while the fishing towns of the south-west of England favour another.

Negotiations are due to open in Brussels and the Scottish Executive, with its particular interest in this field, is invited to play its part in 'assisting Ministers of the Crown', as the Scotland Act provides. The relevant Scottish Minister duly attends preparatory talks to settle the single UK line which will be advanced at the European negotiations. But she faces a quandary. It swiftly becomes clear that the demands of the Scottish fleet are out of step with the rest of the UK. A common UK position cannot be formulated around those demands. Further, the Scottish Minister suspects that the fisheries row may be used by the UK government in a trade-off over another

EU controversy, perhaps of more general relevance to the economy of the UK.

How, then, does our notional Scottish Minister proceed? She can argue strenuously for the Scottish position. In such circumstances, however, the fishing interests of Cornwall and Devon would be bound to complain, with some justification, that they are being thwarted by a Minister they did not elect from an Executive they cannot hold to account in a Scottish Parliament with which they have absolutely no connection. In any event, the UK Minister might well decide that the common state position runs contrary to the Scottish demands. Alternatively, our Minister can hold her peace and sit placidly on the fringe of the eventual Brussels talks as a line perceived to be inimical to the interests of the Scottish fleet is advanced and agreed. In such circumstances, the Minister can expect a relatively warm reception from the Scottish Parliament – and the Scottish fleet – on her return.

I am aware that this is a deliberately extreme example where the interests are polarised. I am aware that most preparatory negotiations will involve an element of give and take. It is, however, by no means inconceivable that a Scottish Minister might be unable to square the apparent interests of her own backyard with the ultimate obligation to pursue a common UK line.

It will be argued that this quandary often confronted Ministers from the territorial departments under the pre-devolutionary system. They frequently found that their 'regional' interest departed to some degree from the wider UK perspective. Certainly, this is true, and it is arguable that matters will continue to proceed smoothly by the customary system of trading off one demand against another, that Scotland, provided its Ministers are energetic and alert, should be able to chalk up as many, or more, successes than concessions. There is, however, I believe, something of a structural difference between the old system and the new.

The Scottish Parliament may be of a different political make-up from Westminster. The May 1999 elections, for example, left Scotland with a coalition in a hung Parliament by contrast with the huge Labour majority at Westminster. The Scottish Parliament will certainly develop its own dynamic, command its own loyalty. In the past, territorial Ministers such as the Scottish Secretary were advancing their demands within a single Cabinet made up of colleagues and were answerable to a common Parliament in which their party, by definition, could reasonably expect support from its own majority.

Now and in the future, Ministers from the Scottish Executive will be haggling with UK Ministers from a different Parliament and, possibly, from a different party. At present, you may find a LibDem Scottish Minister negotiating with a Labour counterpart in Westminster. In future, who knows? A Labour or SNP Scottish Minister in talks with a Westminster Tory? Whatever the political complexion, the UK Ministers will be answerable to and influenced by one set of party political realities. The Scottish Ministers will be governed by another. In practical terms, that means that the doctrine of collective Cabinet responsibility cannot be enforced across the two administrations. Civil servants cannot offer identical, unfettered briefing to both sides. At its simplest, the UK Prime Minister cannot sack the Scottish Rural Affairs Minister.

Unlike Cabinet colleagues, the two sets of Ministers may have no overriding partisan motivation for reaching an agreed deal, for preserving an appearance of unity. It may, indeed, be in their political interests to be seen to be standing up against the other side. Privately, Foreign Office diplomats and Executive insiders are alert to this issue. They mutter that there can be no guarantees of smooth co-operation, say, ten years down the line if the political colour of the administrations in Edinburgh and London is markedly different. However, the same insiders swiftly offer reassurance that the machine coped with the transition to devolution and could, arguably, cope with varying political demands. Finally on this point, never forget the underlying motivation: to cement Scotland into the Union. One should never underestimate the capacity of the state to mould its daily operations to a long-term fundamental objective.

There are, however, clear limits to the operation of this in practice. The Foreign Office works on three levels with regard to preparations for European negotiations. Officials will maintain informal contact between the administrations, on a daily basis if necessary. There may be formal talks in advance of important negotiations in order to establish the common UK line. Finally, if necessary, these preparatory talks may involve the full-scale Joint Ministerial Committee (JMC) that has been established to bring together members of the various executives. A JMC covers each important area of governmental activity where there is cross-over between Whitehall and the devolved administrations.

While it is stressed that this structure is designed to link Whitehall with all the devolved territories, it is tacitly recognised that Scotland may well seek to play a bigger role in European talks, given the nature of the Scottish Parliament and the history of political controversy over this issue in Scotland.

In many ways, of course, this simply replicates the previous arrangements for gathering and assessing the views of the territorial departments like the Scottish and Welsh Offices. Again, though, there is a clear structural difference.

As mentioned above, Ministers from the devolved administrations receive Foreign Office briefing and guidance but not to the same degree as that available to Ministers from Westminster. It has been decided within the Foreign Office that the briefing to devolved Ministers can only be strictly factual, an enhanced version of the information which might be made available, for example, to a British company or public-sector organisation of recognised status. There can be no question of guiding devolved Ministers on policy or discussing strategic possibilities. The problem, again, is that the devolved executives lie beyond the reach of the doctrine of collective responsibility which covers the Westminster government. Further, the Foreign Office might find itself briefing party political opponents of their Westminster bosses. Again from a Foreign Office perspective, it is taken as read from the legislation that UK Ministers will select, lead and guide the negotiating teams in European talks. Ministers from the devolved administrations may well be involved: indeed, given the wider objective, that is seen as a plus. However, that involvement must be within the ambit of an agreed UK line, as the White Paper made clear.

Given the potential requirement to consult three devolved administrations, this seems – to the Foreign Office – to be simple, common sense. As I have argued elsewhere, within the context of a devolved settlement, it is very hard indeed to disagree with that judgement, logically. However, particularly in Scotland, there may well be dissent, politically, either over the practical implications as they affect individual issues and Scottish grievances or over the principle of London control of influence. The Scottish Nationalists, understandably given their viewpoint, do not take kindly to Whitehall's supervisory role.

In a speech before the 1999 elections, the then SNP leader Alex Salmond made that concern explicit.[4] He told the European Institute in Brussels that Scotland would not be satisfied with 'subsumed' involvement in European Union matters. He warned: 'If the UK position is to be given in the Council of Ministers, it must never be given without either an assent from Scotland or a dissent from Scotland. Our democracy demands nothing less.'

Such an approach, if applied rigorously, might end up breaching the approach spelled out in the White Paper and implemented by the Foreign Office. It would risk infringing the confidentiality rule governing preparatory talks and the establishment of a firm, single UK line. Again if fully applied, it might even give the Scottish Executive and Parliament an effective veto over UK proposals that they did not favour.

Self-evidently, such a veto would not be tolerated by the UK administration, and has not, of course, been attempted in practice. Rather, the devolved Executive has worked within the parameters and avenues of influence described earlier. Executive Ministers have repeatedly sought to play down the potential for this to cause friction. As External Affairs Minister, it fell to Jack McConnell to respond to an SNP-instigated debate at Holyrood on 21 June 2001.

The SNP had argued that Scotland's voice was inevitably muted in Europe and in international affairs generally. McConnell argued that Scotland would have 'less influence' by ending the Union because we would be 'divorcing ourselves from the one country that has membership of the G8, the EU, the Commonwealth and NATO, and permanent membership of the United Nations Security Council – the United Kingdom'.

Apart from the now familiar use of the metaphor of divorce – a powerful image for Labour against the SNP – this speech essentially deployed what has become known as the 'Big Stick' argument. By this, I mean the assertion that Scottish interests are best advanced by deploying the diplomatic, negotiating and voting clout of the UK.

This argument was frequently used by Donald Dewar. Delivering a lecture in January 1999, he scorned the suggestion that Scotland might have distinctive interests that might diverge from those of the rest of the UK.[5] Indeed, he listed key issues such as trade policy, the single market, agriculture, fisheries and regional policy, and declared, confidently, that 'in every case Scotland's interest and the interests of the rest of the UK are aligned'.

Dewar went further in this lecture and sought to question the capacity of small member states to influence European decisions in their favour. He derided the claims surrounding the power of such small states as 'the tyranny of the tiny', plainly implying that its impact was overstated. He added: 'The brute fact is that even in today's European Union, the big member states call the shots. Enlargement is likely to see voting power better balanced to share of population. More power to the big. Enlargement is likely to see an extension of majority voting. What use the Scottish veto?'

As I have noted elsewhere, I regard this line of argument, which has been followed in all essential respects by Dewar's successors, as flawed. It may well be true that the accession of other states will alter the voting balance. It is incontestably true that a big state like Germany or the UK has more clout than a small state like Denmark or Ireland. Neither of these statements, however, have particular relevance for a substate nation like Scotland in determining its standpoint within Europe.

While it is true that the UK has more clout than Denmark, it may also be true that Denmark has more direct clout – as a member state with a place at that fabled 'top table' – than Scotland, whose views are filtered through UK membership. It depends on whether we accept the assessment that the UK's interests and those of Scotland are always aligned.

If they are, then Scotland can rest easy, knowing that the muscle of the UK is flexing in its interests. If they are not, and I think it at least feasible they may occasionally diverge, then the potency of the UK may not be of much good to Scotland. Indeed, it is possible that the UK's bargaining clout may end up directed against the narrower interests of Scotland. The key issue is the relative importance attached to individual demands. EU negotiations always involve a trade-off. Germany, for example, will moderate its demand for a reduction in its budgetary contributions, provided France is willing to drop its objection to a trade-liberalisation measure which the Germans are particularly anxious to secure.

In such circumstances, it is at least feasible that Scotland may attach particular importance to some sectoral interest such as fishing

or transport, while UK negotiators may be keener to see movement
on trade reform or EU expansion. It is, again, feasible that the UK
negotiating team will be willing to drop issues that a Scottish team,
from a different standpoint, would wish to pursue.

I am very far from asserting that there is an incontestable case for
autonomous Scottish membership of the European Union. It may
well be that Scotland benefits by being able to borrow a big stick
from Westminster. It is arguable that an independent Scotland would
be sidelined.

Donald Dewar noted in his lecture that no European region has
broken from its member state to assume sovereign membership of
the EU. In passing, it might also be noted, however, that there has
scarcely been a rush of small nation states seeking to merge with
their bigger neighbours to enjoy a share of their negotiating might.

It is not sufficient, I feel, simply to state that the UK carries weight,
and that Scotland intrinsically benefits. This is an assertion which will
require to be tested over a long period while the Scottish Parliament
and Executive continue to settle into their respective roles. It is, at
the very least, arguable. It may, in certain circumstances, be wrong.

What then of the third element which I mentioned at the outset: the future of Europe? What role will a devolved Scotland play
in this debate, if any? Let us remind ourselves briefly of the basics.
A wide-ranging debate on the future of the European Union was
launched at the EU's Intergovernmental Conference (IGC) in Nice
in December 2000. This complemented existing initiatives designed
to make more efficient use of the existing structures of the EU. The
objective is an exchange of ideas leading to the preparation of a plan
for reform to be presented to a further IGC in 2004. As part of this
initiative, EU member states signed the Laeken Declaration on 15
December 2001. This opened with familiarly dignified sentiments
about the European project, before getting down to the core
problem.

Citizens, it was said, 'undoubtedly support the Union's broad
aims' – of security, peace and co-operation – but they did not always
see the link between those goals and the Union's everyday action.
What they wanted, apparently, were 'more results, better responses
to practical issues and not a European superstate or European institutions inveigling their way into every nook and cranny of life'.

The declaration contained plans for a Convention on the future of Europe, convened by Valéry Giscard d'Estaing, the former President of France. It was stated that the Convention, which has since begun work, would consist of fifteen representatives of the heads of state or government, one from each member state; thirty members from 'national Parliaments', two from each member state; sixteen members of the European Parliament; and two Commission representatives. In addition, those countries presently negotiating to join the EU – the accession countries – were to be given membership 'without being able to prevent any consensus which may emerge among the member states'.

Plainly, then, this is a very substantial rethink of the entire EU structure; its ways of working, its links to the voters. This is big, ground-breaking politics, with the potential to influence the decision-making process affecting individuals across the whole of the Union. Is there a role for Scotland, or other devolved territories?

Certainly, key figures at the substate 'regional' level in Europe thought so, and had anticipated the question. On 22 February 2001, the Minister President of Flanders, Patrick Dewael – head of a devolved Belgian territory with significant powers – had convened a colloquium in Brussels to respond to the 'grand debate' begun by the Nice IGC. Present were representatives of North Rhine Westphalia, Bavaria, Salzburg, Wallonia, Catalonia and Scotland.

This initiative led to the signing of the Flanders Declaration in May 2001 by the same seven constitutional regions, as they styled themselves. As First Minister, Henry McLeish signed this declaration on behalf of Scotland. The Flanders document was later endorsed by a much larger gathering of regions with legislative powers, in Liège on 15 November 2001.

The Flanders document is bold. It anticipates the Giscard Convention on the future of Europe and states that the constitutional regions 'demand to participate directly in the preparatory work for the Intergovernmental Conference of 2004'. It notes that the political role of the regions must be strengthened within the European Union. Such regions, Scotland included, are obliged to implement European legislation 'but do not have a sufficient say in preparing and determining European policies and legislation'. This, seemingly, must change.

On the face of it, a blunt demand for action. Flanders and its fellows, it seems, are not content to be represented by member states, big or small. Where, one might ask, is your big stick now? Certainly, that was the interpretation placed on this declaration by the SNP and others. The Nationalists chided Henry McLeish for subsequently turning this bald statement of action into an aspiration, an aim. They mocked, they jeered.

The inside story, however, is somewhat different. The Minister President of Flanders, I am sure, was sincere in seeking to develop a distinct 'regional' element to the debate on the new Europe. The other signatories, Scotland included, were undoubtedly also seeking to advance the debate in their own interests.

It is not accurate, however, to say that McLeish watered down his commitment to Flanders in subsequent statements. That commitment was already fairly liquid when pen was put to paper.

Let us go back to the text of the Flanders Declaration. I am told that Executive civil servants and Ministers 'sweated blood' to get the word 'considered' into the text. Indeed, it features at various points, not least in the final section where the constitutional regions get down to the nub of their aims. Boiling it all down, they want action in three areas: a strengthened Committee of the Regions; better links between regions and the European Parliament; and, crucially, the right for the constitutional regions as well as member states to air grievances in the European Court of Justice.

However, by contrast with the previously bold language, the text says merely that the constitutional regions would 'wish' these topics to 'be considered' among others. Regardless of how others viewed the Declaration, this was key for the Executive. This was the wording which enabled McLeish to sign. It was a request for consideration – not an unalloyed demand for action. This may seem a diplomatic nicety, and certainly other sections of the document read more like a declaration of hostilities than a polite request for a debate. However, the Executive was satisfied that it had obtained a get-out clause. Failing this, McLeish would have had to walk away from the talks.

I am told further that the Executive was unhappy with the notion of direct regional access to the European Court of Justice. Scotland, apparently, preferred the notion of a watchdog body to monitor the operation of subsidiarity, the EU principle by which decisions are meant to be taken at the appropriate level, rather than always shunted to the top. There was also an underlying sense that Scotland did not want to upset the UK government unnecessarily. The Flanders Declaration was signed on 28 May, at the very culmination of the UK General Election campaign.

Although this was never brought to a head, I understand the Foreign Office was nervous about the emerging shape of the Flanders initiative. It was beginning to feature on radar screens as a potential diplomatic blip, an intrinsic challenge to the carefully guarded role of member states in the EU. McLeish, naturally, cleared his stance on Flanders personally with Robin Cook, the Foreign Secretary.

In the event, any difficulty was avoided. The Executive was anxious to work with its fellow 'constitutional regions'. As a relatively new member of the club, it felt frankly flattered at being invited to join the big hitters; at least, 'big' in regional terms. It would not, however, sign a declaration which openly challenged the status of EU member states. Hence that word 'considered'.

There was even a further effort to replace the word 'demand' at various points with the more polite 'ask'. However, weary civil servants acknowledged that 'demand' was merely a transliteration of the French verb *'demander'* – meaning 'to ask'. They gave way. The upper echelons of the EU, no doubt, gave due consideration to this request. But, in practice, little has emerged to date. The Giscard Convention is operating as envisaged, with member state rather than direct regional participation.

Scotland will have representation through, of course, the UK membership; through European Parliamentarians such as Neil MacCormick, who is a member; and, indirectly, through the Committee of the Regions, which has observer status, with six members drawn from Belgium, Italy, Germany, Spain and France.

I said earlier that it is important in Europe to recognise where power does *not* lie. Palpably, it does not reside in the Committee of the Regions. This body, which draws members from organisations ranging from local authorities to large legislative regions, has frankly not delivered upon expectations. Indeed, it is laughable to think that there was once a furious political debate over how many delegates Scotland would be permitted to send to the Committee. It is a useful ventilation point for issues. It can advise, it can chide. But it does not have clout, and the big regions like Flanders know it.

This episode had one entertaining follow-up. David McLetchie, the Scottish Conservative leader, suggested on BBC Radio Scotland's

Politics Tonight programme in January 2002 that Scotland should have an independent voice in the Giscard Convention. This was pursued by the Tory MEP Struan Stevenson, who said: 'States which are not yet members of the EU will have more say on what happens than Scotland – and that's ridiculous.' In response to that, the Labour MEP Bill Miller was quoted as saying: 'It's time Struan took out his SNP card. Scotland will be represented through the UK, and that's fine.'

Certainly the Tories were keenly aware that they were indulging in quasi-nationalist, rebellious talk, somewhat at odds with their support for the status of the United Kingdom. McLetchie told me he was alert to that hazard, but that it was important to make a distinction between 'powerful, legislative regions and wee toon cooncils' in deciding the future of Europe. He would, I feel sure, be a welcome guest in Flanders.

The Tories, of course, were pursuing their objective of rebuilding their credibility as a party capable of standing up for Scottish interests. It would appear, also, that they were impressed by the logic of the Flanders case.

It is important to stress that the Executive went along with part of that logic too. Henry McLeish may have been clear that he was featuring caveats in his support for the Flanders Declaration. But he did sign. He signed willingly. And there have been similar sentiments expressed by other Ministers.

In April 2002, the First Minister Jack McConnell said, 'the governance of the new, enlarged Europe' should be based upon 'strong democratic credentials'.[6] In particular, that meant involving democratic institutions at varying levels.

In response to this speech in Brussels, the First Minister was invited to draft for consideration the formal opinion which will be presented to the Giscard Convention by the Committee of the Regions. McConnell said he would dwell upon economic prosperity, social justice and democracy. The Executive described this task as 'an important role in shaping the new Europe'. The SNP appeared less enthused. They accused McConnell of 'scraping the bottom of the barrel' in an effort to overstate Scotland's European influence. The new role, they said, was 'demeaning to the office of First Minister'.

I believe both comments are wrong. First, the Nationalists are trying to compare pommes with poires in their diagnosis of contemporary Europe. In essence, they are saying that Scotland's devolved First Minister does not support independence in Europe. Understandable from a Nationalist standpoint, but trite and just a fraction churlish. Equally, though, nothing will convince me that the Committee of the Regions as presently constituted is a European powerhouse. I suspect McConnell knows that only too well. Hence his repeated pressure for the substate Parliamentary level to be given a clear voice in the emerging new Europe.

Earlier, as External Affairs Minister, McConnell delivered a speech in Brussels in March 2001.[7] He said he had no wish to undermine the important role of member states but – again deploying a now familiar argument – he noted that 'the impact of European governance on those who have devolved authority to legislate is significant'.

Specifically, McConnell urged three issues: a code of conduct to ensure that Scottish views can be taken into account *before* legislation goes to the European Council and Parliament; a power to allow Scotland to 'implement EU policies in a flexible way that makes sense for Scottish conditions', with particular reference to areas like fisheries policy; and the watchdog on subsidiarity discussed earlier, perhaps involving representation for legislative regional Parliaments.

Of these, the first is partly constitutional structure, but also, arguably, largely a matter of developing custom and practice. If Scotland wants to be in at the ground floor of EU decisions, the Executive and Parliament must continue to sharpen up their act.

I think the second point – flexibility in implementation – is most likely to be troublesome. Arguably, many of the tensions within the EU are presently caused by flexible interpretation of the rules, for example over farm quotas or industrial aid. I think the EU institutions may take some persuading on this point, if it is to be pursued.

The third point, however, policing subsidiarity, is likely to feature in the wider debate over the future of Europe. Jack McConnell expanded upon this particular issue in a Brussels speech on 6 June 2002. The First Minister suggested that the EU establish a 'Subsidiarity Council', with perhaps nine members, linked to existing Parliaments. This body – modelled on arrangements in France for settling constitutional squabbles – would be empowered to rule 'quickly' on whether the EU was acting beyond its powers, whether particular decisions should be devolved to 'regional' Parliaments. McConnell's plans contained provision for appeals to this body before a European law had been adopted.

As ever, there is a macro-political dimension to this question of the relative European status of member states and substate regions. It is important to realise that this is far from being a question that is confined to the UK. Indeed, in some respects, it comes into sharper focus in other member states, notably Spain.

The Spanish regions have very varied powers. Some are little more than enhanced local authorities. Others, like Catalonia and the Basque territory, have substantial autonomy, predicated upon historical and language differences.

The Spanish government, however, is decidedly keen to maintain a degree of central control, particularly when it comes to foreign affairs and relations with the European Union. At a news conference in Madrid in January 2002, the Spanish Prime Minister José Maria Aznar dealt bluntly with the question of regional representation in the EU. He said: 'The EU is a union of States. Each State decides on its own internal organisation. This is the reality.' At the same news conference, the EU Commission President Romano Prodi made plain that the European institutions could not and would not interfere in such sensitive matters. He said: 'Spain has the last word on Basque representation in the EU. The extent to which regions are represented is a matter for the States and is not a matter for the Commission.' Britain's asymmetrical system of devolution differs from that of Spain, where there are provincial governments throughout the country with varying degrees of power, and is substantially different from the system in Germany where the Länder (or regional states) divide responsibilities with the federal government.

Ministers from the Länder, for example, will normally take the lead in European negotiations where the subject matter under discussion falls into their area of responsibility. In such cases, it will be a Minister from one of the sixteen Länder who will speak for Germany, nominated by the Bundesrat, the German upper Parliamentary chamber which represents regional interests.

Further, the Bundesrat has considerable power within Germany to frustrate or delay the programme of the federal government if it does not like the direction advocated by federal Ministers. Obviously, this clout gives the Länder a bargaining tool to obtain concessions, although it is a lever which is best used sparingly and in order to obtain an advance for the entire Länder sector rather than for a single Land.

Länder politicians are big league in Germany: Chancellor Gerhard Schröder was formerly the President of the Bundesrat. They can exercise power on the European stage: former Chancellor Helmut Kohl was obliged to reverse his stand on a proposed deal concerning immigration and justice matters at the European summit in Amsterdam following protests from the Länder who had responsibility for implementing part of the package.

However, even in Germany, there is central suspicion of the peripheral regions. There are influential German voices raised against the power of the Länder. It is claimed that the system is costly, cumbersome and bureaucratic. There is talk that the federal government may seek to re-establish the power of the centre at the expense of regional influence.

So the Executive's call for a stronger regional voice in Europe – even with the Flanders caveats – will not be entirely welcome. It will cause disquiet, and not just in London. If Scotland is serious about pursuing that greater role – and the Executive statements are consistent, if occasionally diluted – then it will be a substantial task.

As with so much in politics, it is impossible to be precise about Scotland's future devolved role in Europe. We may benefit enormously from building new alliances across Europe. Whitehall and the Foreign Office may display a fatherly concern for our progress which produces genuine results. Alternatively, we may find the new structure frustrating and chafe at the constraints on our power.

Notes

1. *Towards Scotland's Parliament*, a report by the Constitutional Convention, presented November 1990.
2. *Scotland's Parliament, Scotland's Right*, Constitutional Convention, November 1995.
3. *Scotland's Parliament*, Government White Paper, the Scottish Office, July 1997.
4. Alex Salmond, Lecture, the European Institute, Brussels, February 1999.
5. Donald Dewar, Lothian European Lecture, Edinburgh, January 1999.
6. Jack McConnell, speech to Committee of the Regions Commission for Constitutional Affairs and Regional Governance, Brussels, 26 April 2002.
7. Jack McConnell, speech to hearing on governance, Brussels, 16 March 2001.

15 The English Question

Towards the end of the nineteenth century, Gladstone attempted to answer the Irish Question. The Parliament now established in Edinburgh is an attempt to address the Scottish Question. It is reasonable to argue that the great conundrum which has yet to be tackled seriously is the question of how to govern England under the reformed constitution of the UK.

Perhaps I should start with a couple of bald statements. The English Question is first and foremost for the people of England to address: that is, if they believe there is a problem at all. In reality, as opposed to perception, the governance of England has not been altered at all by Scottish devolution.

That last remark, I know, risks occasioning an outburst of spluttered indignation. Hasn't England been changed utterly by Scottish devolution? From outraged commentators, we hear tales of Celtic invaders insolently telling the English what to do. All the Scots ever do is whinge. Outrageous. Send them packing. If they want to run Scotland, good luck to them, but why should they run England as well?

For example, there is George Trefgarne in *The Daily Telegraph* with a balanced, thoughtful contribution to the debate.[1] He suggests that London should 'hold on to Gibraltar and get Spain to accept

Scotland instead'. Trefgarne continues: 'Those of us who live in England were first hurt, then bemused and are now angered at the process of Scottish devolution. It is a swindle, whereby the Scots receive better public services at English expense and get to send their tartan army of MPs to Westminster too.' Can you feel Trefgarne's pain, a blend of bafflement and lost Empire? He moans about money but his Gibraltar comparison discloses the real angst about Scotland: yet another colony gone.

However, for me as a Scottish journalist, the most intriguing and entertaining aspect of monitoring the English response to devolution has been that the sharpest, most horror-struck comments have come not from the Tory commentators in *The Telegraph*, but from the liberal Left. I feel sure this has a partisan explanation. The Left fears its cause will suffer from the erosion – or disappearance – of the Scottish vote in UK politics.

As above, much of the right-wing comment has consisted of tedious similes from *Braveheart*, complete elision of the difference between devolution and independence, and world-weary sorrow that the Scots are being misled. The finale is usually a thunderous warning to the people of England to wake up before it is too late.

Occasionally, there is a defiant, even jubilant note. Go, if you must, you Scots. England will be Tory forever! Certainly, Scotland's consistent contribution of large numbers of Labour MPs to the Commons adds a degree of force to such bravado from the Right, although the 1997 and 2001 General Elections, when England also voted Labour in large numbers, are rather inconvenient counterpoints for that argument. In general, though, Conservative commentators console themselves with the notion that Scottish separation, as they invariably style it, might assist the Tory cause in England.

If you want real angst over the consequences of devolution, you must set aside *The Daily Telegraph* and turn to the pages of *The Guardian* or *The Observer*. In contrast with the underlying perspective of the right, I believe the liberal Left fears that its project of reshaping England will be undermined if Scottish votes are withdrawn. It is a concern, consequently, not so much for Britain or England as for the sort of England which the centre Left wants to see.

Certainly, the extent of the concern has been wonderful to witness. Here's David Walker, providing an analysis piece in *The*

Guardian:[2] 'Even in the debate about daylight saving time, there's a new edge of English self-consciousness. Why should clocks be changed for the benefit of kids going to school in Glenrothes?'

Or Hugo Young – one of the most acute of contemporary commentators – also writing in *The Guardian*, before the 1997 General Election.[3] He forecast then that the Tories in the Commons would fight to the last ditch over devolution: this proved to be wrong. He also claimed that Labour would have to play down elements of devolution like the financial subsidy of the Scots in order to get the package through. Then the apocalyptic warning: 'For the purposes of the election, Scotland has to be strung along in the belief that it can have the best of all worlds. But, after that, when the British wake up, it will be a different story.' Presumably by 'British' he means 'English', but the point is made.

Hugo Young again,[4] long after that General Election, warning that the establishment of a Scottish Parliament has made it impossible in practical terms for senior Scots like Gordon Brown to advance their careers further at Westminster. 'The enormity of the price that Scotchness may yet exact must be intolerable to contemplate. It portends a systemic crisis for the working-out of modern Britishness, perhaps some kind of slow crack-up.'

On reading such remarks – and there are many more in similar vein – the casual observer, perhaps from overseas, would undoubtedly be intrigued. What kind of horror is it that has been imposed upon the poor, brave people of England? What are they being forced to endure?

The position is this. In future, now that Scottish devolution is in place, England will be governed exactly as it has been for centuries by a Parliament at Westminster where the vast majority of the MPs come from English seats. The only concrete difference is that, after the next shuffle of boundary constituencies, it has been foreshadowed in legislation that there will be considerably fewer MPs from Scotland. It is also likely that several of the Scottish MPs who remain at Westminster, including the Nationalists, will voluntarily abstain on English issues. The arithmetic of the Commons will consequently be substantially tilted in favour of English interests. There will be no other change to the governance of English matters. This is what is happening in practice, as opposed to what is frequently perceived to be taking place. England's control of its own domestic matters is growing proportionately stronger, not weaker. I thought it pertinent to state the genuine position presently confronting England before conceding that it is the perception which may well drive events.

There is talk again of the West Lothian question. In its original form, it was advanced by the Labour MP Tam Dalyell, whose constituency was formerly called West Lothian. Dalyell asked how it could be fair and just that a Scottish MP at Westminster after devolution could vote upon matters such as education affecting English seats, but that the same MP could not vote on such matters affecting his own constituency because they would have been devolved to a Scottish Parliament.

Mr Dalyell intervened repeatedly during the debates over the 1970s devolution legislation to pose his question. As I recall, and I am aware that I am paraphrasing, he did so by summing up the impact upon communities in his area and similarly named areas in England. 'How could it be right', he would intone in that wonderfully penetrating voice, 'that I as the MP for West Lothian could vote upon schools in Blackburn, Lancashire, but not upon schools in Blackburn in my constituency?'

I have, incidentally, the greatest regard for Tam Dalyell as a Parliamentarian. His persistence over such issues as the Lockerbie inquiry is to be commended. I particularly admire his style in asking supplementary questions. A Minister delivers the opening reply drafted for him by his civil servants and slumps on the front bench hoping for a lengthy and complicated supplementary to allow time to muster the next thought. Up pops Tam to boom simply 'Why?' or 'How much?' Much shuffling of front-bench papers ensues.

The clarity and simplicity of the Dalyell approach has been rather obscured over the passage of time with regard to the West Lothian question. It is now commonly expressed as challenging the right of Scottish MPs at Westminster to vote on English matters when English MPs cannot vote on Scottish affairs. In essence, it is now used as shorthand for the mood I have outlined above: English political resentment at unwarranted Scottish interference. It has become a political cliché to say that there are no answers to the West Lothian question within a Union structure. There are, however, a series of potential rebuttals which mitigate or vary its force.

As noted above, it can be pointed out that the West Lothian

question in its contemporary guise patently does not apply at present.
England has voted Labour by a significant margin at two successive
general elections. Further, the question has applied very infrequently
in the past. By my calculation, the political balance in England has
only been upset by the addition of Scottish members twice in the
post-war period.

In other words, England has twice elected more Conservative
MPs than Labour ones, yet ended up governed by Labour. This
applied to the Labour government between 1964 and 1966 and to
the administration which lasted from February to October 1974.
Every other Labour government has had a majority of seats in
England as well as in Scotland. By contrast, it might be noted that
the other signatory of the Treaty of Union, Scotland, has regularly
voted Labour only to end up governed by the Conservatives. This
applied with perhaps the greatest force to the Conservative administrations of Margaret Thatcher, which applied a new ideological zeal
to politics. I may have missed them but I do not recall anguished
leading articles in the London press over this point.

A second rebuttal to concern over West Lothian, then, is to note
that it has applied to Scotland much more commonly than it has
applied to England. This, I stress, can be advanced as no more than
a plea in mitigation by those who would seek to tackle the West
Lothian challenge. It does not address the concerns of England.

Third, the Labour government case is that Westminster has opted
of its own free will to devolve power to Scotland, to activate the
West Lothian question. It is argued therefore that West Lothian is
not an unforeseen consequence but a tolerable and relatively minor
anomaly created by the sovereign UK Parliament. This argument
has always struck me as a weak case. It ignores the fact that the
'sovereign Westminster Parliament' broadly does what it is told by
the governing party, by the executive. While it is true that Labour
has the power to create whatever anomaly it likes, this is the nega-
tion of reasoned argument. It is almost tantamount to saying that the
government can do anything, however patently stupid or unfair.

Fourth, it is pointed out that there has in the past been a parallel
anomaly when Northern Ireland had its own assembly but continued to send members to Westminster. The particular sensitivities of
Westminster tend to reduce the frequency with which this argument
is deployed. Further, Northern Ireland sends far fewer MPs to

Westminster than Scotland, and consequently has far less capacity to activate a form of West Lothian question.

Finally, there is the practical approach adopted by the Labour government. This is to pave the way for a reduction in the numbers of MPs from Scotland sent to Westminster. The proposal is to reduce the number from the present 72 to 59. This, of course, does not completely answer West Lothian. It will still be the case that Scottish MPs are free to vote upon English matters. It does, however, lessen the chances of Scottish votes outweighing England's political choice.

These arguments, though, are rebuttals, not answers. The most common private reply to the West Lothian question, muttered by Ministers under their breath, is: 'So what?' What difference does it truly make to England if Scotland has devolution? It is not a reply which a politically acute government will want to offer to the English people.

As I have argued above, English governance as a whole will experience no practical impact whatsoever from Scottish devolution. Indeed, Tony Blair's insistence that a Scottish Parliament be accompanied by a cut in Scottish representation at Westminster tilts the balance in England's favour.

Further, it seems to me that it is at the very least questionable that those Conservatives who most vigorously supported an unreformed Union can credibly argue now for further change. They fully backed the governance of Scotland and England by a United Kingdom Parliament. They were prepared to accept that a UK mandate might vary across the border, that England might, infrequently, be governed by a party it did not directly elect and that Scotland might, more regularly, be governed against its apparent electoral wishes.

The Union mandate would apply to both. The Kingdom would be governed in a United fashion. From an undiluted Unionist perspective, this was an entirely consistent standpoint. What has happened now, under devolution, is that Scottish domestic matters will be governed according to a distinctly Scottish mandate, not a UK one. English domestic matters will continue to be governed in exactly the same way – with the exception that the Scottish input will ultimately be less.

Conservative critics of devolution were entirely content for England and Scotland to be governed by the established rules, disregarding a century of complaint from Scottish Home Rule activists. They argued, forcibly, that the system should not be changed. Why then, in logic, should they complain now? England's position has not been altered at all. English legislation will still be processed by the House of Commons, by a Parliament which in future will contain fewer Scottish MPs. England will still be governed by the UK mandate that the Conservatives were seemingly so anxious to maintain for Scotland and England combined. The answer to these questions, of course, is that political debate is not dictated purely by logic. Psychologically, everything has changed. Democratic government operates by consent. If that consent is withdrawn or becomes grudging, then democratic government begins to stutter and fail.

This was the case, I would argue, in nineteenth century Britain before the Reform Act of 1832. This was the case in late twentieth-century Scotland, particularly when the Conservatives continued to govern with shrinking Scottish support. It may become the case in England in the future.

There is, as I have said, no strictly logical reason why it should. Part of the potential for resentment is undoubtedly fostered by the miscomprehension of devolution, enhanced by commentators who confuse Labour's reforms, deliberately or otherwise, with independence for Scotland.

The impression is created in the public mind that Scotland has gone its own way entirely and yet continues to influence English politics. Scotland, of course, is still governed by the UK Parliament in key matters like defence, macro-economics and social security, and is consequently entitled to a democratic say in the formulation of decisions affecting those areas. Scottish MPs are entitled to be at Westminster.

One has only to turn to the issue of defence to negate any impression that devolution equals independence, and that Scottish MPs should, consequently, be sent packing from Westminster. Defence remains a matter reserved to Westminster. Scotland continues to house the Trident nuclear deterrent. Scottish service personnel are still sent into conflict on the orders of the United Kingdom government. That will continue to be the case in the future under devolution, even if the party governing in London is different from the party governing in Edinburgh.

In the context of devolution, that is entirely justifiable and right.

However much certain commentators and politicians may argue otherwise, devolution does not equal the separation of Scotland from the United Kingdom. Therefore under devolution, there can be absolutely no question of removing Scottish influence from the House of Commons entirely. I am aware that I have rather laboured this point but it seems to me that so much comment on the topic of devolution is based upon a misconception of its true nature that it was worth pursuing the question. Under devolution, Scotland remains in the United Kingdom. The only Westminster issue, then, in the developing political relationship between Scotland and England is whether English domestic matters should continue to be affected by Scottish votes. As with so much else in politics, those who address this question are often pursuing a range of issues rather than simply the core question of English governance.

Tory backbenchers in the Commons now routinely complain about Scottish involvement at Westminster. Since 2001, the Scottish Tories have had a solitary representative in the Commons, Peter Duncan from Galloway. He avoids stirring further resentment by voluntarily abstaining from votes on purely English issues. Such abstinence is also practised by the SNP, who say they have no wish to interfere in the governance of England.

The Tories, though, go further and say that all Scottish members should keep out of the division lobbies when the matter in hand affects only England. William Hague, the party's former leader, used to recount how his slogan of 'English votes on English issues' would raise the roof at meetings of the faithful across the Home Counties and further afield in England. Iain Duncan Smith encourages broadly the same approach, although it is my impression that he has tended to make less of this as an issue, concentrating more upon his crusade to re-engage the Conservatives with defence of the vulnerable. In passing, one might note two points. First, the Hague slogan had no impact whatsoever upon his subsequent rout at the polls in England. Second, it is just that, a slogan, not a structured solution to the constitutional conundrum of England.

If the Tories are in favour of an English Parliament or federalism or whatever, then they should say so, providing sufficient detail that their policy can be measured and judged. To be entirely fair to William Hague, he was well aware of this, and uncomfortably aware, too, that fostering a brand of English nationalism sat ill with his party's staunch support for the Union. As a consequence, he seldom went beyond the slogan, and resisted the temptation to play the English card too strongly.

More generally, those back-bench Tories who pursue this issue are often motivated by their residual distaste for the entire devolution project rather than by concrete examples of any consequential problem for England. It is partly a question of a self-fulfilling prophecy. They forecast devolution would be a disaster and consequently have little motivation to play down their complaints now.

Equally, the complaints have become embroiled in a wider issue: the search for a renewed sense of English identity. This in turn is entwined with the arguments over the influence of the European Union. It is no accident – although a fraction ironic – that those who most vigorously condemn Europe's overweening power are also those who resent the transfer of power from Westminster to Edinburgh. They want nothing to alter England's status. This is not purely a question of political structures. For the Tory critics – as for the originators of devolution – it is a question of identity. Quintessential English Tories feel threatened, a little uncertain. They see power and influence leeching away to Brussels on the one hand and to Edinburgh on the other. They wonder: where stands London, where stands England in this uncertain and changing world?

Several writers and commentators have bemoaned the lack of a clear English identity. The poet laureate, Andrew Motion, has argued that it is an issue which requires to be addressed in the aftermath of the assertion of Scottish identity which the Parliament in Edinburgh represents.

Philip Johnston, addressing this question in *The Daily Telegraph*, noted a problem of definition in that 'whereas Scots wave the Saltire with pride, the Cross of St George has become associated with lager louts, bigoted fringe nationalists and Morris dancing'.[5] Arguably, World Cup 2002 will tend to link the flag of St George, more positively, with David Beckham and English football.

But anxiety remains in some quarters. The Campaign for an English Parliament, a minor but zealous organisation, argues in its literature, distributed around party conferences, that 'the most important reason for creating an English Parliament is to help restore confidence and self-respect to the people of England'.

Others use vigorous, even grotesque imagery. Writing in the

Daily Record, Quentin Letts summoned up an image of an emotive political leader attempting to whip up English fervour.[6] In a bizarre and gruesome passage, he added: 'All it would take is a few killings of English children in Scotland. All it could take is an English Salmond to come along and appeal to the Lionheart Factor.'

Such outlandish sentiments, I would suggest, do not remotely represent the feelings of the English people. I lived happily in London for six years, making several close friendships in the process. I have not succumbed to the current Scottish affectation for finding London crowded and distasteful. Rather, I found and still find it one of the most exciting cities in the world, up there with Dundee and New York. My elder son was born in St Thomas's Hospital on the south bank of the Thames. (I am uncomfortably aware that in the preceding paragraph I have begun to sound like those irritating visitors to Scotland who talk patronisingly of their vague Scottish connections.)

Living in the Surrey suburbs, I did not encounter an aggressively assertive people. I did not encounter any dislike of the Scots who made their living in the capital. Rather, I found a pleasant, comfortable populace, perhaps rather insular by contrast with their counterparts among the educated Scottish middle classes who are accustomed to seeking their fortunes more widely. If they thought about their national status at all, they invariably described themselves as English or British interchangeably.

It seems unlikely to me that such a populace will easily be stirred into the vicious resentment forecast by some commentators. It is, however, possible over a longer period that constant repetition of the alleged unfairness of Scottish involvement in Westminster politics will begin to have an impact. Without being fully understood, this may well become part of the conventional wisdom.

As I noted earlier, the liberal Left has a different perspective. It was most succinctly described by the journalist and political analyst Will Hutton in a lecture[7] reported by his newspaper, *The Observer*. Hutton is a renowned advocate of the Third Way political philosophy of free-market, inclusive social democracy pursued by Tony Blair. In his lecture, Hutton warned: 'Scottish independence would be the end of Britain and the end of any idea of constructing a federal Britain. It would also, I argue, gravely weaken the liberal social democratic Left in these islands just when it needs to build international alliances rather than balkanise into separate movements.'

At one level, this can be seen as a plea for the liberal Left in Scotland and England to conjoin in order to advance the reform agenda in both nations. Put more simply, however, that means that England could not be relied upon to continue to vote Labour (or Liberal Democrat) in sufficient numbers to sustain the Blairite project of building a near-permanent centre-left government.

At its crudest, this argument may be said to take the West Lothian question and elevate it to new heights. Scotland must stay in the Union, so that England can have a centre-left reforming government, presumably regardless of England's future voting pattern. I stress again it is a question of perspective. From an English centre-left standpoint, it can be legitimate to argue for common effort. However, it is not in itself a particularly convincing argument to deploy against Scottish independence. A Scottish Nationalist is unlikely to be swayed by an appeal to abandon support for independence in order to protect England from Toryism. To be entirely fair to Hutton, he also voices other, economic anxieties about independence in his lecture.

A third strand of thought – to add to Conservative and liberal Left – has entered the debate about English identity. The Scottish Nationalists assert the sovereign right of the Scottish people to determine their own constitutional future. They are aware, however, that England must have a voice in this, if only because independence would require negotiations with London and legislation through Westminster. Consequently, they have begun to talk in terms of a new relationship between Scotland and England.

In a lecture, the former SNP leader Alex Salmond claimed that there was a 'crisis of identity' in England.[8] As I have argued above, I believe this considerably overstates the true position and was, of course, advanced by Salmond primarily to create an impression that there may be UK-wide pressure for further reform in the direction of breaking the Union. Salmond went on to say: 'We must aspire to a whole new concordat between the two nations, one which adds a new momentum to the process of discovering and securing the identity of both of these nations and defining the best future for both on this island that we share and this continent to which we are tied.'

His successor John Swinney took this further. On St George's Day 2002, he headed for the cultural heart of England. No, not

Stratford-upon-Avon. Nor the Globe Theatre. He went to visit the set of *Coronation Street* in Salford. Now *Corrie* – as the bold Swinney called it – has been through a period of upheaval, with new characters, new plots. So as he strode on set, you could just imagine the stars muttering to themselves: 'My God, now they want us to fit a Scottish accountant into the script! That's it, luv, I'm off!'

But the SNP leader persisted and, with charm, achieved his two principal objectives. He got his picture in every paper between Wick and the Isle of Wight, and he wangled an option on a future cameo role as Hector, the long-lost grandson that Elsie Tanner never knew. Cheap, Brian, cheap. Unworthy. Behind the photo-call and the folksy populism, there was a serious message. Two serious messages, in fact.

First, John Swinney wanted to assert that the SNP is not about separation from shared heritage with England. That means Shakespeare and the glories of literature in the English language, but it also means authentic popular culture. Seemingly, there are troubled souls around Scotland who fear that, post-independence, their tellies will be rigged so that they can no longer see *Corrie* and *EastEnders*, and will be obliged to watch endless reruns of *High Road*. Swinney was offering reassurance: he is never happier, apparently, than when settling down to catch up on the Street or Albert Square.

Second, and more subtly, this was an attempt to place Scottish self-government into a context of UK change. Naturally, the SNP believes in Scottish self-determination but it plainly feels that the outcome of independence will be eased by paying attention to the status of the remainder of the UK. The underlying claim is that England will lose a surly lodger and gain a friendly neighbour.

Swinney's trip to the Street was followed by the publication of a party strategy paper, *Talking Independence*, which included the claim that 'independence is in the interests of better relations between Scotland and England'. The document goes on to argue that 'independence is about redefining and improving the relationship between Scotland and England, not ending it'. In truth, of course, this document is aimed at those in Scotland who fear the consequences of independence. It is about neutralising anxieties which may be stimulated by rival parties. Naturally, again, the SNP's stress is upon Scotland. It is intriguing that party strategists feel the need to encompass the English perspective but, as noted above, they do this

largely for Scottish reasons. They do not expect England to pre-
scribe constitutional solutions for Scotland, and so would not
presume to do the same in reverse.

Therefore it is up to the good people of England to determine
how they wish to be governed: that is, assuming that there is any
substantial degree of anxiety over the question at all.

What then, among the options I have canvassed, is the answer to
the West Lothian question? There are, in reality, only two constitutional solutions that would answer – rather than mitigate – the
question. These are independence or federalism. Neither of these
solutions is presently being advanced by either the UK government
or the principal opposition party at Westminster.

Before addressing these two options, I should note that West
Lothian is not remotely answered by English regionalism, however
extensive. The UK government has established an elected body for
London and has published a White Paper, which I shall look at
shortly, which proposes regional assemblies for England where there
is demand backed up in a referendum. Some argue that this addresses
West Lothian, supplying an English counterbalance to the Scottish
political structure. Certainly, such an English regional dimension –
even initially operating only in those areas like the north where
there is apparent demand – might help to mitigate such envy as
exists towards Scottish autonomy.

It would not, however, answer West Lothian unless it were proposed that these regional bodies should have law-making powers. Such
a notion is explicitly ruled out by the White Paper. So as long as the
law for the south-west, for example, is laid down by Westminster –
and as long as Scottish MPs participate in Westminster votes – then
the south-west is governed by Westminster and Scottish MPs play
their part in that government. West Lothian applies. Establishing an
assembly in Bristol or Plymouth may be regarded as a valuable step
in its own right but it has no impact whatsoever upon legislative
politics and consequently upon the West Lothian question. Until
Bristol can legislate for the south-west – and such a development is
utterly remote from government or popular thinking – then the
regional dimension in England will be, properly, a division of local
government. It will not parallel the Scottish Parliament.

First, West Lothian could self-evidently be answered by Scottish
independence, by breaking the Union, by reducing the number of

MPs from Scotland at Westminster to zero. However, this is steadfastly opposed by Labour, the Liberal Democrats and by the Conservatives, apart from a handful of Tories who believe that it might advance the party's cause in England while allowing Scotland to adopt a zealously, free-market approach, to become the Luxembourg of the British Isles.

Second, West Lothian could be answered by federalism; either a version incorporating English regional legislatures or, more probably, a system whereby Scotland, Wales, Northern Ireland and the whole of England become domestic self-governing units. Such an approach is broadly endorsed by the Liberal Democrats as a longer term aim, although in the meantime they have thrown their weight behind the devolution movement.

There are two problems with federalism. First, there is minimal evidence of a uniform demand in England for regional government – far less for full-scale English federalism. Second, England taken as a whole would far outweigh the size of the other components in any new federal structure. It would be as if the federal United States consisted solely of Iowa, Rhode Island, Delaware – and California.

Consider this future prospect, for example. Labour has formed Britain's federal government on the back of a UK mandate. At the same time, however, the Conservatives can muster enough support to govern the state of England. Is it seriously suggested that a Labour federal Prime Minister would deal with defence and foreign affairs for the UK, while a Conservative English Prime Minister sorted out education, health and other domestic matters for England, for 80 per cent of the UK population? Would they take turns in Downing Street? Would the two administrations take questions in the Commons on alternate days? Would the English state government move to York?

The federal solution which works in the United States and Germany – where no single state is completely dominant – would not easily translate to the UK, where one constituent nation has the vast majority of the population and the firmly established UK capital.

This brings us back to the White Paper on regional government in England.[9] This was delayed, partly because it did not receive high ranking in the government's priority list and partly because senior Ministers harboured significant doubts about the entire enterprise. The driving force for change was John Prescott.

The deputy Prime Minister is easily lampooned. Indeed, some of his more contorted utterances are beyond parody. But the Blairite transformation of the Labour Party would have been much more difficult, arguably impossible, without Prescott, an iron chain to the anchor of Labour traditions. Prescott, however, is more than a convenient token for Blair. He has long believed in reform, and has voiced that belief most substantially through the campaign for English regionalism.

I have heard Prescott speak on this topic several times: in private, at small political events and from conference platforms. Each time the message is the same: there are those inside government who do not want to do this but I am going to make sure that they do. For Prescott, largely sidelined by the main departmental Ministers, this is personal. He believes fervently in regionalism, but, at the same time, he wants to reassert his reforming role at the heart of government.

Without Prescott, English regionalism might have slid still further down the government's agenda. Key Ministers, including Tony Blair, appeared at various times to be bored with the subject and lukewarm towards implementation. Prescott kept at it, but the White Paper that emerged is a masterpiece of Whitehall caution, stating the overall aim of revitalising the regions but also stressing the strict limits to regional power.

In summary, the White Paper traces recent efforts to recognise the regional dimension in England, most notably the establishment in 1999 of eight Regional Development Agencies (RDAs). The document notes in passing that these bodies still face a substantial task in competing with the job-pulling power of Scottish Enterprise.

The government's proposal is that these eight regions, together comprising the map of England outside London, should move at their own pace towards further democratic reform. Everywhere, there will be moves to strengthen the RDAs and the existing central-government offices in the regions. But it will be up to each area to decide whether – and how swiftly – to cap that structure with an elected assembly.

These assemblies would have between twenty-five and thirty-five members each, elected by the Additional Member System on the Scottish model. They would have regional executive and scrutiny functions, but no powers to make law or to usurp the key role of Westminster in governing England.

The document notes: 'As around 84 per cent of the population of the UK lives in England, devolution to an English "Parliament" or national assembly would have relatively little practical effect or benefit. It would not bring people in the English regions any closer to the decision-making process.' Quite. This is regionalism, not national devolution, Scotland style. Without repeating every detail of the White Paper, a number of further analytical points can be made. First, the document repeats *ad nauseam* that the regions will not take powers from local councils. Yet the powers on offer sound remarkably like those of large-scale local government.

The new English regions will be responsible for things like economic development, including fostering local skills; spatial planning; transport; waste targets; housing strategy; health improvement (but not the health service, which remains with Westminster); culture and tourism. Juggle the list a little, borrow a few services from city councils, and you could be talking about Strathclyde or Lothian or any of the big Scottish regions abolished by the Tories. More to the point, you could be talking about Tyne and Wear or any of the big English regions, also abolished by the Tories.

Further, funding for the new regions will come from block grant plus a power to levy a precept upon council taxes. This money would be raised by local authorities and passed to the new assemblies. Sound familiar? It is exactly what happened under the old, defunct regions. It is repeatedly stated that the regions will largely gain powers from central not local government. This is true in as much as they take over the supervisory and administrative role of existing central government offices in the regions. But, by contrast with Scottish devolution, there is no serious derogation from the principal powers retained at Westminster. The White Paper states: 'There will be no change to the responsibilities which Parliament and central government have for UK-wide matters (including defence, foreign policy, relations with international bodies and taxation).' So far, that statement matches the Scottish model.

However, the document adds: 'In addition, responsibility for many policy areas of England-wide importance (such as the National Health Service and schools) will remain on an England-wide basis and Parliament will continue to have responsibility for these matters.' To make matters completely clear, the document notes: 'Parliament will continue to be responsible for legislation for the English regions.'

By stating that the planned bodies sound to me more like large-scale local government, I am neither condemning nor praising the proposal. I am simply arguing that this is not remotely devolution on the Scottish model. However much it is denied, this is a form of regional council. Taken together, these new bodies – even if they are established all across England – will not sit alongside the Scottish Parliament as a uniform, devolved pattern of governance below Westminster.

For one thing, as stated above, their functions are quite different. The Scottish Parliament has the power to make law. It has sole control over most Scottish domestic affairs, including the health service, schools, universities, justice, the courts. For another, the scope of the two bodies is quite different. In the White Paper, it is envisaged for example that a regional assembly for the north-east would be responsible for around £350 million if it were up and running in 2001/2. The total Scottish budget for the same year is just a fraction short of £20 billion. That is, sixty times bigger.

There is, however, a third point which is more significant than the first two. It is implicit in the White Paper that the new English regional bodies will be delivery mechanisms for central government. The assemblies will be funded by a single block grant, but there will be extra money to 'reward' those regions who contrive to attain targets agreed with Westminster. Soothingly, it is noted that these targets would only comprise a 'small number – perhaps six to ten'.

Further, it is noted in the White Paper with regard to the economy that 'central government will retain powers to ensure that elected assemblies and their Regional Development Agencies continue to address national priorities'. Spelling it out, the document notes that central government can require changes to regional policies if they are detrimental to national planning or might impact badly on other regions.

As stated earlier, the government leaves it to regions to determine whether they want to go down the path towards an elected assembly. In effect, Ministers will decide when there is evidence of demand in a particular region and will put that to the test in a regional referendum. The establishment of a regional assembly would involve local government shifting to a single tier.

However, it is plain from reading the White Paper that central government wants to encourage such a move. The document stresses that there will be reforms for all regions – including those who do not opt for assemblies – but adds that there are limits to this approach. Greater devolution of power must be matched by greater accountability.

For the government, there is a further attraction in the new approach. It would sit well with established structures across the EU. The White Paper notes that 'England now includes virtually the only regions within the European Union which don't have the choice of some form of democratic, regional governance.'

To repeat, these planned bodies are not semi-autonomous, devolved Parliaments on the Scottish model. They are large-scale regional authorities with no legislative powers and a specific remit to help deliver economic targets set by Westminster and Whitehall. Again, that is neither to criticise nor condemn. The White Paper diagnoses a problem of sluggish economic growth in areas such as the north of England and proposes to remedy that with a new democratic structure intended to revitalise those areas. It is a worthwhile objective, which may or may not be attained, but virtually nothing to do with Scottish devolution. Except that there are already voices suggesting that English regionalism offers an opportunity to rebalance the UK. The organisation, Campaign for the English Regions (CFER), submitted a document to the government in January 2002, anticipating the White Paper. This body, grounded in the north-east of England, makes plain that it wants to encompass Scottish devolution within the new structure.

The document suggests that the posts of Secretary of State for Scotland and for Wales in the UK Cabinet should be abolished, and replaced by a Secretary of State for the Nations and Regions. This individual would have responsibility for supervising the Scottish Parliament, the Welsh Assembly and the new English regions.

The CFER study talks of the UK government's programme of legislation, and how there must be a conduit of consultation with the regions who will be affected by these proposed new laws. This is, arguably, a splendid notion for the new English regions but completely ignores the fact that the domestic laws in that UK programme of legislation do not apply to Scotland. Further, the document refers briefly to 'regional representation' in a reformed House of Lords. Again, from an English point of view, this may look attractive. It would give the new regions a voice in Parliament, albeit the Upper Chamber. It might help the government by applying a regional veneer of democratic respectability to the Lords. However, viewed from Scotland, this notion can look potentially threatening. The legislative autonomy of the Scottish Parliament is jealously guarded. I do not believe that those who campaigned to prise Scotland away from sole control by the House of Commons would readily return even partial power to the House of Lords.

The government White Paper makes only a passing reference to the House of Lords, noting that decisions on regional representation and other issues will be taken in due course. If there is confusion on this issue in the English regions – and it would seem that there is – I do not believe that confusion is shared by the Leader of the Commons, Robin Cook. As a Scottish MP, he is well aware of Scottish political opinion on this point.

Equally, in constitutional politics, there is often a gap between ambition and outcome. For example, Labour had a grand scheme for directly elected mayors across England. The outcome? A monkey won Hartlepool. A chap who dresses in a monkey suit as mascot for the local football team was elected mayor, commemorating the poor primate hanged by the good people of Hartlepool because they thought it was a Napoleonic spy. I confess I have not laughed so much since I last watched *A Night at the Opera*.

Similarly, it seems unlikely to me that any grand design for UK-wide regional governance, subsuming Scotland, will work in practice. Those who desire neatness in constitutional politics are frequently frustrated, as our friend the monkey will attest. However, the Scottish Parliament and Executive will no doubt monitor such developments with close interest. To return to the main point, the proposed English bodies may or may not have value in themselves. They may assuage regional concerns, but they do not answer the English Question. They do not even address West Lothian, which is primarily concerned with the power to make law.

If you doubt me, think of this. Labour could set up eight regional assemblies in England to add to the existing assembly in London. Imagine that, in future, the Tories were to gain control of every single one of these assemblies. Even then, Labour could still be returned to power at Westminster, with the help of Scottish votes. It would be Labour who made the law for England. It would be Labour who governed England.

As I said at the outset, Scottish devolution does not affect the wider governance of England, other than to reduce Scotland's stake in the Commons. England may remain content to be governed as it has been for centuries by the Union Parliament, dominated naturally by MPs and peers from England. Or it may complain. I, for one, intend to leave it to the people of England to decide.

Notes

1. Article in *The Daily Telegraph*, 7 January 2002.
2. Article in *The Guardian*, 13 April 1999.
3. Article in *The Guardian*, 11 February 1997.
4. Article in *The Guardian*, 4 June 1998.
5. Article in *The Daily Telegraph*, 2 February 1999.
6. Article in the *Daily Record*, 23 April 1999.
7. The John Mackintosh Lecture, Edinburgh University, 19 November 1998.
8. Lecture, London School of Economics, 25 February 1999.
9. White Paper, *Your Region, Your Choice – Revitalising the English Regions*, published by the Cabinet Office and the Department for Transport, Local Government and the Regions, 9 May 2002.

16 A Look to the Future

It was a remarkable event, almost unique. Her Majesty told a funny. Quite a good gag, too. The loyal Parliamentarians duly laughed. The disloyal had tactfully stayed away. The Queen was addressing the Scottish Parliament in Aberdeen on 28 May 2002 as part of her Golden Jubilee tour. The MSPs had sojourned north because their customary accommodation in Edinburgh had been reclaimed by its owners, the Church of Scotland, for the Kirk's General Assembly.

This was a special event in another way. When Her Majesty performs the state opening at Westminster, the MPs are summoned to the Lords, where they stand at the back looking a little lost, like puzzled kids in the family enclosure at a big sporting event. When she first addressed the Scottish Parliament on 1 July 1999, she was similarly initiating proceedings, not joining in the fun.

This was, however, the first speech by the sovereign to a convened session of Parliament since the Union. It was, apparently, standard practice for the Scottish monarchs to take part in the pre-Union Parliament of Scotland. Indeed, I am told (by a historian who should know these things) that it was scarcely possible to get James VI to shut up once debate was under way. This, then, was the subject of the Queen's funny. Not James, the wisest fool in Christendom, but Crown and Parliament. She explained that Aberdeen had previously

All smiles as Sir David Steel invites the Queen to address the Scottish Parliament in Aberdeen.

played host to Scottish Parliamentarians in 1462, during the reign of James III. The city had appended 'somewhat petulantly' the following note to their financial record. 'Towards the arrival of the King in Aberdeen – although he did not come – by mandate of the Treasurer: £20.'

This tale of a regal let-down – and Aberdonian dismay at the cost – had them hooting. I doubt whether Her Majesty will win a Fringe award for stand-up, but then she was scarcely auditioning as a comic. The remainder of the speech had a deeply serious, political purpose. The Queen noted that the devolved Scottish Parliament had suffered from a somewhat troubled start. She argued, however, that Donald Dewar had recognised that 'Scotland was never going to build a new political culture overnight'. Then she added: 'After what might be considered a Parliamentary adjournment of almost three hundred years, that process will inevitably take time. In an age which tends to instant judgements, this is something we would all do well to remember.'

The sovereign went on to express her hope that the new constitutional relationships within the UK – 'unity within diversity' – would strengthen the bonds linking 'the nations and regions of the

United Kingdom, the Commonwealth and Europe'. The entire speech was very carefully worded in order to vaunt the Union without outraging the Nationalists.

Look at that reference to 'a Parliamentary adjournment'. That reflects, directly and deliberately, a Nationalist sentiment. It fell to the SNP's Winnie Ewing, as the oldest member, to call the very first session of the new, devolved Parliament to order, before a presiding officer had been elected. She announced that the independent Parliament which 'adjourned' in 1707 was duly recalled.

Look, too, at the speech more generally, its stress on popular consultation and engagement. Yes, the speech stressed the Union. From the Queen of the United Kingdom, scarcely a surprise. Indeed, it was a primary purpose. On the face of it, the Nationalists might have felt tempted to complain of a partisan intervention against their political standpoint. But that stress on the 'good judgement' of the people gave the Nationalists a get-out clause. It allowed them to say that they were similarly content to trust that the good judgement of the people would eventually lead to independence.

Glancing at my copy of the Aberdeen speech, I see I have scrawled a little note in the margin, in fading shorthand: 'I can never forget that I am Queen of the United Kingdom – 1977.' This was a reminder to myself of the Queen's speech on the occasion of her Silver Jubilee, twenty-five years previously. With those words, delivered in 1977, she had appeared to be casting doubt upon the then Labour government's programme of devolution to Scotland and Wales. That earlier speech was – rightly, in my view – interpreted as a controversial political intervention.

Aberdeen was not an apology for those earlier remarks. Monarchs seldom apologise, and, arguably, events had moved on sufficiently in order to allow a change of emphasis. However, the Aberdeen address was similarly a political intervention, although carefully stripped of any partisan controversy. It was royal approval, British state approval, for Scottish self-government within the Union.

So regal opinion has apparently altered. But might the Scottish Parliament itself change? Might it retrench – or develop further? Is independence likely? I believe, first, that self-government is here to stay. Despite individual criticisms, I do not detect any public mood to reverse the referendum result. I am sure the Scottish mood is: 'Well, they may make a mess of things from time to time but it is our mess.' Far from shrinking in influence, I see the devolved Parliament steadily strengthening its place in Scottish life.

So might the Parliament develop, perhaps towards independence? In opposition, the former Labour leader John Smith described devolution as 'the settled will of the Scottish people'. By this, I believe John Smith meant no more than to argue that Labour was working with the grain of popular opinion in Scotland. His phrase encapsulated Labour's political ambition: to establish devolution firmly as the central position, marginalising by implication the Tories on the one hand and the SNP on the other.

Some occasionally appear to stretch Smith's phrase to imply that the specific scheme implemented by the UK Labour government is close to the last word on the subject, that the governance of Scotland is now fixed. By contrast, I do not believe that the 'settled will' of the people which prompted devolution is necessarily the final will. Equally, I do not believe that there is any specific route map pointing the way ineluctably towards independence.

John Smith frequently deployed another phrase, describing devolution as 'unfinished business'. By that, he meant that Labour in the 1970s, when he was the Minister in charge of the issue, had been unable to implement its devolutionary proposals. Nationalists occasionally like to suggest that the present Parliament represents unfinished business for them, that they will 'complete the powers' of the devolved body and generate independence. I believe it possible that the powers of the Parliament will be altered. Devolution may become evolution. As Donald Dewar was scrupulous in stressing, there is scope for the powers of the Parliament to alter if there is evident demand or evident need. I do not, however, believe that independence, however defined, will *necessarily* follow devolution. It may. It may not. There is no guarantee either way.

For one thing, as already discussed, the definitions of sovereignty and independence may change in an increasingly inter-dependent Continent. It is impossible to be precise about the United Kingdom's future relationship with the EU. Similarly, it is impossible to specify the developing role of the new devolved Scotland within the framework of that broader relationship.

For another, while I believe there may well be changes to the devolutionary package, there are reasons to assume that the pace of any change will be relatively slow. First, I do not detect any great agitation for further change among the non-Nationalist parties in Scotland. To the contrary, Labour and the LibDems are anxious to foster the impression that they are running things well under the present structure. The Tories want to attack the Executive, but, equally, they have a strong motivation to defend the Union, to prevent any drift towards independence. Further, polling history would suggest that the SNP is relatively unlikely to break through to power in its own right. As already discussed, the electoral system is designed to prevent any party from gaining control of the Parliament with a minority of the popular vote. Should the Nationalists win power through a coalition, the impetus for change would, of course, be accelerated. Even then, though, the SNP would require to win a further referendum to gain independence. Even to increase the constitutional powers of the present settlement, the Nationalists would need to oblige Westminster to amend the law.

To avoid any confusion, I am not remotely saying that independence is impossible. As I have repeatedly stressed, I believe that popular opinion carries more weight than the constitutional structure. Should Scotland at any stage declare for independence – clearly and without equivocation – then independence will happen.

At the same time, I am not remotely saying that the present powers of the Parliament are immutable. To the contrary, I believe they will change over time. I am simply stressing that such change may not happen easily or swiftly. The non-Nationalist parties have relatively little motivation to agitate for change themselves: at least for as long as the electoral threat presented by the SNP is contained.

Moreover, there may now be a mood of constitutional inertia. The voters may be weary of the topic. Certainly, Labour is trying to encourage that notion by arguing that Scotland should move from the politics of identity to the politics of social justice. There is a certain audacity about this initiative. First, Labour seemed happy to exploit identity politics when it was striving, successfully, to marginalise the Scottish Tories. Second, it is a little cheeky to suggest that the Nationalists should now abjure such issues, because Labour has achieved its aim of a devolved Parliament.

However, Labour may be swimming with the tide, at least for now. Arguably, there may not be a great public appetite in Scotland for substantial alteration to a structure so recently put together. Also, Westminster would be extremely reluctant to sanction further significant devolution of powers so soon after the detailed negotiations that led to the present set-up. There are structural anomalies, certainly, within the wider devolution settlement. It is anomalous that Scottish MPs can still vote on English business in the Commons. In the longer term, this dilemma may have to be resolved. But I do not detect widespread popular – as opposed to partisan – agitation in England for that issue to be resolved now. I do not believe such agitation will surface seriously unless and until England votes for one party and ends up governed by another when the MPs from Scotland are added in.

I believe there are also underlying problems with the financial settlement and with the Scottish Executive's rights of audience in Europe. I believe those two issues will merit longer term reform. Again, though, there is little sign of early popular agitation for change.

Further, I confess that I expected greater tension between Edinburgh and London than has proved to be the case. There have been sporadic feuds at departmental level, and public rows such as the conflict over the withdrawal of UK benefit cash as a result of the Executive's policy of free personal care for the elderly. Again, such conflict might become endemic if there were an administration of one political colour in London, and an entirely different colour in Edinburgh.

However, the machinery of the state has adjusted relatively well to the disruption and anomalies of devolution. It has coped with Scottish coalition. It has contrived to pay (some) attention to the views of the devolved administrations in formulating European policy. Who is to say the state – with its core objective of maintaining smooth government and the Union – would not find a way of coping with different governing parties north and south of the border?

I believe, in short, that those who advocated devolution – and, more subtly, those who now administer it – will take great care to avoid a climate of conflict, either within the Scottish administration or between Scotland and England, which might foster support for independence. Those who want independence – and they know this only too well – will have to fight for it. It will not fall into their lap.

It may be, though, that the people of Scotland – as the SNP hope – will subsequently seek to extend their new devolved Parliament into a form of independence. Alternatively, it may be that devolution will embed itself comfortably within a reformed United

Kingdom. Like the Queen's audience in Aberdeen, I will let the people decide.

So what about the performance of the devolved Parliament itself? While the Queen's opinion may have moved towards endorsing devolution, there have been pressures upon Scottish popular opinion to move the other way. Devolution has been far from universally successful. There have been the early 'housekeeping' problems, the policy rows such as Section 28, the turmoil inside the Executive, the departure of Henry McLeish and the Holyrood building project. After all that, MSPs voted themselves a 13.5 per cent pay rise on 21 March 2002. This was scarcely calculated to increase their popularity. However, it might be said that most of these controversies reflect a settling-in process for the new politics. The Holyrood building, for example, will presumably be finished one of these years. It will then be judged as architecture, not as an icon for political discontent.

There is even another side to the pay rise. The increase had been suggested by an independent investigation. It still left MSPs paid less than their counterparts at Westminster. Are they *never* to receive a pay rise, just because the rules left them in the invidious position of voting for their own salary? As I said at the time, there are some MSPs who could hold down a senior post in industry or the professions, and some that you would hesitate to send for a message. But are we to reward them all according to the merits of the poorest performers? Pay peanuts – and you get primates.

Further, politics is everywhere in disrepute. If you could choose, you would not open a new venture when its sole product is facing consumer resistance. The Scottish Parliament has suffered from the generally poor reputation of partisan politics.

Yes, I think there have been some spectacular blunders. In that category, the Holyrood building project is awesome, a class apart. It may yet, however, turn out well. In similar fashion, I think we require to judge the Parliament so far according to fundamental questions, rather than fad or froth.

I think there are three such questions. Does it hold the Executive to account? Does it provide a forum to ventilate issues of concern to the people of Scotland? Is it good at making and reforming the law of Scotland? I have tried to deal with these questions throughout this book, and so will simply summarise here.

First, does it hold the Executive to account? Demonstrably, yes.

Ask Henry McLeish. Or Jim Wallace, who has faced close – and challenging – scrutiny over his plans for Scotland's prisons. Ask the previously anonymous senior civil servants who now frequently face trial by Parliamentary committee.

I believe the committees could be, and will be, more subtle and evidence-driven in their approach. I believe the Executive should be obliged to disclose still more detail about the workings of government. I believe opposition parties could do more to sideline tedious point-scoring, and focus upon the authentic Parliamentary or public agenda. I believe Executive backbenchers, especially Labour, should ditch any lingering sycophancy and join in the task of questioning Ministers. However, I believe that the Scottish Parliament successfully scrutinises the Executive.

Next, does it provide a forum for authentic popular concern in Scotland? I believe it does. Naturally anyone with a specific grievance will dissent from that view. Fox hunters will say the Parliament has spent all its days ruining their lives. Dog owners may believe that MSPs should have more to occupy their time than attempting to clear up canine mess. In response, I would say, first, that Parliamentary democracy need not always be confined to the highways. It must occasionally wander down the by-ways of public life. Who is to say what should be the sole or predominant focus of politics? What is critical to one person may seem trivial to another. Spotlight only the major objectives, and minor injustices or problems may go without remedy.

The key is to get the balance right between highways and by-ways. I report upon the workings of Parliament pretty well every day it sits. You can trust me, I am a journalist. Okay, point taken, but you can still trust me. MSPs have not spent their every waking hour saving foxes or wielding legislative pooper scoopers. These are relatively minor members' Bills and receive proportionate attention. By far the greatest time is devoted to significant reforms of the criminal and civil law, and to debates on major concerns, like education, health or the other public services. Equally, I cannot think of a genuine Scottish controversy, a public talking point, which has not featured sooner or later in the Scottish Parliament. So, yes, I think Holyrood is an authentic forum for Scottish concerns.

Third, is it good at making and reforming the law of Scotland? I think here the verdict must be Not Proven. I think Parliament is serious in its intent. I think our law-makers, mostly, work extremely hard at getting matters right. However, as I noted much earlier in this book, I believe there is still an inclination in committee and chamber to pay too much attention to the views of enthusiasts and interested parties, rather than to assess the genuine need for legislation and to provide specific remedies.

Scotland's body politic has yet to accustom itself entirely to its new status, to its capacity to act rather than demand. Instead of simply saying things, our new politicians can do things. That potency is hazardous. I believe that some MSPs are still a little inclined towards gesture politics, even in the legislative field. They prefer laws which symbolise a creed, which demonstrate vision – the ban on smacking toddlers, for example – rather than dull, technical measures that close loopholes or address specific grievances.

To be clear, I am not arguing against visionary legislation. It is, again, a question of balance. Present an MSP with two alternatives: a technical Bill tackling a detailed, specific problem or a grand measure with a grand-sounding title which will delight a pressure group and intrigue the public. Their compass needle still veers, understandably, toward the grand gesture, even although the technical Bill may be the more significant in the long run. I believe that our MSPs are still a little too tempted to ask themselves: 'What shall we do today?' Instead, they should challenge those who press for new laws: 'Why should I do this? And how? And, if I should do this, why now?'

What else might change? I believe that politics more generally requires reform. It must become more mundane, more workaday, less concerned with the fake controversies cooked up across party lines, the rows over process and verbal nit-picking which intrigue the cognoscenti and send the voters running for cover.

By that, I do not mean some form of artificial consensus across party lines. I do not believe that is possible or, indeed, desirable. Arguably, any enforced constraint upon party debate would lessen the choice available to the voters. Rather, I think the parties should ditch their bogus horror at each announcement from the other side. They do not believe that their opponents are the embodiment of all that is evil, and, consequently, should not behave as if they do. The voters have long since stopped paying attention anyway. They might just start listening again if they hear serious, well-argued debate about issues that concern them.

Naturally, these changes are not solely in Holyrood's power. I believe, indeed, that the Scottish Parliament has been more attuned to popular politics than Westminster with its adversarial traditions of artificial angst. I believe, however, that the Scottish Parliament must beware.

By now, politicians will be yelling: fine, Brian, but what about the media? You people only report petty squabbles, you're not interested in serious politics. I believe, to be frank, that the politicians have a point. Some media coverage does tend to trivialise or, more commonly, to exaggerate the extent of any controversy. Politicians can never have a friendly dispute. They must always split, furiously.

To defend my craft, politicians foster this impression by attempting to represent their side of the argument as saints and their rivals as sinners. They may privately concede that the opposition has a case. Put them in front of a camera and they will condemn their critics as fools or knaves or both.

I do not know what initially caused this dislocation between politics and the real world. I do not know who started it, and, to be honest, I do not care all that much. All I know is that the voters seem decidedly sceptical about everything they hear from a politician and everything they read in the press. They seem to look a little more favourably on the broadcast media, but not all that much. We broadcasters should not preen ourselves.

Is it possible to call a truce? For politicians to speak openly about their concerns in return for fair, balanced coverage? You see the problem instantly, of course. You go first. No you. You started it. Did not. Did too. I believe there are hopeful signs. From the Prime Minister down, politicians do seem to be disowning spin, without being able to break the habit entirely. In return, there are journalists who are recognising that defending their craft against all complaints and in all circumstances is counter-productive.

In any event, reform is essential. People, I am sure, are still hugely interested in the big issues like crime or the health service or schools. But more and more voters are turned off by the present nature of partisan politics, and, consequently, by political coverage which deals exclusively with partisan politics.

I am definitely not suggesting an end to party politics. I do not envisage our politicians all sitting together around a large table and sorting out the world after a group hug. For example, Unionists and

Nationalists disagree because they have fundamentally different views of the way Scotland should be governed. Such disagreement cannot be wished away. It is important to present the alternatives to the voting public. But parties should be careful to confine their disagreement to genuine issues, and areas of genuine public concern. I understand the temptation to hurl insults at one another. The Tories, for example, would scarcely be human if they did not complain of Labour 'sleaze' after the hounding which John Major endured.

However, the problem is that the voters do not distinguish between parties. When they tune into contemporary political debate, they may find relatively little which resonates with their particular concerns. They just hear a discordant noise, they just see a heaving bulk of political bodies pressing for power. And they pay less and less attention. In the interests of democracy, there must be change.

Index